Innovation and Individuality
in African Development

**Linking Levels of Analysis**
Emilio F. Moran, Series Editor

# Innovation and Individuality in African Development

## Changing Production Strategies in Rural Mali

Dolores Koenig,
Tiéman Diarra,
*and* Moussa Sow

With Ousmane Diarra, Makan Fofana,
Yaouaga Félix Koné, Halimata Konaté Simaga,
and Fatoumata Maiga Maiga

*Ann Arbor*

THE UNIVERSITY OF MICHIGAN PRESS

Copyright © by the University of Michigan 1998
All rights reserved
Published in the United States of America by
The University of Michigan Press
Manufactured in the United States of America
⊗ Printed on acid-free paper

2001   2000   1999   1998      4   3   2   1

*A CIP catalog record for this book is available from the British Library.*

Library of Congress Cataloging-in-Publication Data

Koenig, Dolores.
  Innovation and individuality in African development : changing
  production strategies in rural Mali / Dolores Koenig, Tieman
  Diarra, and Moussa Sow with Ousmane Diarra . . . [et al.].
    p. cm. — (Linking levels of analysis)
  Includes bibliographical references and index.
  ISBN 0-472-10894-8 (acid-free paper)
   1. Agriculture and State—Mali. 2. Rural development—Mali.
  3. Land settlement—Mali. I. Diarra, Tieman. II. Sow, Moussa.
  III. Title. IV . Series.
  HD2143.5.Z8K63  1998
  338.1′86623—dc21          97-45270
                         CIP

*To the Malians who have left home and kin
to try to create better lives for all Malians.*

# Series Introduction

The series Linking Levels of Analysis focuses on studies that deal with the relationships between local-level systems and larger, more inclusive systems. While we know a great deal about how local and larger systems operate, we know a great deal less about how these levels articulate with each other. It is this kind of research, in all its variety, that Linking Levels of Analysis is designed to publish. Works should contribute to the theoretical understanding of such articulations, create or refine methods appropriate to interlevel analysis, and represent substantive contributions to the social sciences.

The volume before you, *Innovation and Individuality in African Development,* is the product of years of research in Mali by teams of scholars concerned with land settlement and resettlement programs in river blindness areas, and with the challenge of development. It is an important book because it shows with impressive empirical detail the reason for successes and failures in African development. It moves the discourse on development from the traditional focus on development planning and countrywide strategies to one in which the successes are measured in individual lives changed and improved—and in which individual farmers account for much of the success. In short, local, national, and international development agencies emerge as much as constraints as facilitators. Success emerges from the skills of farmers in benefiting from resources made available, and their ability to avoid the often high costs of the plans associated with development.

The choice of Mali is a felicitous one. Mali, one of the world's poorest countries, as measured by per capita GNP, is also poor in rainfall, and many other natural endowments. The authors show how Malians have benefited from donor programs, and they refuse to treat these farmers in the familiar exotic terms that render them powerless. In contrast, they present us with individuals who actively seek to improve their condition through mettle and wit, through critical thinking and personal skill. This demystification of Africans came about in no small part from the intimate role that Malians played in the research itself. For the Malians on the team, the farmers were people simply less fortunate than they were but hardly exotic. This in itself was a notable change from the common practice in development assistance where expatriates are dominant. They also brought a less pessimistic attitude toward efforts at development than their jaded Western counterparts, often schooled in armchair critiques of development that fail to ask the poor how they really feel about foreign assistance. Malian culture and traditions were seen to be far more flexible and changing than outsiders may have recognized. In fact, the authors make the important point that in the very process of changing, the farmers affirmed how they were just "following tradition." Adapting and changing *is* tradition.

The choice of a sample of villages also contributed to the emergence of a view that played down the presence of a unitary culture, and privileged the diversity of communities, and the variability of farmer response. Even within the same ethnic group it was clear that there were important differences in how they farmed, what constituted a large household, and how resources were partitioned among household members. Response to innovation under these conditions was also varied. Just as these farmers manifested classic resistance to externally induced introduction of innovations, they just as vigorously pursued endogenously driven experiments in innovation. This is because local actors valued food self-sufficiency and felt they needed to control the process to ensure their own provisioning. This was best ensured through maintenance of a diversified strategy, rather than promises that through simplification of cropping bumper harvests would result. Farmers have always been suspicious of government promises in this regard, and with good reason. Sahelian farmers know all too well the marginality of their region for agriculture, and value diversification, food security, and other means to ensure that they live to next year. The role of the state in this setting must perforce be a flexible one, just as farmers must stay flexible to cope with unpredictable droughts. Policymakers, development planners, extension agents, and social scientists have a lot to learn from this book.

It is my hope that this volume will be read widely by those who see it as their mission in life to "assist others." Good intentions have never been sufficient to ensure that others are not harmed by our good intentions. Humility in proffering advice to farmers should be the rule rather than the exception, and advice should be given that provides farmers with plenty of room for them to reject it. The awesome responsibility to provide for one's household with needed food should be kept foremost in mind as an antidote for the pretensions of knowledge that need not bear the consequences of erroneous application of knowledge. There is a great deal of wisdom in this book about how farmers in West Africa respond to change, cope with drought and disease, and interact with those who would help them. The sophistication with which people everywhere today are affected by the international global economy and still manage to preserve their dignity and a measure of their autonomy speaks profoundly about the complex linkages and processes that have always made human lives a rich linking of levels of analysis.

We hope this book inspires some readers to submit their work to the series. Please contact the series editor or other members of the editorial board to discuss your work and our possible interest in publishing it.

*Editor*
Emilio F. Moran, Department of Anthropology, Indiana University, Bloomington

*Editorial Board*
John Bowen, Department of Anthropology, Washington University, St. Louis
Conrad Kottak, Department of Anthropology, University of Michigan
Kathleen Newman, Department of Anthropology, Columbia University
Douglas White, Department of Anthropology, University of California, Irvine

# Contents

# Illustrations

Figures

Maps

Tables

# Acknowledgments

The work presented here began as applied research for development purposes. Most of the primary data was gathered under the auspices of two contracts to the Institute for Development Anthropology. The first, funded by the United Nations Development Programme and executed by the World Bank, provided data on five sites and had as its goal a deeper understanding of land-settlement activities in the Onchocerciasis Control Programme (OCP) zones. The second, which funded research at Manantali, was from the United States Agency for International Development (USAID) as part of the Manantali Resettlement Project (625-0955). In addition, the Mellon Fund of the College of Arts and Sciences at American University provided funds to edit French-language site reports. These individual reports formed an important first step toward comparative analysis of change processes in the different zones.

Yet formal funding was not enough. The research could not have been done without the help of many in Mali. First and foremost, we would like to thank the personnel of the OCP Western Zone, Bamako, for doing much to expedite the work, both logistically and by sharing their knowledge of the characteristics of Mali's onchocerciasis zones. We would also like to thank Dr. Issiaka Niambelé, the Malian National Coordinator of the OCP, and Denis Traoré, then Directeur de Cabinet of the Ministry of Plan, who facilitated contacts with other national agencies. Aliou Coulibaly and Soriba Keita of the Cellule Oncho at the Ministry of Plan also shared their experiences and pointed out valuable literature, much in the Ministry's Documentation Center.

In the field, the *commandants de cercle* and *chefs d'arrondissement* of all sites were extremely helpful, as were the village chiefs and councils in all the study villages. We would especially like to thank André Sangaré, Noumoutié Sangaré, and Ali Yalcoué, all particularly helpful in Yanfolila; Soungalo Coulibaly, head of the OCP Sikasso sector; and Youssouf Diarra, head of the Bougouni sector. At Manantali, Garan Konaré, head of the Senegal River Basin Authority office, and Mahamadou Sidibé, then Associate Director of the Direction Nationale de l'Hydraulique et de l'Energie and acting head of the Manantali Resettlement Project, offered much assistance.

For aid in Bamako, we would like to thank Klena Sanogo, Director of the

Institut des Sciences Humaines, and Mamadou Coulibaly and Dennis Bilodeau of USAID, who facilitated many aspects of our research. We also want to thank Idrissa Bagayoko, whose hours behind the wheel driving the teams to and from the research sites allowed us to complete the study within a rather strict time frame. Kalilou Tigana and Mamary Traoré computerized the data very efficiently.

Back in the United States, Vera Beers-Tyler of the Institute for Development Anthropology made sure things ran smoothly. Michael Horowitz, Ted Scudder, and David Brokensha all were instrumental in providing intellectual leadership. Della McMillan and Tom Painter ran the overall project; Della provided much expertise and insight based on her long-term experience in OCP zones, and Tom gave ever-wise counsel. Della also gave many useful comments on the final manuscript. Alice Willard offered a disinterested, critical perspective on several versions of the manuscript as well as many practical editing suggestions.

This work would never have been achieved without the funding from the different donors and the support of these and many other people; we appreciate the many comments and suggestions to improve our work. Ultimately, though, we remain responsible for what is presented here. The views in this work are our own and do not necessarily reflect those of our funders or employers.

# *Acronyms*

AFRAM      Association pour la Formation et la Réinsertion des Africains
           Migrants
           Association for Training and Reintegration of Migrant Africans
AV         Association Villageoise
           Village Association
BCR        Bureau Central de Recensement
           Central Census Bureau
CAF        Cost, insurance, freight
CAMSEL     Coopérative Agricole Multifonctionelle de Selingue
           Multipurpose Agricultural Cooperative of Selingue
CAMUKO     Coopérative Agricole Multifonctionelle de Kokolon
           Multipurpose Agricultural Cooperative of Kokolon
CECI       Centre Canadien d'Etudes et de Coopération Internationale
           Canadian Center for Research and International Cooperation
CFDT       Compagnie Française pour le Développement des Fibres
           Textiles
           French Company for Textile Development
CILSS      Comité Permanent Inter-Etats de Lutte contre la Sécheresse
           dans le Sahel
           Permanent Interstate Committee to Fight
           the Sahel Drought
CMDT       Compagnie Malienne de Développement des Textiles
           Malian Company for Textile Development
COMATEX    Compagnie Malienne des Textiles
           Malian Textile Company
DNAFLA     Direction Nationale de l'Alphabétisation Fonctionnelle et de la
           Linguistique Appliquée
           National Directorate for Functional Literacy and Applied
           Linguistics
DNAS       Direction Nationale des Affaires Sociales
           National Directorate for Social Affairs

| | |
|---|---|
| DNCT | Direction Nationale de la Cartographie et de la Topographie, Mali |
| | National Directorate for Cartography and Topography |
| DNEF | Direction Nationale des Eaux et Forêts |
| | National Directorate for Water and Forests |
| DNHE | Direction Nationale de l'Hydraulique et de l'Energie |
| | National Directorate for Water and Power |
| ECBM | Entreprise pour la Construction du Barrage de Manantali |
| | Enterprise for the Construction of the Manantali Dam |
| FAO | United Nations Food and Agriculture Organization |
| FCFA | African Financial Community franc |
| FF | French franc |
| FM | Malian franc |
| FOB | Free on board |
| IDA | Institute for Development Anthropology |
| IER | Institut d'Economie Rurale |
| | Rural Economy Institute |
| IGN | Institut Géographique National, Paris, France |
| | National Geographic Institute |
| IMF | International Monetary Fund |
| ISH | Institut des Sciences Humaines |
| | Institute of Human Sciences |
| MATDB | Ministère de l'Administration Territoriale et du Développement à la Base |
| | Ministry of Territorial Administration and Local Development |
| NGO | Nongovernmental organization |
| OA | Opération Arachide |
| | Operation Peanut |
| OACV | Opération Arachide et Cultures Vivrières |
| | Operation Peanut and Food Crops |
| OCP | Onchocerciasis Control Programme |
| ODIMO | Opération de Développement Intégré du Mali Ouest |
| | Integrated Development Operation of Western Mali |
| ODIPAC | Opération de Développement Intégré des Productions Arachidières et Céréalières |
| | Integrated Development Operation for Peanut and Cereal Production |
| ODR | Opération de Développement Rural |
| | Rural Development Operation |

| | |
|---|---|
| OECD | Organization for Economic Cooperation and Development |
| OERHN | Office de l'Exploitation des Ressources de Haut Niger |
| | Office for the Exploitation of the Resources of the Upper Niger |
| OHV(N) | Opération de la Haute Vallée (du Niger) |
| | Operation of the Upper Valley of the Niger |
| OMVS | Organisation pour la Mise en Valeur du Fleuve Sénégal |
| | Senegal River Basin Authority |
| OPAM | Office des Produits Agricoles du Mali |
| | Office of Malian Agricultural Products |
| PIRT | Projet Inventaire des Ressources Terrestres |
| | Project to Inventory Land Resources |
| PRM | Projet pour la Réinstallation des Populations de Manantali |
| | Manantali Resettlement Project |
| PRMC | Programme de Restructuration du Marché Céréalier |
| | Program to Restructure the Cereal Market |
| SCAER | Société du Crédit Agricole et de l'Equipement Rural |
| | Society for Agricultural Credit and Rural Equipment |
| SECAMA | Secours Catholique du Mali |
| | Catholic Relief in Mali |
| SEPOM | Société pour l'Exploitation des Produits Oléagineux du Mali |
| | Society for the Exploitation of Malian Oil Products |
| SOMIEX | Société Malienne d'Importation et d'Exportation |
| | Malian Import and Export Society |
| TAMS | Tippetts-Abbett-McCarthy-Stratton |
| UDPM | Union Démocratique du Peuple Malien |
| | Democratic Union of the Malian People |
| UNDP | United Nations Development Programme |
| UNJM | Union National des Jeunes du Mali |
| | National Union of Malian Youth |
| USAID | United States Agency for International Development |
| WFP | United Nations World Food Programme |
| WHO | World Health Organization |

Map 1. International and regional boundaries of Mali. (From IGN 3615, Map of Mali 1:2,000,000 [1993]. Copyright IGN, Paris, and DNCT, Bamako.)

Chapter 1

# Demystifying African Farmers

African countries remain among the world's poorest and least developed even though national governments and international agencies have pursued a variety of development strategies since at least 1960, when many African countries became independent. Although each initiative began with great hope, few have proven successful over the long term, leading both intellectuals and practitioners to question the development process. We offer this book in the belief that development remains possible but needs new perspectives to link analysis and action.

This study looks at a group of related successes and failures to see what insights they can offer to improve analysis and ameliorate action. In particular, it suggests the importance of a renewed emphasis on human agency and individual choice. While existing frameworks show how structures constrain actions through historic and contemporary processes, they have deemphasized the scope for human initiative and choice. Yet individuals choose, negotiate, and innovate, even within the constraints imposed by local, national, and international structures. In this volume, we use an extended case study of agricultural production in Mali, one of the world's poorest countries, to show how the use of complementary perspectives can increase our understanding and lead to better development theory and practice. As practitioners who believe that development is not only possible but essential, we think that this expanded analytic framework brings into focus issues crucial to the future of African agriculture and suggests new solutions to continuing problems.

This introductory chapter begins by discussing some of the limits to the major frameworks used thus far by anthropologists to analyze rural development. We then turn to the methodological elements that underpinned our theoretical approach. This leads to a discussion of the major concepts that oriented data analysis and presentation, and an alternative framework for looking at rural change. We end with a summary of the major issues in contemporary African agriculture that we will address, and we outline the following chapters.

## Anthropological Approaches to Development

Textbooks on the anthropology and sociology of development commonly describe two major analytic frameworks, modernization and underdevelopment theories (Long 1977; Harrison 1988; Gabriel 1991). Inspired by the classical social theories of Durkheim and Weber, modernization theory assumed explicitly or implicitly the superiority of the Western capitalist system. The goal of development programs was to encourage a country to undertake internal sociocultural and economic changes that would permit it to follow the Western model. Development was usually measured by growth in national GDP, industrialization, urbanization, and agricultural commercialization. Anthropologists expected these economic changes to be linked to sociocultural changes, such as increasing structural differentiation or new Western values (Smelser 1959; McClelland 1976). Modernization theory was criticized for its use of Western societies and economies as positive models, as well as its disregard for external historical influences. Anthropologists also criticized it for its view of traditional societies as cohesive, homogeneous, and static units antithetical to "modern" values, and its focus on the obstacles to social change (Harrison 1988, 29; Long 1977, 32).

Drawing upon Marx for inspiration, underdevelopment theorists formulated an alternative model that focused on the dynamic historical processes of capitalist exploitation and the continuing interrelationship of capitalist core and underdeveloped periphery (Frank 1967; UN 1964; Wallerstein 1979).[1] Underdevelopment theorists stressed that it was important to distribute new resources equitably, not simply to generate new wealth to be monopolized by elites. These approaches have come to dominate the development literature (Ferguson 1990), as the use of a historical framework to explain the evolution and continuing importance of the power differences between the developed and developing countries proved particularly attractive. Also compelling was the theoretical focus on inequality, class stratification, and poverty. Modernization theory per se has come to be treated mostly as an historic artifact.

Nevertheless, underdevelopment perspectives have also been criticized, first because they often said too little about "real people doing real things" (Ortner, cited in Roseberry 1988, 162). Because they focused on the actions of the West, especially colonialism and capitalist penetration, as the prime explanatory factor, external events rather than internal deficiencies were the major barriers to local development in the Third World (Roseberry 1988). Although the poor peoples of developing countries were no longer blamed for their own condition, the framework nevertheless led to a pessimistic outlook about the possibilities for positive local change (Gabriel 1991).

To meet these criticisms, two recent offshoots of underdevelopment theory have grown. First has been concerted pragmatism, focusing on local priorities and grassroots initiatives to improve local conditions, with the hope that over the long run these might lead to empowerment as well (Gran 1983). A second, somewhat newer approach, with very different consequences for activism, has been the analysis of the "discourse of development" to complement economic and social analysis (Escobar 1995; Ferguson 1990).

This section looks at three contemporary perspectives: underdevelopment theory, pragmatism, and discourse, as they have been used by development anthropologists, both analysts and practitioners. From our perspective, a major failure of all of them has been that they overwhelmingly privilege the experiences of the West as a way to understand paths of change in developing countries. By doing so, they continue to contribute to a vision of the people of developing countries as relatively homogeneous, stable, and cohesive, in ways similar to modernization theory, which they purport to critique. They continue to exoticize Third World people and construct them as "others" rather than fellow human beings.

*Underdevelopment Theory*

The emphasis of underdevelopment theory on international power relations and the external factors of colonialism and imperialism is usually seen as a contribution to deemphasizing the cultural and social differences between the First and Third Worlds. However, the emphasis on powerlessness within this paradigm has rendered those in developing countries, but the poor especially, different and exotic. This is especially clear in broad synthetic works with the explicit goal of understanding the ways in which peripheral societies were subordinated, destroyed, or absorbed by industrial capitalism. Eric Wolf's synthesis, *Europe and the People without History* (1982), for example, kept the focus clearly on the West, since its activities were the impetus for the growth of the global capitalist system. For example, Wolf's discussion of Africa centered primarily on the slave trade and secondarily on selected areas where cash-cropping became important in the early twentieth century. Since the work concerned as much the way the slave trade affected the Americas as Africa, the history of Africa was seen through an Americanized lens. The role of slavery within African societies prior to the transatlantic trade was explored only minimally and the effects of other forces during the period (e.g., the rise of Islamic revolutionary movements) not at all. Hence, the history of the zone became meaningful only as it related to a core, and people's lives in terms of their own trajectories appeared to be of little interest. Although the West was not positively evaluated, it continued to have primary importance, particularly in syntheses, which were, to be sure, about the development of the world-system it dominated. Since the depth and breadth of synthesis require a certain level of generalization, perhaps case studies might better acknowledge the ways in which local groups interacted with capitalist structures in ways that transformed them not only for the capitalist world economy, but also for themselves.

Some case studies used the concept of exploitation to focus analysis, which continued the emphasis on the core, either the capitalist West or the indigenous elite. For example, *Seeds of Famine* showed how colonial and postcolonial policies brought about the conditions leading to the Sahelian drought of 1968–74 (Franke and Chasin 1980). Contemporary production systems based on cash crops (e.g., peanuts, vegetables) were geared to the short-term profits of states and investors, the authors argued, rather than to long-term economic growth or environmental sustainability. The use of the technical improvements these systems encouraged (e.g., fertilizers, herbicides, irrigation) were seen to lead to the impoverishment of local populations and environmental degradation. Although people were willing to change, the results benefited only the Sahelian elite and the countries of the capitalist core. Despite the existence of slavery and farmer-herder tensions in precolonial societies, contemporary stratification was seen as a marked contrast to earlier "relatively prosperous and stable communities" (Franke and Chasin 1980, 61). In general, stability was evaluated more positively than change generated by capitalist growth, and technological progress was considered highly problematic. Since the growth of a capitalist world-system prevented the powerless from gaining benefits from national growth and change, the reader could conclude that it was better to avoid change and try to reconstruct precolonial patterns of action. In other words, it would be best for the rural poor of the Third World to accentuate their differences from the First World.

To introduce greater human agency into their explanatory frameworks, others working within the underdevelopment paradigm used resistance as an orienting concept. Lewis (1979), for example, saw the collective production systems of Bambara villagers in Mali as a form of resistance against the precolonial Segou state. To avoid enslavement, villagers created gerontocratic forms of labor control that allowed them to produce sufficient surplus to pay taxes. The consequent value placed on control over labor was in conflict with the contemporary world, where the adoption of new technology such as plows accentuated the accumulation of goods (i.e., crops) over labor. Their desire to conserve their ability to control labor made Bambara villages significantly less likely than their non-Bambara neighbors to adopt plows or use small-farmer credit schemes (Lewis 1978). Moreover, egalitarianism among household heads allowed them to remain successful food producers (Lewis 1979). This analysis appears to assume that food self-sufficiency at the household level is superior to crop commercialization and that egalitarianism should be more highly valued than stratification. In other words, the ideal developing country community would look very different from one in the capitalist First World. Moreover, the focus on cultural values grounded in the past may suggest that people cannot respond to new conditions or incentives, creating the impression of allegiance to tradition in a manner quite similar to what modernization theorists saw as cultural obstacles to development (Long 1977).

Practicing development anthropologists have tended to be more drawn to the concept of resistance than exploitation, possibly because it suggests more practical approaches to action. Many oriented studies around the question of why poorer populations (small farmers, small herders, etc.) refused to accept the allegedly superior practices of "modern" agriculture (Hoben 1986; Horowitz 1979; Painter 1986; Waldstein 1986). While some of these analyses focused on the specific ecological and economic conditions within developing countries that made suggested changes ineffective (Netting, Cleveland, and Stier 1980), others stressed social and cultural resistance to, or incompatibility with, new technologies (Kottak 1991). The latter approach continued to stress the differences between the rural poor in the developing world and other people. The focus on refusal to adopt new technologies, versus a more in-depth study of nonadopters alongside those who did adopt, lent itself to a view of rural Third World residents as essentially different from those in the First World.

*The Pragmatic Perspective*

Many development practitioners, persuaded by the descriptive analyses of underdevelopment theory, were nevertheless dispirited by its prescriptions. Committed to the belief that conditions could improve in developing countries, they found themselves in a quandary: how to accept the inequalities between the First and Third Worlds while nonetheless moving toward better quality of life in the latter. How could the inhabitants of the Third World gain the advantages of technological progress and industrial growth faced with an antagonistic superstructure? Thus began the search for a more pragmatic "third way" to approach development. Although there were many varieties of this approach, most emphasized working from the bottom up, that is, from the priorities and capacities of those it intended to benefit.

Among the best known of these approaches were those that stressed local participation (Uphoff 1991) and the use of indigenous knowledge (Brokensha, Warren, and Werner 1980; Richards 1985). As a practical strategy, many suggested working small, using local resources (Franke and Chasin 1980) and existing forms of local organization (Gran 1983). Anthropologists and sociologists were likely to recommend building on their empirical field traditions as a route to a more "realistic" approach (Harrison 1988; Gabriel 1991). Many cited the success of the Grameen bank as an example of the long-term potential for change inherent in this approach (Holcombe 1995).

Many who used this approach accepted the historical analyses presented by underdevelopment theories but pinned their designs for future development more on cultural independence than economic autonomy. Linking his proposals to earlier African thinkers who proposed basing development on specifically African institutions (e.g., Nyerere 1968), Mazrui (1986, 295) suggested that Africa needed to look inward toward its ancestors even while gaining inspiration from the wider world. Practitioners also linked suggested actions to an underlying assumption that local systems of thought were different from those used by developers. For example, indigenous technical knowledge could be contrasted with scientific knowledge. The former was more "concrete" and relied almost exclusively on intuition and evidence of direct senses, while science had a greater ability to break down and reassemble its data. Science was an "open system," while indigenous technical knowledge was closed, and showed a lack of awareness of other ways of seeing the world (Howes and Chambers 1979, 5). As Gran stated, "Foreigners have different world models" (1983, 32).

By stressing the cultural differences between First and Third World, many of these approaches ended up with a perspective similar to earlier modernization theorists. Although authors generally worked from a framework that stressed the historical growth of inequalities between First and Third World, they stressed sociocultural obstacles to development at least as often as political resistance to change. Swanson (1980, 67), for example, said that "new developments must be based on Gourma perceptions, not on foreign concepts, if they are to succeed." He continued, "programs should not include elements of risk or experimentation, as failure would encourage people to believe their destiny was against such activities." Kottak maintained that the goals and values of subsistence-oriented smallholders were different from those who produced for cash: "Their goals are not abstractions such as 'learning a better way,' 'progressing,' 'increasing technical know-how,' 'improving efficiency,' 'adopting modern techniques' or 'preserving biodiversity.' Rather, their objectives are concrete, limited, and specific" (1991, 438). The evidence for these generalizations was not always clear.

This approach differed from earlier modernization theory in its positive valuation of "tradition" and the past. Where modernization theorists had seen traditional values implicitly or explicitly as inferior, contemporary advocates of cultural difference found them at least equivalent and sometimes superior. Gran (1983, 287), for example, could say, "it is the peasants who are rational, not the planners."

There were other voices among those using bottom-up approaches. Richards (1985), for example, emphasized the ways in which indigenous and scientific knowledges could build on and support one another, while Swift (1979, 43) stressed that rural people needed also to gain an adequate grasp of modern knowledge and technology. Brokensha and Riley (1980, 127) noted that not all local beliefs were valid. Yet enough analysts used the allegedly pragmatic analysis of sociocultural traditions in ways that romanticized or reified "tradition" and the past that the trend toward exoticizing rather than humanizing the rural poor continued. The emphasis on a shared cultural past also continued the trend of looking at past societies as cohesive, homogeneous, and stable. People were often viewed primarily as members of groups, rather than as individuals, ignoring the importance of human choice in cultural stability and change.

## The Discourse of Development

Recently, anthropologists focusing on "the discourse of development" have tried more explicitly to meld the recognition of historical political inequality with a respect for cultures, both "traditional" and "modern." Inspired by Foucault's work, these authors (Escobar 1995; Ferguson 1990) attempted to understand how projects that purportedly intended to achieve one goal, development, arrived instead at contradictory results. While many underdevelopment theorists located the failure of development initiatives in the hidden agendas and interests of international donors and national elites, theorists concentrating on the discourse of development are inclined to accept that many development practitioners believe in their stated goals. They show, instead, how the dominant discourse produced a structure of knowledge that permitted only some problems to be seen and, hence, addressed.

From this perspective, a significant source of inequality in development initiatives came from the political control exercised by those who structured the discourse, namely, development economists and planners from international institutions like the World Bank (Escobar 1995), bilateral donor countries, or national governments (Ferguson 1990). Program results reflected international and domestic political-economic inequalities and allowed for further penetration of state and capitalist market relations into rural areas. Local people often resisted this incorporation, using the tools available to them, often aspects of "traditional" cultural repertoires. One of the strengths of this approach is the way that it revealed certain seemingly "traditional" practices to be rooted in strikingly contemporary situations. Ferguson's (1990) discussion of the "bovine mystique," for example, showed that the reluctance of Basotho rural inhabitants to sell cattle was linked not only to ongoing conflicts between men and women, youth and elderly, but also to the way in which migrant wage laborers constituted a retirement fund.

The discourse of development was able to hide the political ramifications of its actions, however, because it was framed in neutral terminology that depoliticized interventions (Ferguson 1990). The growth of development economics as a "science" produced a structure that created "underdeveloped" economies and the problems within them (poverty, environmental degradation, etc.) that only "experts" could attempt to solve (Escobar 1995). It is questionable, however, whether the discourse of development masked power issues as effectively as its proponents have argued. Ferguson (1990) indeed made a strong case for depoliticization in rural Lesotho, but both Malian peasants and elites were very clear about the political consequences of development initiatives. As we will discuss in chapter 3, Malian agricultural policy has been clearly oriented around two forms of national control: the peasantry on the one hand, and donor-furnished resources on the other.

The discourse approach problematizes the concepts of modernity, science, technology, and the state, a worthy enterprise to be sure, since modern technology and scientific progress should not be regarded uncritically. Yet both Escobar (1995) and Ferguson (1990) criticized new resources, technology, and state power in terms quite foreign to many poor, even though Escobar (1995, 145) did note that some people's lives improved in light of development interventions. Rural Malians seemed rather more ready to appreciate what they saw as the benefits of both technology and the state. Infant mortality decreased from 204 per thousand births in 1973 to 157 per thousand in 1993 because of better health services, mostly provided by donors and the state, while adult literacy increased from 10 percent in 1976 to 32 percent in 1990 because of state-provided primary schools and adult education programs (World Bank 1981b, 134; 1995, 162, 214).

Clearly, there is room for political debate about the best course for future social change, but the way the discourse of development argument has been phrased seems to have once again had the effect of exoticizing and rendering different the people of developing countries, despite intentions to the contrary. Not only are the poor simply less powerful than elites, but they become powerless (Ferguson 1990). Group action through progressive social movements, for example, is again valorized over, rather than alongside, individual attempts to create better lives. Hybrid cultures, created by people who resist by mixing new and old, dominant and resistant, may be a possible alternative to capitalist hegemony (Escobar 1995), but it is not clear how this process is any different from the cultural syntheses peoples universally engage in when they have multiple cultural repertoires with which to work. Focusing on those aspects of culture that divide the poor from the rich and the center from the periphery accentuates difference, conflict, and resistance as opposed to cooperation, collaboration, or working for mutual self-interest. Moreover, common humanity is lost.

*Toward a New Synthesis*

Any approach that exoticizes the citizens of developing countries is theoretically deficient because it continues an anthropological stance that objectifies research subjects. As the discourse of development perspective suggests, these approaches are also pragmatically deficient because they render researchers and practitioners blind to aspects of social life that do not correspond to accepted knowledge structures. They ignore, as already stated, "real people doing real things" (Ortner, cited in Roseberry 1988, 162), and real individuals making real-life decisions and choices.

As historical description, theories that focus on economic and symbolic inequality do provide a suitable framework for beginning to understand the range of choices open to people in different parts of the world-system. However, they underestimate the possibilities for, and effects of, individual choice within structures of domination as well as among those dominated. No single group is ever in complete control of the system, no single discourse completely dominant. Individuals in more powerful places often contest among themselves system goals as well as the strategies to reach them. Discord among the more powerful can create niches for action among those with less power, making the range of possible actions greater than the structure or the discourse might suggest. Individual, as well as group, attempts to make use of autonomous spaces sometimes have consequences for the system as a whole, both to the benefit and detriment of those at the bottom.

Practitioners who argue that pragmatic bottom-up approaches create development possibilities among those who thus far have reaped the least benefits have also begun to reorient development programs in a useful way. However, these approaches too would benefit from an increased focus on human agency and a perspective that sees individuals manipulating and contesting their own cultural systems. Groups at the bottom are not necessarily cohesive or stable but are composed of living, active human beings confronted with and making choices about their lives. They negotiate with others, experiment with new technical and social forms, and sometimes make changes that have larger societal impacts.

We have tried to develop a conceptual framework that captures the specific experiences of rural Malians and their place in the global world-system while simultaneously recognizing the common human problems they confront and the individual and collective ways they have dealt with them. The remainder of this chapter addresses this approach. We begin with an overview of the study and then turn to methodological and analytic issues.

Study Background and Context

This study began as applied research whose goal was to provide information to the Onchocerciasis Control Programme (OCP) so that it could improve its own socioeconomic development initiatives. The OCP, funded by multiple donors and implemented primarily through the World Health Organization (WHO), began in 1974 as a program to control the spread of one chronic disease, onchocerciasis, or river blindness, found in much of savanna West Africa. The first phase, which concentrated on chemical spraying to kill the major disease vector, black fly, took place in seven West African countries, including Mali. OCP strategies for fly control changed over time, as the project moved from more toxic (e.g., DDT) to less toxic, biodegradable chemicals. In 1986, the area covered by the OCP expanded to include more areas in existing countries and four new ones. Disease prevention strategies changed in the 1980s as well, as the development of the drug ivermectin for humans led the OCP to begin patient treatment alongside fly control (Eckholm 1989).

The OCP was not interested in disease control simply for its own sake but also wanted to improve the possibilities for socioeconomic development in the West Africa savanna by rendering underpopulated river basins habitable. Some countries, for example, Burkina Faso, began settlement and economic-development programs in the onchocerciasis-controlled zones, attracting significant donor investment (McMillan 1983; J. Murphy and Sprey 1980). In 1986, donors and participating countries approved a systematic assessment of the nature and scope of development opportunities resulting from onchocerciasis control. A preparatory study was undertaken by Hunting Technical Services (1988) and completed in 1988. This was followed by other studies to describe existing settlement experiences and make recommendations for new initiatives, funded by the United Nations Development Programme (UNDP) and executed by the World Bank. Carried out by the Institute for Development Anthropology (IDA), the studies looked in depth at four countries (Burkina Faso, Togo, Ghana, and Mali) and more cursorily at the experiences of the other seven (McMillan, Painter, and Scudder 1990). One goal was to use these as the basis for further national development studies in each of the participating countries.

Based on the IDA Mali study, this book draws upon the same data as the initial reports (T. Diarra et al. 1989; Koenig 1990). Dolores Koenig was hired by IDA to organize this work, carried out by the Institut des Sciences Humaines (ISH), a research organization of the Malian government, now part of the Ministry of Secondary and Higher Education and Scientific Research. Koenig and the ISH social scientists designed the study collaboratively, and Tiéman Diarra, head of the ISH Ethno-Sociology Department, served as team leader. He and Moussa Sow, then ISH associate director, were responsible for site selection and study organization. The team worked in at least three villages at each of five sites with different settlement contexts during May and June 1989. All reports, and this book as well, included a sixth settlement site, Manantali, where dam resettlement had been studied in the mid-1980s by IDA anthropologists (including Koenig) as well as ISH social scientists (T. Diarra et al. 1990; Horowitz et al. 1993).[2]

In addition to the country-level study, the team produced six individual site reports: Yanfolila (T. Diarra, Simaga, and Koenig 1992); Finkolo (Koné, Maiga, and Koenig 1992); Tienfala (Sow and Koenig 1992); Selingue (Fofana, Simaga, and Koenig 1992); Dioïla (O. Diarra and Koenig 1992); and Manantali (Koenig 1992). These made information from the study more widely available in Mali. The team believed, however, that insights from the study would be valuable to a wider audience beyond those interested in onchocerciasis or Malian agriculture. As the only native speaker of English, Koenig took on the task of turning the various pieces into a single book in English.

Mali was chosen for in-depth study because its experiences were quite different from what the OCP imagined the typical development situation to be. Most notably, there were no large free tracts of land waiting to be settled by farmers once onchocerciasis was controlled. In fact, most of the Malian population (59 percent) already lived in zones with onchocerciasis. The OCP zones included what was by far the most developed part of rural Mali, the area in which agricultural extension was carried out by the Compagnie Malienne de Développement des Textiles (CMDT). Most people appeared to assume that blindness was a typical characteristic of old people, especially old men, although they did avoid settling in pockets of severe onchocerciasis. Despite the lack of "empty land," there was substantial immigration into Mali's OCP areas for reasons unrelated to onchocerciasis control, including drought conditions further north, the repatriation of Malians previously working in foreign countries, and the continual search for better economic opportunities. Hence, the study zones offered a chance for a cross-sectional study of rural-to-rural migration in contemporary Mali.

Research design and data collection parameters were specified by the OCP, and research and analysis were done under rather strict financial and time constraints. The study directors elaborated a core of information to be collected in a relatively structured fashion to facilitate comparison among different sites in Mali, as well as among the four different countries. Each site was staffed by one or two ISH social scientists working with interviewers. Insofar as possible, samples were selected randomly from all migrant households (or, in a few cases, all indigenous households) in a village. The focus was on agricultural production and associated livestock and off-farm activities, but teams also gathered information on household demographics and migration histories. They carried out group interviews on village-level issues with women and men separately. In many ways, this study methodology was quite standard for agricultural production and development studies in the West African savanna.

Yet sites were chosen to maximize diversity, and within sites, villages were chosen purposefully to capture a variety of situations. Although households were the major unit of inquiry, the team worked under the assumption that they were heterogeneous units, with multiple field owners, multiple budgets, and potentially different sets of vested interests. Information was gathered about women and their fields as well as about men and theirs, and some attempt was made to gather individual budgets. On the teams where women were included, they did most of the research on women. Researchers kept informal field notes to help interpret the structured information on the questionnaires and to pursue particular research concerns. Team members also complemented this core methodology to pursue their own interests and to capture a richer set of data. The agricultural economist on the team, for example, collected more technical agricultural information, while the geographer did more mapping and descriptions of village landscapes. More detailed information on the structure and content of the study will be presented in chapter 4 when we address study data directly.

Methodological Perspectives

Our search for new perspectives began with a desire to counter the popular image of Africa as exotic, a place perceived not only as different, but also difficult to know. The popular media reflect this exoticism in images that focus on the extraordinary, either positive or negative. On the positive side, Mali may be known for its past, the "glorious age in Africa" (Chu and Skinner 1965), since the boundaries of the contemporary country overlap those of the historic savanna empires of Ghana, Mali, and Songhay. The city of Timbuktu, at the southern edge of the Sahara desert, and once a center of Islamic learning, continues to symbolize the different and exotic. For example, one West African travel guide notes that "Timbuktu was (and still is) the terminus of a camel caravan route across the Sahara that has linked Arabia with black Africa since ancient times" (Newton and Else 1995, 519). On the negative side, Africa is seen as a center of civil disturbance, famine, and natural disaster. Mali sometimes made it into the popular press through its natural disasters, for example, the Sahel drought followed by a plague of locusts (Ellis 1987). Sometimes, people knew it because of its poverty, high infant mortality, growing deforestation, and economic difficulties. Whether positive or negative, the images accentuated the differences between Malians and Westerners.

Since the popular media used these exotic images to generate audience interest, one might expect that academics and development practitioners would stress more mundane ones. Yet much of contemporary social science has also used images of exoticism and difference, and as Ferguson (1990) has noted, so too has the project of development. How, then do we deexoticize them? We began with research strategies that pushed us toward a view of Malian activities as everyday and banal. These strategies were (1) the international nature of the team; (2) long-term field experience; and (3) the inclusion of multiple sites in the study.

*International Collaborative Research*

The collaborative nature of the study design and data analysis helped pull the team as a whole toward an analytic approach that deemphasized the exoticism of rural Malians. For the Malian researchers on the team, rural Malians were not exotic, but poorer members of their own country and culture, a perspective consistent with much of Malian social science. Using the same range of analytic paradigms as their Western counterparts, African social scientists have tried to tie the differences they found between urban and rural Africans, or between Africans and Westerners, to concrete explanatory factors rather than images of difference. The writings of some earlier Malian researchers elucidate the distinctive approaches of local researchers, who often worked within the same paradigms used by Western social scientists during the same time period.

Bokar N'Diayé, one of Mali's first social scientists, used the general framework of structural functionalism. One of his major publications, *Groupes Ethniques au Mali,* dedicated a chapter to each of Mali's major ethnic groups, drawing primarily on already published work by other historians and anthropologists (N'Diayé 1970). In ways quite in line with the paradigm, each chapter touched briefly in turn on language, political organization, legal traditions, social organization, marriage, inheritance, beliefs, ceremonies, production systems, and so forth, and finally on "characteristic traits" of each group. He stressed the homogeneity within each group, most notably in each concluding section on characteristic traits, which sometimes led to stereotyping, for example, "The Bambara is by nature very enthusiastic" (142). However, while his approach drew on the distinction between "traditional" and "modern" used by Western authors, he departed from them in two significant ways.

First, he paid much more attention to history and began each chapter with a discussion of the origins and precolonial history of the group. These were presented not as legends, but as possible historical fact, with concrete dates where possible. Although he recognized that some of the history was distorted or unprovable, he did not suggest that these were simply imagined charters of origin. Secondly, he evaluated modern and traditional Africans quite differently than did Western anthropologists. For example, the French anthropologist Griaule (1965, 1) had been attracted by the isolation and backwardness of the Dogon he studied. He preferred the richness of tradition or "'authentic' custom" and found African intellectuals "no longer authentically African" (Clifford 1988, 88). In contrast, although N'Diayé (1970, 476, 477) feared that Malians had lost their traditional moral emphasis on human dignity and solidarity, he was strongly in favor of greater social equality and scientific and technical progress. He envisaged a transformed Mali, where traditional social divisions had been suppressed, an industrial base had transformed artisanal production, women were emancipated, information could circulate freely, and people had a new consciousness of themselves as Malians, rather than as Bambara, Dogon, and so on (N'Diayé 1970, 475). Struggling with an intellectual paradigm that stressed the gap between the traditional and the modern, however, he could only offer Malians the hope that they would somehow find a way to blend the best of both worlds. He refused to exoticize contemporary Malian rural traditions, but in so doing, his paradigm required him to accentuate the differences between them and the past.

With the growth of underdevelopment theory, most Malian social scientists, like others in the Third World, turned to it as the most useful analytic framework. However, they tended to concentrate much more on the Malian political experience than on inequalities with the West, as shown by the collection of essays *Mali: Le paysan et l'état* (Jacquemot 1981), whose four authors focused on the inequalities in their own country. For example, when Dembélé (1981, 120) wanted to understand why many Malian farmers refused to cultivate cash crops, he looked at the actions of the "petit bourgeois" who allied with farmers before independence but turned around to exploit them afterward. Kébé (1981) and Dembélé (1981) both analyzed the ways that farmers financially supported the administration through the high fees imposed by cash crops, while M. Cissé (1981) showed that state enterprises created a new kind of feudalism through corruption, despite socialist ideals. These authors saw farmer and administrator as part of the same national culture; economic conflicts of interest between them were indicative of class struggle rather than cultural differences (Dembélé 1981, 129).

Secondly, unlike some outsiders who appeared to evaluate positively resistance to technological change, the authors of the essays generally valued both change and technological progress highly. Despite the fact that capitalist expansion gave Mali few benefits, the authors nevertheless pinned their hope for the country's future on new technology, including irrigated agriculture to provide food security (Kébé 1981, 40; Dembélé 1981, 117). Kébé (1981) noted the importance of agricultural equipment and chemical inputs to improve production and approved of the growth in peasant farmer consumption (through the purchase of bicycles or radios) and investment in livestock. They also refused to romanticize their past; Dembélé (1981, 105) in particular criticized the "quasi-idyllic exaltation of the village community by Malian nationalists."

Malian social scientists, like Western ones, also struggled with the pessimism inherent in underdevelopment approaches and looked for pragmatic alternatives. By the 1980s, some were committed to locally generated bottom-up development, an approach that appeared officially in Mali's 1981–85 Five-Year Plan as "développement à la base" (Cellule Oncho 1984, 12). The Malian approach to *développement à la base* crystallized around discussions about the potential of the *ton,* a local institution, as a means to generate development. In many areas of Mali, unmarried and married men to approximately the age of 35, as well as unmarried women (generally less than 20 years old, since most were married by then) performed collective agricultural work using this organization. Older male members ran it; younger men did the physical labor; and young women brought food to workers, often dancing or singing to urge them to greater effort. The money the *ton* earned for their work was often used at the end of the year for a villagewide celebration.[3]

Believing that collective development efforts were politically and economically preferable, Malian socialists in the 1960s tried to use the *ton* to institute collective production and pave the way to collectivized socialist agriculture. Although this attempt was a dismal failure (Jones 1976),[4] the idea of using the *ton* for development goals did not die. In the 1980s, when development organizations began to experiment with group lending, they looked again to the *ton* as an existing local institution that could be adapted to new ends. This new *ton* was different from the traditional one, as it included mainly heads of households, but like it was meant to express villagewide solidarity and include all village households. Local social scientists entered the discussion about what local institutions could be adapted to new ends, but they rarely either romanticized or reified local "traditional" community structures.

Some saw the use of local community structures simply as an effective practical strategy to reach wider development goals (such as more effective use of commercial credit to increase production) where the local resource base was poor. The *ton* was only one of a number of old and new associations that could carry out development initiatives, such as local land management or identification and implementation of pilot projects (Cellule Oncho 1984; I. Cissé, Coulibaly, and Sow 1989; S. Traoré 1989). Others noted that local, indigenously developed institutions were a response to specific local constraints, likely to change when those constraints did. Kassogué (1990), for example, showed how use of soil and water conservation techniques on the Dogon plateau waxed and waned with rainfall, much used when rainfall was short but not when it increased. Others were critical of the use of local organizations. Dembélé (1981) discussed the contradictions inherent in the idea that the *ton* could be a real vehicle for local development while it was simultaneously directed by the party apparatus. He saw its rehabilitation by the Union Démocratique du Peuple Malien (UDPM), the single legal party during Moussa Traoré's regime, as yet another piece of evidence for the class struggle between elites and the Malian people.

Only rarely did an author suggest that it was "important to return to old African principles" of social versus individual organization (Coulibaly 1986, 129). Much more commonly, Malian social scientists saw rural institutions as part of a contemporary cultural repertoire that included new and old together. While they valued and recognized their own history more than did foreign social scientists, they were also less likely to idealize it. For them, Malian "tradition" was as subject to flexibility, change, and inequality as were more specifically "modern" institutions. They recognized international inequalities but preferred to focus on an arena where they could have an impact, their own country.

The emphasis by Malian social scientists on the centrality of their own national experience was continued by the Malian team members here. Since they shared a national culture and language, Malian farmers did not appear exotic to them. In turn, Malian social scientists did not appear particularly exotic to the American since we shared professional interests and language. These separate linkages created the context for the American social scientist to perceive the ordinariness of Malian farmers and their problems as well.

Working together as a team also had pragmatic advantages. The varying skills of the team members increased the scope of data available. Many activities in rural Mali remain highly sex-segregated, and the mix of male and female team members allowed the team access to both men and women. The Malian team members all had impeccable local-language skills, so that interpreters were not necessary. Each Malian team member also had an individual social network that allowed access to a variety of administrative sources, while the American team member's English-language skills and status as a foreigner gave access to yet another set. The diverse networks allowed us to get background information in a more efficient fashion than if any one of us had done it alone. The same multiplier effects occurred in data analysis, as team members brought a diverse set of theoretical and methodological orientations. The fact that we were all conversant with the language and issues of modern social science gave us an international language of disciplinary discourse and created fertile ground for discussion, increasing the analytic perspectives considered.

Nevertheless, the single most important effect of working on an international team with local social scientists was to make the Malian experience the center of our analysis. Although we all recognized the historical development of the capitalist world-system and its resulting inequalities as one factor limiting possibilities in contemporary Mali, we looked closely at other, more Mali-centered factors as well.

*Long-Term Field Experience*

The second aspect of study methodology that pushed us to see certain aspects of rural society was the depth of experience of the team members, most of whom had been working in rural Mali for at least 10 years. To be sure, none of us had done so continuously, for our field styles were dictated by the contemporary working conditions of applied anthropologists. In contrast to more academically oriented anthropologists, development practitioners, both international consultants and national experts, tend to go to the field for short periods of time, but often. This fieldwork style does limit the ability to get certain kinds of data (Finan and van Willigen 1991). It is, for example, difficult to follow closely a single dispute through its various stages to a resolution, investigating thoroughly the different points of view. It can also be difficult to gauge the reliability of different informants or sort effectively through different versions of a single account. Nevertheless, intermittent long-term fieldwork does have advantages, both practical and intellectual.

The depth of field experience allowed us to spend less time on preliminaries and to begin data collection quickly. We all had developed acceptable cultural styles for putting rural Malians at ease, mainly because both researchers and informants could work within one cultural framework of discourse.[5] When confronted with outliers, we could relatively accurately differentiate among interviewer mistakes, interesting innovations, and areas where we needed more information. Our long-term experience led us to understand better the patterned ways in which people were likely to overestimate or, more commonly, underestimate. Previous experience had given us all much knowledge about the larger institutional and political structures affecting rural Malians that we could use to interpret quantitative and qualitative information collected during a single field period. Again teamwork was important, for these evaluations were rarely based on the judgment of one team member only.

Long-term experience also had the potential to create a perspective on anthropological subjects quite different from that of traditional individual participant observation. It allowed a researcher to move from the phase of learning about a culture like a child, an analogy often used by American researchers, to that of interacting in the culture like an adult (Clifford 1988). This had the effect of making culture appear less cohesive and made variation and heterogeneity more apparent. Using the words of development projects, it led us to view culture as a framework rather than a blueprint. Culture gave people a series of parameters within and across which they negotiated, but it was by no means determinative of their actions. People regularly disregarded and acted counter to cultural ideals, leading to a significant amount of behavioral variation. We could see more clearly the ways in which people manipulated rather than followed their cultural categories.

Recognition of variation led in turn to a greater focus on individuals as active choosers, who often chose change. It is sometimes difficult to see informants in this role, since people often maintain that they are not changing their behavior when they are actually doing so quite radically. Scudder and Colson (1979) observed this stance among the Gwembe Tonga, and it was quite marked in Mali as well, as Malians throughout the country often said that they were simply following tradition, while they were trying all kinds of new things. We began to see the extent to which change was banal and normal.

Long-term field experience also underlined the fact that data were gathered in "a constructive negotiation involving at least two, and usually more, conscious, politically significant subjects" Clifford (1988, 41). The team was conscious of the fact that most rural Malians did not present themselves naively either to interviewers or government administrators. Rather, they presented the calculated self that they felt would be to their advantage in future dealings.

*Multiple Research Sites*

Since donors often prefer multiple-site studies to get a better grasp of the generalizability of findings, pragmatism demanded that we look at several different sites simultaneously. This strategy intensified the effects of long-term research and working with a multinational team, again making us more sensitive to variation and diversity. Levels of commercialization, kinds of technologies, and crop mixes all varied substantially from one site to another. While we did miss the depth that case studies of individual regions or ethnic groups can provide (e.g., Lewis 1979; Toulmin 1992), looking at multiple sites helped avoid overgeneralization. For example, people of the same ethnic group living in different sites often farmed quite differently, pushing us to see heterogeneity.

Moreover, looking at different systems in juxtaposition to one another elucidated certain aspects that did not seem problematic until we realized that similar terms were being used quite differently across groups. For example, what a "large" household was, what a "diversified" cropping system looked like, when "intensification" occurred all could vary, depending on the group. Looking at terminology among different groups helped us to clarify some of the key issues. Looking at six different zones also allowed us to understand better how national and regional factors variably impacted local production systems. Some of the detail available from individual case studies was lost, but the approach gave a more diverse picture of Malian agriculture.

Analytical Concepts

Our methods pushed us toward a framework that could look simultaneously at similarity and difference, and toward analytic concepts that could highlight the role of human agency while continuing to recognize the structural constraints that affected people's choices. At the level of structure, we made analyses more Mali-focused by integrating national and regional structures as well as international ones and by paying greater attention to local history. To understand the microlevel decisions of farmers, access to resources was the link between structural context and individual choice and remained a key concept in our analysis, since one result of recent population movements was to increase or decrease access to resources. Three complementary concepts were essential in making existing approaches more actor-centered: an understanding of the negotiability of human relationships, the role of individual choice, and innovation.

## Mali-Centered History

While Western colonialism and imperialism did influence social change in the region that became Mali, a more Mali-centered approach sees it as one factor among many. Emphasizing rural history is one aspect of making a historical perspective more Mali-centered. Most Malian villages had individuals who kept track of their histories, providing a context for understanding who they had become and how they lived now. Like outside analysts, these histories did sometimes romanticize this past, but they rarely presented it as static tradition. Often, it was remarkably full of change: population movements, changing alliances, and so forth. Although some groups traced their origins back to the "glorious" kingdoms of Ghana, Mali or Songhay, village histories often spoke in more detail of the nineteenth and twentieth centuries.

These histories underlined the fact that since at least A.D. 700, rural Malians had to deal with one form or another of state penetration. Changing configurations of power often implied new dominant groups and changing forms of conflict and inequality, which in turn meant changing demands on local populations. These elicited varying responses from those at the bottom, but clearly, one of the elements of farmers' social knowledge with some time depth was how to deal with state pressures for taxes or tribute and other attempts at control. Resistance to state demands, and manipulation and exploitation of state resources, were things that rural Malians have done in many ways for a long time.

Nevertheless, history suggests that some individuals and groups were able to use changing circumstances for upward social mobility. As new invaders came through, individuals and local groups had to choose, inevitably with incomplete knowledge, whether to ally or resist. Rural survival placed a premium upon assessing change and then adapting to the new political environment. Unchanging adherence to tradition was usually less adaptive than an ability to justify change in terms of existing cultural values and symbols. The extent to which political changes were accompanied by technical or social organizational change is an open question that needs to be explicitly addressed.

The optimal approach to Mali-centered history would involve linking village histories to the larger regional and countrywide trends. This would involve a separate study, far beyond what we were able to accomplish here. Nevertheless, the extraordinary productivity of Africanist historians in recent years has enabled us to understand better the national and regional context in which individuals and households made decisions about agricultural production. We address these issues in more detail in the next chapter.

*Access to Resources*

Access to the resources of land, labor, and capital is essential for successful agricultural production, yet it was influenced by a variety of outside factors, including national and international policies. Local groupings and categories, such as class, gender, and ethnicity also constrained access for some and facilitated it for others. Individual characteristics also affected ability to get resources. Technical and environmental knowledge, awareness of the political climate and rules (e.g. of Malian land law), and the ability to manipulate social networks all proved to be important. As Berry (1993) has shown elsewhere, people were quite creative in using varied social networks to get access to a range of resources.

Of particular interest here was the fact that historically and today, Africans often changed potential access to resources by moving, a pattern more common than popular views of African society might suggest. Individually, hunters and traders often went in search of new sites for their activities; in the social arena, witchcraft accusations, inheritance disagreements, and succession struggles all led people, usually the disgruntled losers, to move (Kopytoff 1987). Classic household and lineage segmentation (Fortes 1953; Toulmin 1992) also incited some to move. At the societal level, famines, civil and international wars, ethnic rivalries, and despotic regimes led to population movement in the past as well as today (Kopytoff 1987, 7). Segmentary lineage structures sometimes facilitated expansion into areas held by neighbors (Bohannon 1954).

Despite the interest of historians and anthropologists in population movement, the extent to which it remains important for development initiatives has been minimally investigated, even though there are studies of some at least quasi-voluntary settlement initiatives in Africa (J. Brain 1976; Hansen 1982; Jacobs 1989). While the poverty of many West African savanna countries has been instrumental in pushing their inhabitants into large-scale migration, much more attention has been paid to rural-urban or international migration than rural-to-rural migration. Yet the latter is not uncommon and may be done explicitly to increase access to resources. Despite the importance of structured access to resources, people similarly situated within structures often had a vari-

ety of responses to constraints, leading to differential economic success. This
led us to look more closely at the role of individual agency.

*Integrating the Human Actor*

Although structures constrain choice, and shared language, norms, and cultural
symbols provide a framework for decisions, people use these in a variety of
ways to create individual lives. Some forty years ago, Leach (1965) described
how Kachin with different backgrounds interpreted the same genealogical information in varied ways and used different resources to gain power in their society. More recently, Rosen (1984) has shown how Moroccans constructed,
through negotiation, social identities and personal networks. Hopkins's discussion (1972) of 1960s politics in small-town Mali suggests that this approach
might be useful there as well. Although he attempted to use the role of classes
and ethnic groups to understand why Kita residents had lost belief in Mali's socialist future and adopted "pork-barrel politics," he found that "the explanatory
model that works best is one that assumes that each individual in the political
field was able to decide what to do on the basis of his own personal interpretation of his advantage, and acted accordingly" (Hopkins 1972, 219, 222). Three
interlinked variables help clarify how individual choice works within social and
cultural constraints: negotiability, individuality, and innovation.

*Negotiability*
Among the three concepts, the negotiability of social relationships and rules has
been most used by recent authors on Africa. Berry (1993), for example, showed
how negotiation was important in determining contemporary ethnic identity
and customary law in much of English-speaking Africa, in turn affecting access
to land and agricultural productivity. Our field experience suggested that although people could formulate relatively clear rules, they did not necessarily
follow them. Interaction among groups and individuals, and hence negotiation,
was important in determining which rules were most observed and which relationships became most critical.

Malian villagers did often try to present a seamless, cohesive view of their
culture in group interviews. They also commonly used two opposed ideal types
to frame and think about alternatives. For example, people commonly talked as
if there was a clear distinction between autochthonous groups and migrants.[6]
In theory, the autochthonous were those who settled first and the village
founders. Yet village histories revealed that if an incoming group conquered
and/or enslaved a group already living there, the politically dominant group

might take on "autochthonous" status (cf. Kopytoff 1987). Moreover, the status of migrant or stranger could gradually change over time, and very new migrants were differentiated from migrant families who had spent 20 years in a village. Access to resources even varied quite widely among migrants who were settled for equivalent periods of time. Rather than seeing these oppositions as representing real groupings, they are more usefully seen as idealized categories used to negotiate actual relationships among village residents.

Moreover, interviews with individuals about their own lives consistently showed substantial variation from the seamless view presented in public fora. For example, farmers might present a theoretical crop rotation sequence, but field histories with individuals might not find a single field that fit the ideal. The gap between cultural ideal and actual behavior was clearly quite large, and in many cases, no one seemed particularly concerned about it. Fieldwork showed that people interpreted rules differently and used their interpretations to gain access to things that they desired. They appeared to have a pragmatic approach to their cultural resources, using "traditional" and "modern" ones indiscriminately, depending on which was more advantageous in the particular situation.

*Individuality*

If people get access to resources in many and varied ways, by actively constructing and negotiating economic possibilities, then we would expect to see high levels of individual variation. Yet analysts have tended to focus on group action and choices. Development practitioners have discussed the pragmatic advantages of group social action (Cernea 1991, 359), while those hoping for more transformative change have looked at the potential of collective social movements (Escobar 1995; Ferguson 1990). Strategies for action have been linked to sociological analyses that stress the traditions of community identity and responsibility within Africa (Nyerere 1968). Yet case studies have found a strong sense of individual autonomy and enterprise as well, even to the point that "individualism, enterprise, and pride in autonomy" become an essential component of village-level community spirit (Cesara 1982, 163; Clark 1994).

In Mali, pressing economic need often pushed young rural men to undertake wage labor migration before settling down in their natal villages to farm, but villagers also attached positive value to the ability to take advantage of new, nonlocal resources presented to one while away. In our study, a number of individuals seemed quite willing to experiment with very specialized economic niches. Some specialized in a single crop rarely found in their neighbors' fields, such as watermelon or sesame, while others tried innovative combinations of agriculture and nonfarm activities that optimized household income by building on the particular strengths of the individuals in that family. Some of these activities were probably successful precisely because they were not carried out by large groups but only one or two individuals. Some have suggested that individuals who manipulate or transform existing resources as either innovators or brokers become entrepreneurs (Long 1977), but our data suggest that the manipulation and transformation of existing resources was carried out by many, not just those who would conventionally be identified as entrepreneurs or innovators.

Serious study of individual choice and its consequences requires in-depth study. This is especially true because individual desires and achievements are in conscious tension with group responsibility and identity. While Malians value individual achievement and autonomy, most would claim that individualism is arrogant and egotistical, for it implies subordination of group desires to those of the individual. The individual is meant to choose and achieve for the good of the group, not him- or herself. Needless to say, this is not always the case. In situations with much variation and no clear relationship between production patterns and other structural factors, we believe that individual choice played an important role. This is, however, a question that demands more focused research.

*Innovation*

Using the negotiability of social relationships and individuality as key analytical concepts led us to look more seriously at innovation as well. Individuals innovated as they put resources together in new ways. Since each individual had a somewhat different configuration of human and financial resources available, the potential for both variation and innovation was significant. Many innovations were probably not successful, in terms of improving the lives of the innovators. When one was, however, it could be adopted quite readily by others. Rural people watched each other's experiments and evaluated them in terms of their own human and financial resources in deciding whether to try them.

The emphasis on local resistance to the adoption of innovations introduced from outside has blinded researchers to local processes of innovation, including the ways in which locals take outside resources and adapt them to their own needs. For example, a few farmers in a village north of Segou first bought plows on an experimental basis in the 1950s. Local blacksmiths then adapted the original design to make a lighter, less expensive plow, which led in turn to mass adoption by the 1980s (Toulmin 1992). Among us, T. Diarra (1989) looked at processes by which village-level technical innovations spread. Practitioners have suggested that local innovations in agricultural practice could be used to formulate more broad-based programs (Dommen 1988).

Locally generated innovations are not only technological and economic, but may be social and cultural as well. Many, of course, have noted that social organizational change often accompanies technological change (Netting, Cleveland, and Stier 1980; Venema 1986), but few have looked at the ways in which households may consciously decide to change their organization to take advantage of resources. One exception was Toulmin (1992), who discussed the ways that large households changed the expected relationship between generations in an effort to encourage the younger generation to remain home. Our study found conscious innovation in both household and village political organization. Although not all social change is due to conscious choice or innovation, an emphasis on human agency raises this possibility as a question in each case.

Implications for African Agriculture

Our interest in innovation, individuality, and negotiation is not simply academic. We believe that bringing these concepts explicitly into models of rural social change will lead to better development programs. Here we outline some of the major issues confronted by contemporary African agriculture, which must become more productive if it is to feed the continent's growing population over the next 50 years. It will need to become even more so if it is also to generate the foreign exchange needed to develop other sectors of the economy as well. But even though there is general agreement that increased productivity should not come at significant social-welfare cost, the best strategies to increase production are not clear. This study will address a few controversial aspects of important economic and social issues.

*Economy: Self-Sufficiency, Diversification, and Intensification*

National food self-sufficiency has long been a goal of the Malian government, usually supported by major international donors. Even the World Bank, which preferred the concept of food security to food self-sufficiency, recognized that most African countries needed simultaneously to increase local food *and* cash crop production (World Bank 1989, 92–93). However, it is important not to confuse national food self-sufficiency with regional, local, or household self-sufficiency. The tendency to see international markets as most important has blinded some analysts to the role of local markets and their potential role in local food security. Some appeared to translate national self-sufficiency into regional or even household self-sufficiency. Lewis (1979), for example, appeared to evaluate more positively the household that produced more of its own grain, while

Gran (1983) emphasized self-reliance, use of local resources, and selective re-sistance to specialized production. Yet food security, the ability to provide food regularly in some manner, and not food self-sufficiency appeared to be the main strategy for household survival among most rural Malians. Perhaps individu-als, households, or even localized regions can or should develop comparative advantage in the specialized production of certain crops for domestic markets. A more Mali-centered approach has the potential to look at domestic and re-gional markets as well as international ones and investigate the value of local self-sufficiency.

The role of diversification in agricultural-production strategies is another major issue facing Sahelian farmers. It has been relatively easy to develop large-scale programs that concentrate on a single cash crop, such as cotton or peanuts. As we shall discuss in chapter 3, the cotton operation has been the most effective by far in increasing both national and farmer income, but relying on a single cash crop for either is highly problematic. Sahelian countries need to diversify agricultural production for both international and domestic markets and to buffer themselves against the volatility of any single international mar-ket, as well as to serve growing domestic consumer needs. Yet again, the way in which a national strategy is translated at the local level is important and might well begin with an examination of how farmers already diversify. In Mali, there appeared to be a variety of strategies associated with different kinds of market integration (Koenig 1990; Toulmin 1992). Growing an array of crops does not mean pulling away from the market but may mean serving different kinds of markets. The relationship of social stratification to patterns of rural diversifica-tion needs also to be explored in greater depth.

Ecological considerations, including deforestation and desertification, have led African countries to encourage intensification of existing farm prac-tices. Intensification, the move toward more continuous cultivation of the same land areas, means that growing populations can occupy the same surface area without incursions on forest or fallow. Mali has explicitly adopted a policy of intensification, commonly referred to as "sedentarization," as a means to curb environmental degradation. Yet these strategies also demand some way of returning nutrients to the soil, to maintain soil fertility and existing agricultural productivity. Some practices depend on commercialized inputs supplied through international market channels, while others rely on "traditional" prac-tices using local resources. In between these two extremes is a wide variety of practices that mix commercialized inputs and local resources. Many have sug-gested that new agricultural intensification techniques should be based on those that farmers already use (Dommen 1988; Netting, Cleveland, and Stier 1980), and a perspective that looks at local innovation should emphasize these.

Our framework leads us to ask new questions about these issues. How, for example, do individuals innovate and find niches for diversification or intensification? If individuals can find agricultural, ecological, or market niches to exploit, how is this expressed in individualized production strategies, given the variable levels and mixes of resources that they possess? Finally, if individual variation is indeed widespread, then there are likely to be many intervention points, rather than simply a single best strategy for helping farmers increase production. An explicit recognition of farmer variation will require new approaches by agricultural-extension services and make increased demands on their skills.

*Society: Gender Division of Labor and the Role of the State*

Two sociopolitical issues are of particular importance in sub-Saharan Africa: the changing gender division of labor and the future role of the state. Many have suggested that virtually all changes in African economic structures have been to women's detriment (Gladwin 1991a). If their role in agriculture decreases, they are seen as shut out of major production activities. If, in contrast, it increases, especially through more work on men's crops, then the focus is on their increased workload and decreased autonomy. Boserup's characterization (1970) of Africa as a continent of women farmers has led to neglect of the many farming systems, common in the West African savanna, where men do much farmwork, including production of food crops. A focus on the negotiability of social roles should lead to questions about variation among households in the gender division of labor. Some of our data suggest that family organization can be quite diverse, as household members look for ways to exploit more effectively the particular configurations of labor available to them. In some cases, families appear to have made quite conscious, sometimes innovative, choices about the deployment of their labor. We need to look empirically at the implications of these for women's economic or social position. A view of family and household organization that focuses on its flexibility may lead to the formulation of different kinds of programs aimed at women.

A final issue of great interest is the appropriate role for the African state. Both neocapitalists and more radical analysts have become quite skeptical of state activities. While organizations like the World Bank have focused on the putative greater efficiency of the market over central planning, the latter have focused on the exploitation accompanying increased state control. Both of these approaches could benefit from greater empirical study of services the state provides and how people perceive the benefits and costs of them. Moreover, the use of two ideal types (high levels vs. minimal state intervention) prevents us from looking at whether a mix (i.e., high intervention in some areas and minimal in others) might not be more effective. In fact, the general recognition that the first generation of structural-adjustment programs had serious human costs led to a greater emphasis on state-sponsored social-welfare programs (O'Brien 1991), and others have argued for specific government subsidies to achieve particular goals (Gladwin 1991b; Reardon et al. 1995). This study's review of the ways in which farm households used state services generates recommendations for specific state activities.

Outline of Chapters

We begin with a review of the domestic and international contexts that have structured access to local-level resources. Chapter 2 looks at precolonial history, with an emphasis on the immediate precolonial period from the 1700s to 1890, followed by a discussion of the colonial era from 1890 to 1960. For both periods, we look at the major state structures and patterns of negotiation within them to see better the results, both positive and negative, of attempts to extend state control. The third chapter focuses on national agricultural policy since independence in 1960. We look at the goals of Mali's different regimes, and the degree to which they were constrained by international actions, environmental conditions, and local custom and traditions. We end the chapter with a look at Mali's rural-development operations, the primary way in which farmers have been linked to the state.

The remaining chapters turn to our study data on contemporary rural production systems. In chapter 4, we begin with a discussion of major patterns of contemporary rural-to-rural migration and some of the overall characteristics of the study sample. We then look at the specific situations at each of the six sites.

Chapters 5 and 6 focus on rural production systems in the study areas. Chapter 5 concentrates on agriculture, a major activity in all sites, and the most important economic activity in most of them. The first part of the chapter looks at access to the necessary resources of land, labor, and capital. Of particular interest are differential land rights among migrants and indigenous people, access to unwaged household and salaried labor, and patterns of access to agricultural technology, including equipment and inputs. We then turn to the effects of resource access on agricultural production. Production levels are evaluated in absolute terms through comparison with subsistence norms as well as in light of diverse farmer goals. Of special interest is variation—across sites, among different households within sites, and among various household members.

Savanna farmers cannot survive on crop agriculture alone, so chapter 6 looks at complementary economic activities: livestock and nonfarm income sources. While there were some general patterns, households deployed family members in quite innovative, yet individualized, ways to take advantage of particular configurations of local opportunity. The diversity of individual nonfarm activities in particular reflected choices to exploit distinctive economic niches, and people used both "traditional" and "modern" means to create innovative production strategies.

Chapter 7 looks at issues that transcend village and household, primarily the relationships created by new migrants with both indigenous villagers and other migrants on the one hand, and government and nongovernmental organizations on the other. The focus is on negotiation and innovation in social relationships as people attempted to make structures more directly meet their perceived needs.

Finally, the concluding chapter looks at the implications of our findings for development theory and practice. We suggest an approach to development that is simultaneously pragmatic and theoretical. We assess the effectiveness of our alternative framework for better understanding contemporary African agriculture and make recommendations for restructuring agricultural-development programs.

Chapter 2

# Innovation and Change
# in Malian History

This chapter looks at the interaction between structure and human action in the immediate precolonial and colonial periods. Prior to colonialism, the West affected the path of African change primarily through the slave trade, but Malian states followed their own trajectories as well. The French colonial government later became the major state structure, but its local administrative representatives did not derive their identity uniquely from a metropolitan conception of colonial enterprise. During both eras, there was room for negotiation of rules, social mobility, and innovation. Local governments manipulated larger national and international structures, while simultaneously, individuals responded to many different possibilities created by rapid changes in economy and polity.

Our interpretations follow from the proposition that "the idea of timeless African structures or institutions is a historical myth with no real substance" (Diagne 1992, 23). The accounts of Africanist historians are full of self-conscious actors making choices among alternatives. In many cases, the alternatives reflected an uneven playing field with Africa at the lower and bumpier end, but people nevertheless made creative use of resources, and individuals and cultures changed in significant ways. This chapter is divided into two sections, one on precolonial changes and the other on the colonial era.

Precolonial Mali

Some of the best-known African states existed in or overlapped the area of contemporary Mali. Ghana (ca. 850–1100), Mali (ca. 1200–1450), and Songhay (ca. 1450–1591) all were located here, in the savanna, on trade routes between the Sahara and the forest. As Europeans began to make contact with Africans at the coast from the 1400s, more economic interaction began to occur there, and coastal trading centers grew. From 1500 onward, transatlantic demands for slaves had a profound effect, as an estimated 18 to 22 million Africans were forcibly made to migrate across the Atlantic, eastward across the Indian Ocean,

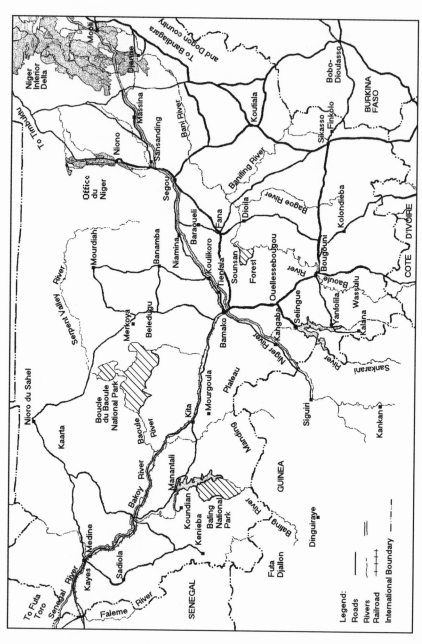

Map 2. Key sites. (From IGN 3615, Map of Mali 1:2,000,000 [1993]. Copyright IGN, Paris, and DNCT, Bamako.)

or within Africa in the different slave trades (Manning 1990, 84; Inikori 1992). The slave trade also stimulated the growth of new African states based on the capture and use of slaves.

What is now contemporary Mali was apparently not a major source of slaves (Inikori 1992, 105; Manning 1990); rather, important slave-raiding and slave-using states were formed here in the eighteenth and nineteenth centuries. From Africa's perspective, the slave trade created both victims and successes, as some individuals used the trade to increase wealth and productivity. Although the impetus for a major part of the trade came from the exterior, powerful Africans used this situation to create new possibilities for themselves and their societies, albeit at significant human cost (Manning 1990).

In light of the changes brought about by the growing importance of the coast and the disruption of the slave trade, historians have sought to understand the social and economic conditions in the West African savanna, particularly during the eighteenth and nineteenth centuries. Some have argued that the period from the fall of Songhay to 1800 was one of widespread poverty, as the countryside and agricultural production declined and ruling elites pushed rural farmers for more taxes (Diagne 1992, 37–39). Alongside this economic decline was natural disaster, a series of drought and plague years during the late seventeenth and eighteenth centuries (Lovejoy 1985, 675, 676). In contrast, others have argued for greater stability, claiming that despite political upheavals, trade along the Niger River was sufficiently established to survive both the Moroccan conquest of Songhay in 1591 and the growing European trade on the coast (Abitbol 1992, 319). There is little evidence to suggest that Islamic learning declined from 1600 to 1800, and, in many cases, the effects of drought and famine were episodic (Willis 1985, 558, 565). Historians more generally concur that growing Islamic reformist movements led to rejuvenation in the savanna in the nineteenth century, although the jihads led by these leaders led to social and economic disruption as well.

The eighteenth and nineteenth centuries saw the rise and fall of three major warrior states in central Mali: the Segou Bambara[1] state (ca. 1712–1861), the Toucouleur state created by El Hadj Umar Tall (1849–91), and Samory Toure's state (1871–98). Other smaller states existed within Mali (e.g., Massina, Kenedugu), and there were other major states in neighboring zones (e.g., Futa Toro, the Mossi state, Kong, etc.). On the fringes of areas of state formation were noncentralized regions. Within Mali, the most notable were the Dogon zones, where non-Islamized, noncentralized groups lived on cliffs. Although some have seen the Dogon as an example of pristine African tradition (Griaule 1965), the Dogon zone is better viewed as a region of refuge for different peoples, trying to escape the depredations of warfare (Palau Marti 1957; N'Diayé 1970).

The three warrior states of the eighteenth and nineteenth centuries had similar structures. All relied on large armies, sometimes with tens of thousands of soldiers, to incorporate new areas and to raid for slaves. Some captives were sold to other groups to generate funds, while others were kept for internal use. Slaves were put to work at various tasks, but many of the soldiers were slaves, and other captives (especially women and children) were given to soldiers as booty. Some were sold to professional merchants, important in all these societies. Merchants, involved in long-distance trade, usually came from distinctive Islamized trade diasporas, with links to a number of different states.

In these hierarchical polities, tension existed between merchants who controlled trade and ruling groups who controlled warfare and production. The beginning of the Segou state has been characterized as a peasant revolt on the part of Bambara farmer-warriors against the Marka traders' increasing wealth (Abitbol 1992), while Samory's state was one of many where Djula traders took an increasingly important political role as trade with the coast grew (Person 1971, 1989).[2] Nevertheless, all three states were multiethnic in the sense that the ruling group welcomed those who were willing to adhere to its ideology and fight for it (Batran 1989; Ly-Tall 1989). Armies in particular welcomed volunteers (Izard and Ki-Zerbo 1992). The Segou rulers retained their traditional religion yet needed Muslim traders; the Toucouleur state, in contrast, was based on Islam, yet those who converted were integrated (D. Robinson 1985). Ethnic and religious identification were flexible, and there was some scope for social mobility.

All states were relatively fragile, however, and depended upon continued conquest for strength and viability. The Segou state managed to survive until it was defeated by the Toucouleurs, and both the Toucouleurs and Samory were defeated by the French army, which had a base in western Mali by the 1850s. French conquest was by no means easy, but the French received aid from groups defeated by the two later African states. African states also had to cope with independent resistance movements, often led by those they had defeated (D. Robinson 1985). The continued disturbances created by nineteenth-century warfare meant that neither the Toucouleur state nor Samory's state was able to implement viable administrative structures, including taxation systems (D. Robinson 1985).[3] In general, the conditions under which most rural Malians lived in the two centuries prior to direct colonial control in the 1890s were neither stable nor pacific.

The rest of this section looks at specific examples of the interplay between access to resources and possibilities for human action. Given our focus on agricultural and rural development, it would be useful to have a social history of the eighteenth and nineteenth centuries. It is clear, for example, that crop choices changed substantially and relatively quickly after European contact, with the adoption of American crops such as maize, cassava, peanuts, tomatoes, and hot peppers (Grigg 1974, 287, 288). However, available sources are biased toward the activities of elites, military history, the evolution of African slavery and the slave trade, and interactions between Europeans and Africans. To get detailed examples, we have made this our focus as well, even though it would have been more useful to follow changes among farmers.

## Access to Resources

Even when their explicit ideologies were focused elsewhere (e.g., Islamic conversion), states wanted to increase access to resources. Labor was the most important resource, and leaders not only used armies to increase populations by theft (i.e., slave raiding) but also encouraged voluntary immigration. Technology was a second important resource, and states made conscious efforts to increase access to it.

Although states were concerned about viable agricultural production, access to land per se was not particularly problematic throughout these centuries, as population density remained relatively low. Ruling groups did want access to relatively well-watered lands, including river valleys where flood recession cultivation was possible. Umar sent his Toucouleur forces toward the Bambara capital of Segou in part for its better agricultural zones, with more rain than the area of northwest Mali, the Kaarta, that he already held (D. Robinson 1985). Nevertheless, access to land appears not to have been a key factor in state expansion.

Rather, the goal of gaining labor oriented the strategies of those who would create states. During this period, the primary means to increase the labor pool was through slavery. The growth of the transatlantic slave trade stimulated African societies to develop enslavement mechanisms that made enslaved persons more available, not only for trade but for their own states as well. The transatlantic trade declined in the early nineteenth century following the British abolition of the trade in 1807, but African polities did not stop slaving. They used the captured slaves to increase their own populations.

Slavery existed in Africa since at least the medieval era, but in most states, slaves had been relatively few and their uses relatively circumscribed. Most lived in the households of rulers although they performed a range of functions.

At one extreme, they worked in productive activities, including farming to feed aristocrats. At the other, they might become soldiers or elite government officials. Since slaves were defined by their status as aliens, they lacked kinship ties and associated obligations, and they could give absolute loyalty to the ruler (Kopytoff and Miers 1977; Meillassoux 1991). Few slaves ended up in nonaristocratic households, but when they did, they were usually slowly integrated, often appearing in genealogies as junior branches of founding lineages.

The increase in slave keeping during the eighteenth and especially the nineteenth centuries meant that the percentage of slaves in West African savanna societies grew to be quite high at the beginning of the colonial period. Manning (1990, 75) suggested that about 20 percent of the entire population of Senegambia and the Western Sudan were slaves, somewhat fewer in the societies from which slaves were taken, and higher in those where they worked. Klein (1990, 240) suggested figures as high as two-thirds for some societies. With these numbers, slave ownership was no longer confined to the aristocracy, and wealthier members of these societies could have many slaves (Meillassoux 1991). A larger proportion of slaves came to be used in agriculture. Soldiers of conquering armies typically received slaves as a part of their booty, and many used them to begin small plantations (Manning 1990; Klein 1990). Wealthy elites could create large plantations, often keeping slaves in separate slave villages. Evidence suggests that much early cash crop production in the West African savanna, especially peanuts and gum, was done on slave estates (Klein 1990).

In addition to slave raiding, other forms of population movement also increased or decreased labor availability in particular areas. Armies encouraged individuals to join. Mamary Coulibaly, the first Segou Bambara ruler, offered to pay fines owned by debtors, condemned men, and prisoners who had broken their parole as an incentive to join his army; he also attracted young adventurers with the promise of booty (Izard and Ki-Zerbo 1992, 335). Umar encouraged Toucouleur youth from his homeland on the Senegal River in Futa Toro to join his army; this zone may have lost 20 percent of its population as a consequence (Person 1985, 216). The Toucouleur army was further swelled by mercenaries, ready to fight for whoever would pay them well (Oloruntimehin 1972, 171). It is difficult to estimate what percentage of the population was involved in the military, but it may have been substantial. D. Robinson (1985, 260, 267) estimated the Segou army at 35,000, the same size as its capital. The total population of the Segou heartland was only about 200,000.

As the populations of successful state centers grew, those of other areas fell. Indigenous people often moved out before armies entered, or in response to the destruction caused by war. When Umar's forces moved from western

Mali toward Segou, he devastated decentralized Malinke villages on the way. Some defeated villagers had to sell themselves into slavery to get food for those remaining in the conquered area (D. Robinson 1985). Samory forced his subjects to leave their homes as the French came in so that the French would have no populations to support them (Person 1971, 136). Since productive states depended on a viable population, those without were lacking an essential resource.

Some occupations, for example, trade, herding, fishing, and transport, required movement across large areas. Others, most notably the Islamic marabouts (teachers), often were itinerant as well (Willis 1985). Rulers believed that conquest would be short-lived unless the conquered region was thoroughly changed; one way to do this was to encourage colonization by individuals from the conqueror's homeland. After the conquest of Songhay, the Moroccan ruler sent Moroccans to key regions (Abitbol 1992, 306). Umar and his successor, Ahmadu, made special efforts to encourage Islamized African artisans from European settlements on the coast to join the Umarian movement (Kanya-Forstner 1971, 57) and invited settlers from the Senegal River valley to come live in Kaarta and Segou (D. Robinson 1985). Today, certain villages around Nioro du Sahel still recognize their Toucouleur roots.

In addition to labor, new technology and information were also crucial resources for building and maintaining states. Modern weaponry was the foremost new technology consciously adopted by African states and will be discussed in the section on innovation below. Knowledge of new resources was essential for their use; itinerant traders and traveling marabouts not only moved goods and Islamic knowledge but also brought practical information and new ideas (Abitbol 1992).

*Negotiating Social Relationships*

The most notable change in status during this period was the large-scale decline among those taken as slaves. However, other information suggests that statuses, including slavery, could be negotiated in some circumstances. Warfare and adherence to new states clearly formed an arena in which status negotiation occurred. A successful warrior could build a following and move up within his state's hierarchy, albeit at relatively great risk. The military nature of these states favored male social mobility, but women gained some influence through their control of domestic institutions, especially when men were at war. Nevertheless, social relationships tied to ethnic identity and the institution of slavery provide the most salient examples of status negotiation.

Most slaves were at the bottom of the status hierarchy, drudge-slaves, as Meillassoux (1991) called them, but a few were in positions that allowed upward social mobility. Captives, individuals given in tribute, and others who joined slave armies could move up in the hierarchy if they were very lucky and good warriors. The most notable example was Ngolo Diarra, sent by his village as tribute to the Segou Bambara king when they had nothing else. When Mamary Coulibaly's heirs were no longer able create a stable government, Ngolo, now a soldier-slave, led the *ton-jon* (the slave army) in a coup. He created the second Segou Bambara dynasty, and his descendants ruled for years after him. Less notable examples of slave warriors who became important administrative officials came from many states. After the Moroccans defeated and ruled Songhay, slaves filled some administrative offices (Willis 1985, 541). Umar appointed slaves as garrison commanders and governors (D. Robinson 1985, 338).

Izard and Ki-Zerbo (1992, 362) have argued that the stigma of slave background was never lost, saying that Ngolo Diarra was taunted by the nobly born Bambara, his family unable to eradicate the memory of the servile status of their ancestor. However, given the complexity of individual backgrounds, it seems more likely that any enemy could find something to fault in a person's background, while that individual could in turn find noble predecessors and salutary acts as well.

Although most slaves appear to have become so involuntarily, there were cases in which people chose to enslave themselves. While some of these people were on the verge of famine and saw no other viable options (D. Robinson 1985), others were only relatively poor and saw possibilities for social mobility otherwise closed to them (Izard and Ki-Zerbo 1992, 335; Willis 1985, 544). Not all mobility was upward however. The Segou state also offers a most significant example of downward mobility, when Mamary Coulibaly created a state hierarchy by forcing free members of his theoretically egalitarian raiding group to become *ton-jon,* or slave soldiers.

Slaves did not passively accept their condition and sometimes resisted. There were many slave revolts, and African masters did not have the same degree of control as did those in the New World (Manning 1990, 144). Once slaves became an identifiable group, for example, on separate estates, they began to negotiate as such to improve conditions (Manning 1990). They were able to decrease the amount of production owed their owners, sometimes changing it to a proportional amount from a fixed quantity. In some areas, this indicated a change from slavery to a relationship approaching serfdom (Manning 1990; Meillassoux 1991). In our study sites in southern Mali, French abolition allowed former slaves to move elsewhere and become independent peasants.

Ethnic identification also illustrated the ability of individuals to negotiate social status. In this region, flexibility of ethnic identification was linked to high levels of ethnic interaction. Although ethnic interaction was in part due to the conquest of one group by another, armies were almost always interethnic, partly because of their tendency to take on volunteers, partly due to the fact that many members were themselves captives from elsewhere. The Segou army had members of virtually every social, ethnic, and geographic background (Izard and Ki-Zerbo 1992, 337). A former captive could command notables, and FulBe could command Bambara. The same was true of Umar's and Samory's armies.

The interethnic mixing in the army was complemented by what appears to have been a relatively high degree of interethnic sexual liaisons, including marriage. To be sure, many of these interethnic sexual liaisons were between warriors and women captives that they received as booty; between these people, the quality of interaction likely varied quite widely. Nevertheless, under Islamic law, a woman who bore a child to her master gained not only freedom for herself but also for her child (Klein 1983, 86).[4] Women, who had fewer options for upward mobility than did men, often chose this route if it was offered. Information about formal marriages does exist for some leaders. Samory supposedly chose his wives very carefully to maximize their political utility (Person, cited in D. Robinson 1985, 335). Umar's three major wives were from Bornu and Sokoto in what is now northern Nigeria. His concubines also came from a variety of places, including northern Nigeria, the Futa Djallon, and Kaarta, but none were from his own home, Futa Toro. While his wives gave Umar strong links to the Islamic states in northern Nigeria, D. Robinson (1985) could not determine if he had an explicit marital strategy.

Since virtually all these savanna societies were patrilineal, children formally took on the ethnic identification of their fathers. Yet since many men were away at war for significant periods of time, women were primarily responsible for raising their children. Many of Umar's children were raised virtually single-handedly by their mothers, many of whom remained in Dinguiraye in what is now northern Guinea while Umar was fighting in Mali (D. Robinson 1985, 338). We are not aware of specific studies that show what difference it made to a child to have parents of different ethnic traditions, but it almost surely gave an individual cultural resources from several traditions on which to draw, no matter the formal ethnic identification.

Several examples suggest substantial flexibility in ethnic identification. Many nineteenth-century jihads, including Umar's, were begun by individuals generally identified as FulBe or Toucouleur from Futa Toro. Yet whether these self-identified FulBe all had FulBe roots is debatable. Some researchers believe that the Torodbe (FulBe class of Islamic scholars) were drawn from FulBe,

Wolof, Mande, Hausa, and Berber origins as well as from all levels of the class hierarchy (Batran 1989, 541). They became FulBe when they identified with FulBe values, spoke Fulfulde, and married FulBe women. The Segou state included state FulBe who guarded state herds, but only a minority of them were apparently ethnic FulBe (Izard and Ki-Zerbo 1992, 338). In the northern Côte d'Ivoire, people who had previously identified themselves as Keita and Coulibaly (ethnically identified clan names) became Wattara when political conditions changed (Izard and Ki-Zerbo 1992, 358).

Africans continued this process of negotiation with the French when they met, presenting their pasts in ways calculated to improve their position. This introduced bias into French sources; for example the French got information about Umar mostly from his enemies (D. Robinson 1985, 38). There was little evidence that Malians (or for that matter, Africans or humans in general) naively accepted the identities ascribed to them by other individuals with whom they interacted. Using the social resources available to them, they worked to elaborate, contest, and/or change these identities, depending on the options available to them as individuals or groups.

*Individuality*

Oral and written traditions about the ways in which people took old and new resources and mixed them in individualized ways to improve their futures are hard to come by. Most historical data were biased toward the elite, and stories of women were extremely rare. Since the elite by definition had greater access to resources, they probably had greater possibilities to innovate than did ordinary people. Nevertheless, their stories are indicative of the ways in which Malians of the time were thinking.

One common theme concerned an individual's ability to make the most of particular resources. For example, one early Bambara leader of Kaarta in northwest Mali, Massa (ca. 1666), was said to have married his daughters to poor men rather than princes. Princes would maintain their independence, but he could make poor affines live with, work for, and raid alongside him (Izard and Ki-Zerbo 1992, 332). In the nineteenth century, a common theme concerned individuals who attempted to manipulate the French to their own advantage. There was, for example, Dama Coulibaly, a son of the last strong Bambara ruler of Kaarta (D. Robinson 1985, 353). As Umar entered Kaarta, Dama left for what is now southern Mauritania and sought out French support. Moving with many family members and slave warriors, he created a "microcosm of the old Bambara court," raiding but also using his slave workforce to cultivate peanuts. Realizing that he could not displace the Umarians on his own, he supported the French advance and carried out a running correspondence with their commander, Archinard, about the liberation of his homeland. In so doing, he influenced the French views of Umar and his state. This strategy evidently worked, for Archinard approved his reinstallation as ruler of Kaarta after the French had taken his home area in the 1890s.

Some Umarians also attempted to collaborate with the French when they saw that French rule was inevitable. The most successful was Aguibou, one of Umar's sons and a rival to Ahmadu, Umar's heir. The French put him in control of the eastern third of the empire, whose capital, Bandiagara, remained his family's fief well into the twentieth century (D. Robinson 1985, 30). Aware of coming changes, Aguibou's descendants attended French schools and acquired positions of influence both within the colonial administration and independent Mali.

Below these elevated levels, talented individuals were sometimes able to exploit specific niches. Among the best known was the Soninke blacksmith Samba Ndiaye Bathily, who had enlisted in Umar's army after previously working as a mason at St. Louis, on the Senegalese coast. He was architect and engineer for Umar, responsible for keeping his vast array of modern weaponry in working order. After Umar's death, his talents were recognized by Ahmadu as well, who put him on his advisory council (D. Robinson 1985; Ọlọruntimẹhin 1972, 159). Another success was Arsec, a captive warrior from Segou, who ultimately became Ahmadu's barber, cook, and executioner and an influential counselor of the inner circle (D. Robinson 1985, 358).

At the popular level, many Africans who considered themselves enemies of existing African states joined the French army. In 1857, the French created the *tirailleurs sénégalais,* regular troops, by no means all Senegalese, to assist in their conquest of the continent (Hargreaves 1985). The regulars were usually accompanied by other African allies, hoping to take booty or get back at old enemies. The French force attacking Segou had only 103 European officers and specialists in contrast to 400 *tirailleurs,* 234 other regular African troops, four African officers, 545 noncombatant Africans, 1466 African auxiliaries, and 818 porters (Hargreaves 1985, 267). French ethnocentrism restricted the ability of most to achieve significant upward mobility, but many tried.

Women's options appear quite restricted. Rarely are women mentioned. Mariam Diawara, a captured Soninke aristocrat who later married one of Ahmadu's counselors, was apparently influential in his court (D. Robinson 1985, 195). A certain Aissatu, presumably a woman, appeared on the list of members of Ahmadu's supreme council (Ọlọruntimẹhin 1972, 159). In these war-oriented patriarchal states, women's influence likely made itself felt in the public sphere primarily through informal means, as women worked to influence the men with whom they were in contact domestically. Whether they were able to have any significant impact in this way is difficult to know since French ethnocentrism made it unlikely that women's impact would be recognized in written sources.

*Innovation*

Key innovations could have widespread effects, in light of the injection of new resources, the ability of eighteenth- and nineteenth-century Malians to negotiate social relationships, and individual attempts to use old resources in new ways. At the technological level, the most important change was the adoption of modern weaponry, an innovation consciously embraced by African rulers. Ideological innovation also occurred as people tried to change their societies. At the social level, the changing relationships between slave and free groups have already been noted; it is likely that relationships between men and women also changed. Although some short-term changes were consciously pursued by individuals, other societal innovations were at least partly the unanticipated consequences of earlier choices.

Strategies for modernizing armies predated the acquisition of European weapons. After the Moroccans defeated Songhay, others, for example, the Bambara, began to adopt Moroccan fighting methods (Abitbol 1992, 312). Efforts were made to increase the use of horses in battle; for example, the Kong rulers fattened cavalry horses in the northern savanna during the nineteenth century (Abitbol 1992, 318). But modern European weapons were the most significant technological change adopted by African armies. By the end of the eighteenth century, Mande blacksmiths were repairing imported firearms (Diagne 1992, 32), and in the nineteenth century Samory's smiths were able to copy the main types of weapons (Person 1971, 123). Nevertheless, many leaders found European-made weapons superior and made great efforts to build inventories of imports, both to resist the French and to conquer other African states. Umar used two howitzers to reduce the fortifications of his African enemies. Modern breech-loading rifles reached West African markets during the 1870s, and after 1890 Samory imported some 6,000 modern Gras rifles through Freetown (Hargreaves 1985, 266).

French authorities attempted to control arms imports, but African leaders still managed to get them. Umar for example, took his two howitzers from the French army when they met in battle at Medine, and bought some fifteen hundred to eighteen hundred small arms annually in his active years (D. Robinson

1985, 331). Samory spent enormous effort to keep open trade routes from his state south to Freetown where British and African merchants sold arms. Both slaves and other goods were sold to get the money to buy arms (Manning 1990, 100). Elsewhere in Africa, states started large-scale state armaments industries (Diagne 1992, 32).

To be sure, the short-term effect of this technological change was to increase the level of violence, but it also illustrated the openness of Africans to technological change. The nineteenth-century states were too short-lived to see if rulers would have consciously used technology to increase production, although a few indications are suggestive. Umar brought a small group of farmers and blacksmiths from Morocco so that his subjects could learn plow agriculture (D. Robinson 1985, 272). The speed with which Africans adopted cash crops when they could indicates their openness to change that had potentially favorable results. Gold Coast farmers were planting cocoa by the 1880s (Hargreaves 1985, 262), and Senegalese farmers exported 83,000 tons of peanuts in 1882 (Person 1985, 211).

Rulers adopted ideologies that furthered their goals. Mamary Coulibaly changed the egalitarian *ton-jon* raiding group into the warriors of an hierarchical state. Umar used the teachings of Tijaniyya Islam to create a core of disciples at the center of his jihad and later state (Ly-Tall 1989). While Samory did not create an Islamic theocracy, he did recruit an Islamic military class to run the state and used Islam as a means to unify the people. Many of these ideological changes did not penetrate very deeply. Nonetheless, social changes did come about.

The major societal change was the increase in the slave mode of production already discussed above. This had impacts beyond changing social stratification. One of the major effects seems to have been changing household structures, most notably, the growth of polygyny within savanna states. Most societies showed a clear preference for female and child slaves, often justified by references to women's docility, but patriarchal and polygynous societies also had the ability to absorb indefinite numbers of women (Klein 1983). Women had important roles in production and reproduction, providing both food and children for their families. They were an important component of the booty offered warriors, as warriors who were often slaves themselves had a better life if they had women to farm and cook for them (Klein 1990, 238).[5]

A systematic study of the household-level social changes that ensued from the increased level of slavery has yet to be done, but the possibilities are interesting. When a state captured large numbers of women, sex ratios between men and women became uneven. Although polygyny among elites had long existed in African societies, nineteenth-century conditions made it possible for more men to have more wives, at least in the first generation of captivity. As raiding decreased, sex ratios evened out and young men found themselves in competition with older ones for wives, which may have increased age stratification (Manning 1990, 142). Second, as men became more involved in warfare, dependence on female farming activities may have grown in importance (Manning 1990, 132). Africa's reputation as a center of female farming may result from specific and relatively recent historic events. Many who have worked in Africa have remarked on the great extent to which economic transactions accompany relationships, particularly male-female ones. Manning (1990, 123) attributed this commodification of human relationships to the slave trade era, when every human being had a price.

Much work remains to be done to discover which social institutions now presented as tradition were innovations in the eighteenth and nineteenth centuries (Manning 1990). Moreover, there is no reason to believe that innovation stopped after the precolonial period, so that certain innovations of this period might have left few traces if they were later replaced. It is clear, however, that Africans were willing to adopt both technological and social changes that they found to their advantage.

None of the data on the eighteenth and nineteenth centuries suggests stable or timeless tradition. Rather, this was a period of rapid change, some induced externally, some created internally, where people, as groups and individuals, sought ways to improve their life chances. Certainly not all changes were adopted by all people, and when the changes were disadvantageous, people resisted, often in creative ways, as Lewis (1979) has shown. Yet many changes did occur, and those during the precolonial period were followed by others during the colonial period as the French began to administer directly their colony of Soudan.

Colonial Mali

The colonial period formally began in the late 1890s as conquest brought areas of Mali under direct French control. Although the colonial period was relatively short, from about 1898 to 1960, it had profound effects. Both the structure of the world economy and the activities of the French state in Africa marginalized Mali to a much greater degree than during the precolonial period. Nevertheless, capitalist penetration was far from uniform. In the African interior, Malians attempted to profit from the particular forms of colonialism that they encountered, and some were able to do so. This section looks first at salient aspects of colonial rule and then turns to issues of interest for our study.

*French Colonial Policies*

France's African colonies were part of a policy to rebuild empire and improve France's political status, especially in comparison to Britain. They were also meant to contribute to economic growth, by providing raw materials for French industry and markets for finished products. But the French generally wanted these benefits without making substantial investments in the colonies, a strategy of "hegemony on a shoestring," in Berry's words (1993). This led to unanticipated consequences and inevitable disjuncture between intent and results. France's African colonies were not among natural centers of international or even African wealth (Manning 1988, 56), and substantial return from them could come only if significant investments were made. Yet, France's net contribution to West Africa was regularly less than what the government received from debt repayment and contributions to government costs (Coquery-Vidrovitch 1986, 368). Moreover, the colonial government was extremely conservative in its fiscal management and only began to invest via deficit spending in the 1950s (Manning 1988, 127, 128).

When the French did invest, they concentrated funds in areas calculated to give maximum returns, usually areas of high resource availability, where previous infrastructure investments ensured lower transport costs. By 1940, the French government had adopted a "dualist strategy," whereby capital investment was concentrated in the most accessible zones. Other areas had to content themselves with any windfalls that might occur (Coquery-Vidrovitch 1986, 381). In French West Africa (its federation of West African colonies), investment and growth were concentrated along the coasts, especially in Dakar, its capital, and to a somewhat lesser extent along the railroad lines into the interior. Hinterlands and interior colonies got much less investment and remained underdeveloped in comparison (Wrigley 1986, 83). Among these was the landlocked Soudan, the colony that later became Mali.[6]

Although colonial centers had more power than their colonies, they too were subject to constraints of international economy and politics. France was never free simply to carry out colonial activities as its government saw fit. World War I, the Great Depression, and then World War II all limited what a metropole could extract from its colonies. Neither colonizer nor colonized, for example, had great control over the cost of African exports. The demand for primary products rose and fell in generalized harmony with an irregular rate of industrial expansion in capitalist countries, and in only rare cases could countries regulate supply or prices (Wrigley 1986, 129).

As world economic conditions changed, booms came to Africa, first in the decade preceding 1913 (Wrigley 1986, 130) and then in a relatively long period from about 1945 to about 1965 (Manning 1988, 112). During these periods, terms of trade often improved for Africans. Imports and exports both rose (Manning 1988, 123), and there was increasing domestic and international trade. The boom after World War II was fueled in part by aid funds sent to Europe; American Marshall Plan funds, for example, specified that a certain percentage had to be spent in French colonies.

In between the booms were periods of economic decline. Terms of trade for African products declined from 1914 to 1920 (Wrigley 1986, 131). In the early years of the Great Depression (1929–34), prices for African commodities fell precipitously while the effective tax rate increased (Manning 1988, 51). There were other effects as well. After 1930, the gap between French and African wages began to widen, although the two levels had earlier followed the same general trends (Coquery-Vidrovitch 1986, 386). The post–World War II boom, in turn, ended with the world oil crisis, after most African countries had become independent. These world economic cycles were outside of the control of either colonizer or colonized; individuals in both center and periphery tried to benefit from upturns and had to cope with downturns.

Changing world ideas about appropriate international behavior, based on political considerations, also led to variation in French colonial activities over time. The general approval of imperialism during the late nineteenth and early twentieth centuries allowed colonial governments more freedom to pursue extractive policies. Then, as post–World War II independence movements began, the French government began to realize that the end of colonialism was inevitable. It tried to improve conditions in its sub-Saharan African colonies and increased investment.[7]

French colonial activities were carried out by a variety of actors: soldiers, civilian administrators, private businessmen, missionaries, few of whom had the same agendas. In the realm of policy, different constituencies in favor of colonialism had varying perspectives, interpretations of laws, and strategies for action. This made French colonialism far from a monolithic project. Moreover, the low level of financing gave local French and Africans a relatively wide field of action. Administrators in Africa, for example, appear to have spent significant effort in creatively figuring out how to avoid directives from the metropole. Systematic description of the contestation and overlapping coalitions and collaboration that developed during the colonial era would require its own study. We offer only a few illustrative examples.

European merchants and administrators, for example, were divided over the role of free versus protected trade. In the late nineteenth century, political sentiments in favor of free trade were widespread, and the original agreements among the European powers for the partition of Africa specified that different tariff rates were not to be used on similar articles from different sources (Wrigley 1986, 114). Through the early 1900s, the administration did not restrain commercial liberty (R. Roberts 1987, 167), a policy contested by European merchants, who often complained about being undercut by African traders and wanted the latter excluded from trade in certain goods. In Mali, African merchants were quite active (Manning 1988, 48), and international protection appeared only when growing economic problems in the 1920s led to a 1928 colonial customs union that created protective tariffs between France and her colonies. From 1929 to 1935, the share of African exports going to France rose from 62 percent to 80 percent (Coquery-Vidrovitch 1986, 381). Although protective tariffs led to greater dependence of the colonies on the mother country, they evidently mitigated some of the worst economic effects of the Great Depression as well.

French attitudes toward slavery in their colonies also reflected differing agendas among various parts of the colonial administration and contradictory coalitions. The French metropole was ambivalent about slavery: abolishing it in 1794, reinstituting it in 1802, and finally outlawing it definitively in 1848 (Manning 1988, 27). Although the law theoretically applied to both metropole and colonies (R. Roberts 1987, 175), French colonial authorities in Africa did their best to limit its impact on African polities neighboring French territories (Klein 1988, 188). Until 1905 conquest was their top priority, and soldiers dominated the administration (Manning 1988, 67, 68). Due to lack of funding, the French military depended on African troops and independent African allies, both of whom were slaveholders. It ran its army much along the lines of an African precolonial army, using booty to keep troops loyal, and hence was willing to tolerate a certain amount of slave raiding as well as ownership (R. Roberts 1987).

The colonial administration was one of the few groups consistently in favor of colonial expansion and increased support for the colonies. In contrast, the metropolitan government was divided. So colonial administrators sought support from the more ardent metropolitan advocates of imperial expansion, among whom were prominent abolitionists, making odd partners and leading to some fancy verbal footwork. Faidherbe, governor of French West Africa in the mid-1800s, for example, argued that the inhabitants of newly conquered territories were subjects, not citizens, and thus not bound by abolition (R. Roberts 1987, 176). Civilians in the colonies were less tolerant of slavery than the army and, moreover, saw abolition as a way to undermine the role of the French military and a strategy to increase civilian control of the administration (R. Roberts 1987, 181). These differing attitudes led to partial and complex moves toward abolition, which did not effectively occur until the 1920s in many places, despite the law.

Because their investment was modest and the various colonial constituencies and goals worked sometimes at cross-purposes to one another, the degree of French penetration into the interior was limited and Malians had spaces in which to pursue their own goals. To be sure, the French did not ignore Mali completely. They eventually stopped warfare and abolished slavery, began to levy taxes, and recruited labor. They tried to develop export crops like cotton and peanuts and began a large irrigation scheme, the Office du Niger. However, European settlement was rare, as were the large-scale concessions to European entrepreneurs common in central Africa; few people were displaced from their land. Compared to many other colonies, direct penetration was low.

Moreover, low funding and control meant that implementation of many policies was incomplete. Despite administrators' goals to use taxes to increase production (Crowder 1970), they remained relatively low in French West Africa for a long time. In 1914, for example, the head tax was about 2 to 5 francs per year during a period when the average wage earner got 20 to 50 francs per month; taxes were simply insufficient by themselves to achieve government goals (Coquery-Vidrovitch 1986, 338). In addition, tax collection was limited to coastal and urban regions during the early years of colonization, even though taxes were theoretically to be collected from all (Coquery-Vidrovitch 1986, 329). Attempts to develop export crops foundered because transport costs made them financially unfeasible unless producer prices were very low, so low that Malians were unwilling to accept them except under threat of force.

Many Malians resisted French initiatives by moving away or by apathetic participation; as often as not, the French simply moved on to deal with more vulnerable populations. Other rural Malians turned to more lucrative activities, including labor migration and production for local, rather than international, markets. The relative neglect of the colony meant that certain aspects of the precolonial economy, most notably the continuation of African regional trade based on north-south ecological specialization, remained resilient and offered opportunities for economic profit to some Africans (R. Roberts 1987). The

French even recognized the importance of internal trade, orienting the Office du Niger more toward grain production for African consumers than intercontinental export crops.

Some have argued that development was actively blocked so that Mali might become a labor reserve for core capitalist enterprises (Meillassoux 1981). Indeed, the relatively high degree of wage labor migration supports this notion. However, other evidence suggests that underdevelopment was created not so much by active predation as by stagnation. As other areas grew, the interior was ignored and its relative status declined. As the French invested elsewhere, they created relative underdevelopment by their policies toward the interior. Mali became a backwater rather than an island of locally generated development.

Colonial policy was not coherent enough, nor did colonial administrations exert sufficient control, to block local development efforts consistently, and many people manipulated or ignored interventions. Because French colonialism was never a unified project, Malians were able to find niches they could use to improve their lives and their societies. A Mali-centered perspective demands that we understand these as well as the processes of capitalist domination initiated by French colonialism. The following sections look at some of the social processes brought about by the interaction of French penetration and Malian responses.

## Access to Resources

Access to labor changed significantly during the colonial period as people moved in response to policy changes. Colonialism also brought new forms of information and its dissemination, creating new options for social networks. In contrast, the effects of new technologies in transport and agriculture were less striking, while access to the major resource of agricultural land changed only minimally. In fact, a general population decline in the West African colonies between 1900 and 1921 (Coquery-Vidrovitch 1986, 358) led to decreased rural land pressure. Even areas with substantial immigration rarely experienced land pressure because population densities were usually already low. Private rural land tenure did not develop in most of rural Mali, and finding land did not prove problematic for those who wanted to increase farm areas.[8] This section concentrates on the two major areas of changing resource access: labor and information networks.

Pressures on labor came from French policies that led to population movements out of some areas and into others, creating some areas of high population in contrast to those of lower density. Other incentives moved labor out of agriculture into other activities. Different policies sometimes worked at cross-purposes to one another.

Abolition of slavery led directly to the first wave of population movements. As noted above, the late 1800s saw the growth of elite-owned plantations worked by slaves, and the French military continued to tolerate slave ownership in the early 1900s. In fact, they benefited directly from it.[9] When the French took Bamako (later to become Mali's capital) in 1883, they had a choice of bringing in provisions from the coast at high cost or nurturing a local grain market. They eventually chose the latter course, since they needed much millet to feed European and African troops. By 1894, the town of Banamba, north of Bamako, one of the major slave markets of the late nineteenth century, had developed into a major grain-producing center.

This boom proved to be short-lived. Banamba elites had increased their slave workforce when Samory and others sold them slaves to buy new weapons, but defeat cut off the supply of new slaves. Plantation owners had to adapt production strategies to use existing labor. Lacking any technological breakthroughs to raise production, they increased the amount of work required from their slaves, and sometimes ceased to give them sufficient food to eat. In turn the slaves resisted. Escapes increased, facilitated by the French military presence, which made travel safer. Small rebellions and revolts also occurred. Despite French colonial ambivalence about enforcing abolition, news of changing metropolitan attitudes reached slaves. In 1905, on the eve of planting, large numbers of Banamba slaves simply began to leave and return to their home areas. French authorities met with representatives of owner and slave groups, negotiating better working conditions for the 1905 season. In 1906, however, the slaves began to leave again, and the local French administration, under increased metropolitan pressure to ensure personal liberty, did not interfere. By 1911, Governor Ponty claimed that some 500,000 slaves throughout the federation had liberated themselves, a figure somewhat inaccurate but indicative (R. Roberts 1987, 197). Some began new independent villages in the regions where they had been enslaved, but recent captives who remembered their origins often returned home.

The loss of population in zones of old slave estates was balanced by gains in areas of immigration. Many of the Banamba slaves had been taken from the Wassulu in southern Mali by Samory in the late 1800s when his scorched-earth retreat depopulated it. In 1894, an initial French census found 6,709 inhabitants in Bougouni, one of the main Wassulu *cercles,* but by 1913 population had increased to 162,343 (Klein 1988, 209). While some of the increase may have been due to better counting procedures (Klein 1988) as well as decreased fear on the part of the locals, the increase was nevertheless quite striking, and clearly due in part to the return of freed slaves.

Other French policies contributed to population movements as well and meant that recently freed slaves did not always stay long in home areas. Investment created poles of economic growth that drew migrants to areas around towns, mines, and costal plantations. The relative economic stagnation of the interior, the need of newly freed slaves and soldiers without wars to earn income, and growing tensions between fathers and sons all pushed young men to migrate there. For example, in 1910, 2,000 young men left Bamako for the mines at Siguiri in Guinea or to work on the Côte d'Ivoire railroad (R. Roberts 1987, 200), and others went to Guinea to work as porters in rubber transport (Klein 1988, 207). In Gambia, immigrants, presumably to peanut farms, increased from 4,657 in 1904 to 21,979 in 1914 (Klein 1988, 206); many went to Senegal as well. Cocoa farms in Côte d'Ivoire and Ghana were also popular destinations. In Côte d'Ivoire, African planters hiring migratory laborers were among the major proponents of a free labor market, for they could not requisition labor the way that French planters could (Manning 1988, 118).

There was also movement to urban centers as towns grew between 1880 and 1940 (Manning 1988). Although the French administration in Bamako was concerned about lack of labor in the late nineteenth century, they began to complain of too many unemployed by the early 1900s, especially after an influx of freed slaves. Evidently, of those who chose neither to go home nor to stay where they were, a significant number moved to towns (R. Roberts 1987).

Furthermore, the French administration requisitioned labor, if sufficient workers did not come voluntarily to build infrastructure, including railroads. At first, villagers sometimes supplied slaves in response to labor requisitions, even buying them for this purpose (Coquery-Vidrovitch 1986, 353). The French also attempted to profit from the rapidly changing situation in regard to slaves by setting up liberty villages *(villages de liberté)* to harbor escaped slaves, strategically placing them along the railroad to ensure labor for construction and porterage. Malians often referred to residents of these villages as "slaves of the commandant." Liberty villages were not very popular among Malians, who tended to use them to help escape but moved quickly out of them.

The French requisitioned goods as well as labor. Most notably, they required West Africa to provide some 400,000 tons of peanuts to feed troops during the World War I (Coquery-Vidrovitch 1986, 354). These varying pressures on labor led to complementary out-migration from some areas. An estimated 80,000–100,000 Voltaics fled to Côte d'Ivoire and Ghana to avoid compulsory cultivation schemes (Coquery-Vidrovitch 1986, 367). Equivalent figures are not available for Mali, but the total numbers were likely somewhat less, since Mali was less densely populated.

The net result of these different policies was to decrease labor availability during an era of increased demands upon it. People were encouraged to produce more, requiring more labor, but also were compelled and enticed to move into nonagricultural activities. Population declined, caused in part by emigration of people fleeing labor requisitions. People were not in principle against new forms of labor but were looking for activities that would offer the best return. Since authorities were always tempted to offer low prices for African goods and work, in part to offset high transport costs, people searched for ways to avoid both local labor obligations and production schemes. They preferred to control their own labor.

Nevertheless, the combination of new demands on labor and the disappearance of old sources set into motion a restructuring of labor within the household, most notable among those parts of the population that had relied heavily on slaves. When the slaves walked off the Marka plantations of Banamba, Marka who wished to continue to farm had to do it themselves. Heads of households turned to sons and wives to provide a labor force, asserting their authority. Sons, faced by what they viewed as increasing exploitation, a decrease in heritable property (since the household no longer owned slaves), and new employment opportunities, often simply left to take up new kinds of work elsewhere (R. Roberts 1987, 200). Women had fewer opportunities to leave and had little choice but to work for their husbands, but they increasingly complained to authorities of ill treatment. Forms of rural extrahousehold labor also changed. Some agricultural areas, again, for example, around Banamba, saw a growth of collective wage labor. Village-level labor groups (the *tonw*) may have begun to work outside as well as within their villages, and labor gangs managed by entrepreneurs appeared (R. Roberts 1987, 203). In other areas, each household stressed its independence and village-level wage labor was rare.

Much work remains to be done on the changing terms of labor availability during this period, but the general lines are clear. Labor was not in surplus in the Soudan, and Africans actively searched for attractive returns to it. Both African and French elites attempted to control the terms at which labor was supplied, to the detriment of laborers. Laborers, in turn, resisted furnishing labor at those terms and developed a number of strategies, including migration, to find better ones. Migration from one colony to another was facilitated by the federation structure of French West Africa, which allowed relatively easy movement between individual colonies.

Large-scale forced and voluntary migration, complemented by new transport infrastructure and new political and social institutions, led to the second major resource change: changing information and communication linkages. The federation structure of French West Africa brought together Africans for a number of reasons. Among the most important were the military and education.

After pacification, the French continued to recruit colonial troops, and during World War I, some 140,000 African troops fought in Europe (Coquery-Vidrovitch 1986). In World War II, some 10 percent of the French troops at the front in 1940 were Africans (Manning 1988, 137), many of whom spent the war in German prisoner-of-war camps. African soldiers not only went to Europe, but also to Algeria and Vietnam in later years, and these cosmopolitan experiences exposed them to diverse perspectives and gave them a chance to compare their own societies with others. Veterans often questioned and criticized both the colonial administration and the traditional order in their own societies (Coquery-Vidrovitch 1986, 356).

The federation also facilitated population movement among elites. Africans who worked in the French administration or for private commercial firms often traveled throughout the federation (A. Roberts 1986, 225). The boundary between Mali and Senegal appears to have been especially fluid, since precolonial population movements meant that many persons had relatives living in both. Higher education usually necessitated travel. Secondary and postsecondary education were offered only in Dakar and a few other cities. The concentration of facilities limited access but increased the possibilities for the new francophone African elite to interact with one another. Many of the first generation of leaders knew one another from their days together at William Ponty Normal School, a teacher-training college in Dakar. For advanced university training, Africans were sent to France. In the 1920s, 23 local graduates went to Paris for teacher training, and soon afterward, 9 were sent to universities, mostly for veterinary studies (A. Roberts 1986, 230). Among them was Leopold Sedar Senghor, future president of Senegal, the only one to study arts and letters. He then taught in France from 1936 to 1940, a pattern followed by many francophone Africans.

The colonial educational system encouraged its subjects to use France and its civilization as a frame of reference. This was linked to the French policy of assimilation, by which Africans could become French citizens, even though the qualifications were so difficult to achieve that only a very limited number did so. Nonetheless, Paris became a center for elite French-speaking Africans, and by the 1930s, some frequented a salon run by a black Martiniquan woman (A. Roberts 1986, 260). The few French citizens from Africa elected a mixed-race representative as deputy to the French parliament in 1902, and a black, Blaise Diagne, in 1914 (Coquery-Vidrovitch 1986, 351).

As Africans met in Paris and talked to one another, they also entered the dialogue about colonialism taking place in metropolitan France. Many of the first African-led protests against colonial rule took place in Paris rather than the colonies (Coquery-Vidrovitch 1986, 378). The concentration of activities in a few centers further peripheralized the areas without comparable institutions, but it presented powerful new ideas to those who found themselves at the center. For many, their experiences led to critiques of racism and underdevelopment, and the formulation of alternative visions for the future. When Africans returned home, these ideas began to be heard in colonies as well.

*Negotiating Social Relationships*

Pacification ended warfare as a major path to social mobility. New forms of status negotiation depended on new ideas and forms of communication and interacted with forms of status negotiation based on earlier social hierarchies and ethnic identities. Negotiation also continued within households, continuing to favor men over women.

Africans, mostly men, used new European institutions as a way to provide social mobility for themselves and their families. The French administration depended on a large number of minor African employees, for example, postal and railroad workers, porters, and foremen (Coquery-Vidrovitch 1986, 349), and some were able to use these admittedly minor posts to their immediate advantage and to secure better education and jobs for their children. African soldiers used their military service to gain entry into positions in the colonies as French agents, guards, and even chiefs (Coquery-Vidrovitch 1986, 359).

Yet even as they used colonial institutions to achieve new status, Africans also used new resources and ways of thinking to resist the inequities of colonialism and to subvert its aims. Returned African soldiers became active promoters of social change (Coquery-Vidrovitch 1986, 359). Railroad workers led strikes in 1925, 1938, and 1947–48. In 1937 when collective bargaining was authorized in the colonies, some 42 unions and 16 professional associations with 8,000 members appeared (Coquery-Vidrovitch 1986, 390). Pan-Africanism grew, as did links with those of African background throughout the diaspora. As racism became a coherent ideology in the late nineteenth century, so also did those oppressed by it develop consciousness of their common ancestry as a way to fight against it (Boahen 1989).

Islam, so important during the nineteenth century, retained a central role, in part because it responded to the desires of many Africans for an ideology that was modern yet non-Western. By 1940, perhaps half of sub-Saharan Africa was at least nominally Muslim (Stewart 1986, 208). Islamic ideology and organization changed in light of the new conditions. By the early twentieth century, many African Muslims saw jihad as an anachronism and sought other ways to spread Islam (Stewart 1986, 200). Muslims started their own schools, providing an important educational alternative to official schools, at least at the beginning of the century. Because Islam is not centralized, new brotherhoods, so important in recruitment, were easily created. Many of them put forth distinctive interpretations of Islam and became vehicles for trying out new ideas (Stewart 1986). For example, one group, founded by a Soninke from the Senegal River valley in 1929, advocated absolute equality among believers, regardless of sex, age, or social status (Stewart 1986, 211, 212).

Ideas could be spread through improved transport and communication networks. As the ease and security of travel across the desert improved, more West African Muslims were able to go to Mecca for the hajj, and Saudi Arabia replaced Istanbul as the spiritual center of contemporary Islam (Stewart 1986, 215). Many smaller groups settled on the overland route to Mecca from West Africa, often offering services to other hajjis. When the hajj was prohibited in 1940 because of World War II, there were hajjis in most major Islamic communities on the continent (Stewart 1986, 215). This of course facilitated migration for Muslims, who could easily find a welcoming community in a new area (Stewart 1986).

The dispersion of West African Muslims, followed by new concentrations in Islamic centers, facilitated pan-Islamic initiatives alongside pan-Africanism. The best students from Islamic schools in Djenne and Timbuktu in Mali continued their education at the Islamic center of Al-Azhar in Cairo, where they met students from throughout the Islamic world. Others settled in Saudi Arabia, including descendants of Umar Tall, who first fled to Sokoto in northern Nigeria at his defeat. Continuing further eastward with colonial expansion, one descendent, Alfa Hashim, spiritual head of the Tijanniya brotherhood, eventually arrived in Saudi Arabia, where he had considerable influence on West African pilgrims (Stewart 1986, 201). Participation in this growing pan-Islamic network allowed people to create new statuses for themselves as well as to learn new ideas. Sometimes, pan-Islamic networks were used to confront colonial powers, as when a Tuareg resistance group in what is now Niger gained help from those further east (Stewart 1986, 199), but most benefits were intellectual and economic.

As new ways to negotiate status appeared, old ways underwent changes as well. Certain aspects of precolonial status hierarchy continued to be important in Malian villages, most notably the preservation of occupational caste identifications among blacksmiths and griots (oral historians and praise singers). Yet, the identification of some as former slaves almost disappeared, a tribute to the ability of rural Malians to renegotiate social positions and roles successfully. It is possible to carry out a study of smallholder agriculture in central Mali today without realizing that only 100 years earlier there existed a strikingly different mode of production, depending on extensive slave labor.[10]

Ethnicity could be used to provide solidarity among and within groups. For example, Bambara soldiers refused to march against their coethnic strikers in 1925 (Coquery-Vidrovitch 1986, 378). When freed slaves returned to home areas with the goal of reconstituting village life, there may have been a rebirth of ethnic pride and encouragement to marry within the group. Yet old patterns of flexibility continued as well. Because of labor migration, men continued to travel extensively and to enter a variety of relationships with diverse women. Individuals could still change their ethnic identity if circumstances warranted; for example, Nigerien Tuareg became Hausa when they settled down to cultivate, while Hausa became Tuareg when they took up nomadic herding (Manning 1988, 42).

Possibilities for negotiation within households appeared to be linked to labor availability. In areas of labor loss, heads of households attempted to increase control over other members, as discussed above. Young men were more likely to leave on labor migration rather than to push for renegotiation of household roles with their elders. Tensions between elders and juniors over labor allocations have still not been elaborated into a new ideal, but remain individually negotiated. Women had fewer economic opportunities to leave. Moreover, they hesitated to leave husbands if they had children, for patrilineal customs meant that the children would have to stay. Even women slaves were less likely to return to their areas of origin than were their male counterparts (R. Roberts 1987, 198). Women had few resources with which to negotiate improvements in their status. Moreover, they received little help from French authorities, who generally had no interest in liberating wives (Klein 1988, 201).

Yet in areas of new settlement, women's labor was crucial. In particular, women in areas with many returned slaves may have had the chance to renegotiate conditions of greater equality as all family members worked to make a success in their new homes. In many of the new villages, men and women worked side by side, disregarding the established gender division of labor (R. Roberts 1987, 198). Because intrahousehold responsibilities remained open to negotiation, the size and composition of households as well as tasks allocated to members were not uniform over ethnic group or region. As in the precolonial period, more information is needed on the history of changes in household labor allocation during this era. However, these examples suggest that those who see colonial changes as simply an increase in patriarchy have oversimplified complex changes.

*Individuality*

As in the precolonial period, examples of individuals able to use new resources to find new niches are biased toward the elite, whose biographies are better known. Yet some were more successful than others at taking advantage of new opportunities, and French power could check elite initiatives in significant ways. This section begins with the stories of a few individuals and ends with some examples of group innovation.

Although the French were less favorably inclined toward indirect rule than the English, manpower shortages forced the early colonial administration to work through African rulers. The attempts of local rulers installed by the French to adapt to new times are indicative of the limits of innovation as well as the possibilities for success. When the French commander, Archinard, took Segou from the Umarians, he placed Mari Diarra, a descendent of the Segou Bambara kings, on the throne. The French put significant restrictions on his rule; Mari had to allow free trade, and he could not independently go to war. Both these cut into the income by which he could ensure the loyalty of his followers, so he continued to let his warriors pillage both sides of the Niger. Less than a year later, the French accused him of conspiring to assassinate the French resident and declare himself independent; he and his close advisors were summarily executed (R. Roberts 1987, 154–57). This experience was encouraging to neither French nor African exponents of indirect rule.

The French also tried using handpicked individuals with proven loyalty, regardless of background. In 1891, they placed Mademba Sy, a Toucouleur aristocrat from Futa Toro and a French citizen who had been to France, on the throne of Sansanding, downstream from Segou. Mademba had worked for the colonial post and telegraph service, had been in the West African campaigns, and had served as a political officer. However, he had no standing with his new subjects, who saw him as another Umarian because of his Toucouleur background. After only a year, he had to request help from French troops because a revolt had imprisoned him. Nevertheless, he remained in power until his death in 1919. His son rose to the rank of captain in the French army in World War I, and later generations gained important positions in independent Senegal and Mali (Manning 1988, 73; R. Roberts 1987, 156, 157).

Some used their new resources to resist colonialism. Among them was Tiemoko Garan Kouyate, born in the Soudan in 1902. Sent to France on a scholarship, he became a Young Communist leader in 1927, organized black workers in French ports, and published newspapers in Europe and Africa. He developed links with other black activists, including Marcus Garvey and George Padmore, a Trinidadian who led the African section of Comintern in Moscow. He eventually broke with the Communist Party in 1933, when he decided that it did not sufficiently emphasize African interests. Returning to Dakar, he created the League for the Struggle for Liberty of the Peoples of Senegal and Soudan, which called for national independence. He died in Paris, a victim of the Nazis, in 1942 (Coquery-Vidrovitch 1986, 391; Manning 1988, 81, 82; A. Roberts 1986, 262). The next generation of African leaders owed its success to the work of innovators like him who began to talk of independence.

Among nonelites, there were examples of group movement into new niches. The Moors, herders with Mauritanian origins, moved quickly into overland porterage from rail stations inland and along other interior routes. They hauled goods from Banamba to Bamako, between Bamako and Côte d'Ivoire, and to the Siguiri mines (R. Roberts 1987, 162, 163, 166). The Somono, who had controlled Niger River transport in the precolonial states, reaped immediate benefits from the increased commercial activity following French penetration. When French merchants began to compete in transport, the Somono were quick to diversify, entering weaving, tobacco cultivation, and grain speculation (R. Roberts 1987, 205).

*Innovation*

One of the goals of the colonial enterprise was to encourage growth in export crops. In Mali, this was relatively unsuccessful, the failure often being attributed to problems inherent in adapting existing social institutions to new ends. Yet the problem was primarily economic. The French were usually willing to offer only very low prices for export crops because of the high costs of overland transport. Faced with no economic benefit, Malian cultivators often resisted colonial advice and programs.

French ethnocentrism blinded them to many aspects of local innovation in other spheres. Malians did grow new crops and use new techniques when they could profit. Many of these crops were for local and regional markets, where transport costs were less of a barrier. As a prelude to contemporary agricultural change, this section will consider developments in two major crops, cotton and food grains, to illustrate patterns of resistance to, and adoption of, new agricultural practices.

The development of food grain production for the Bamako market, referred to above, showed that Malians were willing and able to innovate in crop production to meet new opportunities. In December 1889 and January 1890, for example, Bamako received 56 metric tons of millet and 38.5 metric tons of rice from growers in the hinterland (R. Roberts 1987, 150). Malian farmers also sent grain to Guinea for workers gathering rubber and at the mines (R. Roberts 1987, 167). In 1908, 955 metric tons of rice and 580 metric tons of millet were exported by rail; Senegal with its numerous workers in commercial peanut agriculture was a major market. The growth in indigenous grain production was noted by the French; a colonial report from 1905 claimed, for example, that rice from the Niger valley had an almost unlimited market in neighboring countries. Grain marketing was accompanied by speculation, and a futures market for grains appeared in Bamako by 1903 (R. Roberts 1987, 166, 167).

Some of the early grain boom depended on conditions that soon passed. Abolition decreased production among large-scale farmers, and the continued colonial labor requisitions almost surely also had negative impact. Yet total production did not decrease (R. Roberts 1987, 201), and the French began to envisage an "island of prosperity" (DeWilde 1967, 245) in the middle Niger that would provide food for all of French West Africa. By the 1920s, they were planning a series of dams to irrigate 50,000 hectares northeast of Segou, the Office du Niger. Created in 1932 as a French public enterprise, the Office infrastructure was virtually complete by 1945, with more than 20,000 persons settled on some 22,000 hectares. Presumably the French felt free to encourage the growth of this market since it did not compete with either French industry or agriculture.

The Office was plagued by problems from the start. Adequate technical studies were not done, and farmers had to cope with water flow, drainage, and leveling problems. The administration assumed that colonists would simply come from areas of high population density in the Soudan because of increased economic opportunity. There were, however, few areas of high population density, so they coerced migrants to come from densely populated areas of what was then Upper Volta. When the French stopped labor recruitment in 1945, many of these settlers returned home.

Settlers were to grow rice and cotton on the perimeters, following Office programs and strategies to increase production. Yet farmers, even those who settled voluntarily, were skeptical of official programs and continually tried to subvert the imposed conditions and turn them to greater advantage. Farmers consistently resisted Office proposals to transplant rice as a way to increase yields, because they got equivalent returns with less work by planting extensively on a larger land area (DeWilde 1967). Most of the time, the Office supported owner-operators and discouraged or prohibited absentee landowners, even though some settlers thought they could make a better living by hiring all their labor. One innovation settlers did support was mechanization, increasingly common after the 1940s when the Office bought tractors with Marshall Plan funds. By 1955, tractors prepared land in about 75 percent of the rice and 60 percent of the cotton areas, as farmers called on them to lessen their workloads (DeWilde 1967, 279). Yet mechanization cost more than it earned, and the mechanization division was abolished in 1960 when settlers were encouraged to use animal traction instead.

Clearly the settlers and the administration had different goals for the Office. While farmers were concerned about their own incomes and well-being, the administration was more concerned about return to its investment and appeared to have been guided by ideas about appropriate behavior for small-scale African farmers as well. Yet neither group was able to made a success of the Office; by the late 1960s, it had never earned a return sufficient to amortize the public capital investment (DeWilde 1967, 246, 247). Yet investment in it continued, in part because of the large capital investment already made, but also because irrigation offered production security in a drought-prone land.

Attempts to grow cotton also had their ups and downs. By 1900, the French were interested in increasing cotton exports, when administrators purchased it from existing farms and ginned and pressed it in Bamako. In 1904–5, some 20,000 kg of exotic cotton seed were brought to Mali, mostly from the Americas, and distributed to villagers. Although cotton had been grown in West Africa for a long time, Malians appeared resistant to its increased cultivation for export, complaining about administrative demands. They preferred to sell to a large local textile industry, which spun and wove indigenous cotton, and whose prices were higher. In 1938, for example, the French rarely offered more than .80 francs/kg to producers, to maintain their export profit, while the domestic market offered 2.5–3 francs/kg (R. Roberts 1987, 168–73).

Locally produced cloth was exported regionally to Senegal and Guinea. While the cheapest local cottons were probably replaced by imports, more expensive varieties of local cloth continued to compete favorably (R. Roberts 1987, 171). Many newly freed slaves had learned to weave before abolition and used their skill as independent weavers to supplement agricultural income. Although the French wanted to provide their metropolitan industry with raw cotton, they gave up on large-scale cotton production in 1939 because of Malian resistance. For whatever reason, they appear to have simply ignored the local textile industry rather than actively trying to suppress it, and it thrived (R. Roberts 1995). They encouraged large-scale attempts to cultivate cotton again only when a new organization appeared.

In 1952, the Compagnie Française pour le Développement des Fibres Textiles (CFDT) began a new program of cash crop development based on cotton cultivation by small farmers. The larger economic context and the technical aspects of cotton growing had changed, and farmers could realize quite substantial returns for relatively small investment (DeWilde 1967). They rapidly adopted cotton cultivation in areas of CFDT extension. Most of this cotton was meant for export, although farmers continued to retain some for sale and processing in the local market.

The patterns are clear. Where there were niches for agricultural entrepreneurship, Malians entered them. When they were offered new "opportunities" to which the returns were negligible, they resisted, often by refusing to cultivate more than minimal quotas. Because of the high transport costs in moving goods from the interior to the coast and then overseas even after railroad construction, returns were rarely sufficiently high to make export to the metropole attractive. In contrast, growing specialization within West Africa meant that Malian farmers could exploit the ecological specialization that began precolonially, by growing food grains and cotton for domestic and regional markets (R. Roberts 1987). In addition to these crops, the savanna specialized in cattle production, which expanded as many Malians who might earlier have invested in slaves moved into livestock (R. Roberts 1987, 206). By 1959, Mali was exporting approximately 100,000 head of cattle annually into neighboring forest areas (Jones 1976, 29). Where returns were sufficiently good, Malians did not hesitate to adopt either new crops or new markets.

They innovated not only in agriculture, but in nonagricultural activities as well. Freed slaves were especially active here, particularly during the first few years of freedom when survival was often difficult (Klein 1988; R. Roberts 1987). The number of people entering trade increased as travel conditions became more secure. Previous ethnic specialization in particular occupations began to weaken as more people entered a greater variety of jobs (R. Roberts 1987, 207).

## Conclusion

Although many have seen the possibilities for positive transformation in Africa beginning with independence, postindependence Mali followed hundreds of years in which change was already the norm. French colonial policies and the growing capitalist world economy may have constrained the possibilities open to Malians, but a Mali-centered view of group and individual action illustrates that Malians tried in many ways to increase access to social and economic resources and to make the most of what they had.

During the precolonial era, many Malians participated in highly specialized economies and stratified political systems. Malian leaders eagerly adopted new technologies and activities that they thought would benefit them, and possibilities for upward social mobility were open to a wide variety of mostly male risk takers. Colonial conquest impacted negatively on the dynamism of certain parts of Malian economy and society as the French first attempted to make their colonies benefit the metropole, and then gave up on some, like Mali, that promised them few benefits, even with extensive investment. This created a backwater where one had not been before; specialized commercial agriculture decreased in some sectors. But for some Malians, including many who had been disenfranchised in the precolonial period, the colonial era offered new paths of mobility. Commercial dynamism thrived in niches that the French ignored. Malians built themselves a new culture that harkened back to "tradition" while simultaneously tapping new technologies and ideas.

The patterns prior to independence laid the groundwork for Malian responses to contemporary structural constraints. Local structures were constrained but not determined by international actions. Individuals used new structures to create access to both new and old resources and looked for niches where they could profit. We turn now to contemporary trends, beginning with a discussion of the national and international context.

Chapter 3

# *The Contemporary Context of Rural Production*

This chapter looks at three contemporary constraints on the actions of Malian farmers: the physical and international political environment, national policies, and their own customs and traditions of resource allocation. The chapter begins with the larger environment, both physical and political-economic, and the constraints it placed on local action. It then considers national agricultural policy, which provided a formal context for access to land, labor, capital, and markets. Finally, individual action was constrained by cultural ideologies and social institutions.

The different structural levels did not affect farmer action independently but also influenced one another. Most notably, the effectiveness of particular government policies was limited both by the international context and the willingness of the population to be guided by them. In addition, actors at each level negotiated with one another and sometimes worked at cross-purposes. This meant that the nature of constraints faced by farmers was far from seamless or static. The final section of the chapter examines local extension organizations, which illustrate these interactions and were also how most farmers experienced state constraints.

## External Constraints

External factors and actors limited both national government policy and individual choice. Mali is a poor country in a hazardous environment, lacking significant quantities of high-value resources to finance development. Any development initiatives had to take account of the limits imposed by the physical environment. Moreover, policy choices were influenced in two different ways by the international political-economic context: through the nature of international commodity markets and the policies of foreign donors who provided funds to meet national government expenditures. This section examines each of these constraints in turn.

*The Natural Environment*

As a Sahelian country, Mali has been susceptible to drought, deforestation, and other forms of environmental degradation. In addition, other environmental characteristics have limited the ability of state programs and farmer initiatives to generate satisfactory returns. For example, Mali's landlocked location and its vast area led to high transport costs. Prices of exports, both crops and minerals, were not competitive when neighboring coastal countries produced the same good at similar cost. Transport difficulties also made costs of imported goods relatively high. Governments, independent as well as colonial, were constantly tempted to increase exports through low producer prices, which typically induced local resistance. They were also forced to put much money into route infrastructure, although it was rarely enough, and transport remains inadequate.

The colonial railroad from Bamako to the port at Dakar in Senegal provided Mali's main outlet to the sea as well as internal transport in Mali's isolated western First Region. Derailments were common during the rainy season, cutting off this area from the rest of the country. Rail traffic was also subject to political disruption. When Mali and Senegal broke diplomatic relations in the early 1960s, the railroad was out of service for almost three years (Jones 1976, 85). Mali was forced to find alternative routes to the sea, which it did by developing the road south to Côte d'Ivoire, and its port, Abidjan. Over the long term, this route proved to cost one-third to one-half more than the train. Yet because it was more expeditious and flexible, both imports and exports continued to move this way even when the railroad reopened in July 1963 (Steedman et al. 1976).[1]

Internal transport was also problematic, leading many agricultural-extension programs to build feeder roads. To increase returns, these were often biased toward areas already producing significant cash crops, although better transport invigorated existing activities (Koenig 1986). In areas without adequate roads or public transport, people used bicycles or donkey-drawn carts, or carried produce to market on their heads. Inferior feeder roads made farm-to-market costs very high; at times in the mid-1970s, transport costs exceeded producer prices. When break-even transport costs exceeded government-set transport prices, truckers simply refused to risk their equipment (Steedman et al. 1976, 53). Without better roads, recent liberalization of transport costs may help goods flow more freely but cannot lower costs for consumers or raise producer prices. Recent programs to improve route infrastructure have already had major impacts south of the capital, and further improvements in the road network may lower transport costs further, but much remains to be done. Until then high transport prices will continue to constrain development.

Mali also hoped to generate development funds through exploitation of its mineral wealth, in the style of its neighbor, Niger, which earned much during its uranium boom. Yet most of Mali's minerals (iron ore, bauxite, copper, manganese, uranium, and perhaps petroleum) could not be exploited competitively, because there were significant quantities in other countries with easier transport (M. Traoré 1980, 42). Some minerals were exploited for internal use, including salt and gold from sources known since medieval times, and phosphates processed domestically for fertilizer. Most gold mining was small-scale placer mining in the dry season, carried out by women and men to earn additional income, although the government opened industrial mines, one in the 1970s and another in 1990, with foreign investment (M. Traoré 1980, 42; Cronje 1993, 108). The government recently has begun to earn significant foreign exchange from gold exports, which contributed 20.6 percent of export value in 1988 and 18.0 percent in 1993 (Encyclopaedia Britannica *Book of the Year* 1992, 652; 1996, 663). Exploration has continued, and by 1994 there was talk of another strike, in the west; by 1995, plans were underway for a major mine there. Both the Malian government and individual miners dreamed of potential riches. At the time of this study, the government had not yet earned much from its mines, nor had many individuals struck it rich.

Mali remained dependent on primary agricultural production and livestock to feed itself locally and to buy imports. These depended on sufficient rainfall and arable land to provide food security and generate adequate foreign exchange. Mali has better environmental conditions than many of its Sahelian neighbors, but it too suffered from droughts in the 1970s and 1980s and other forms of environmental degradation. Although climatic conditions are a constraint, they are in turn affected by people's land use practices. To create better environmental conditions, both national and donor policies have attempted to encourage practices that conserve the land base.

Unpredictable rainfall was the climatic constraint foremost in people's minds. While human activity may have played some part in declining rainfall levels, cyclical and long-term climate changes not easily amenable to human intervention also played a role in the unpredictability and variability of savanna rainfall. Coping strategies have involved both adaptation to unpredictability and attempts to control it. Malian farmers, the vast majority of whom depended on rainfed agriculture, grew multiple varieties and crops with different water requirements. Where rainfall was particularly low, they developed water con-servation technologies. Much Malian agricultural research has been oriented around the development of short-cycle varieties. Malian governments have consistently encouraged investments in irrigation and water control to render agricultural production more secure in low-rainfall years.

Some strategies to cope with uncertain rainfall created further environ-mental constraints. As rainfall decreased and became more unpredictable in northern Mali, people moved south to better-watered areas with more pre-dictable rains. This led to increasing population density in areas with good rain-fall, arable land, and access to surface and ground water, in turn raising concern about the development of ecological problems linked to denser settlement, in-cluding the destruction of forests and bush, and soil degradation. To put new land in cultivation, farmers cleared trees and bush and planted existing pastures, pushing herders into remaining forest, where they in turn cut branches and trees for fodder. Meanwhile, growing urban centers stimulated demand for wood fuel and building wood. An estimated 36,000 hectares per year were deforested dur-ing the 1980s (World Bank 1989, 280). These activities also led to conflict be-tween different forest users, for example, herders versus hunters and those who gathered plants and wood.

To address deforestation over the short term, the Malian government put limits on forest exploitation and the clearing of new lands (DNEF 1986). This led farmers to increase their use of lands already under cultivation, leading to shortened fallow periods and decreasing natural soil fertility. Soil degradation poses a significant threat to the more developed areas of Mali, despite conser-vation efforts. Recent estimates of soil loss in southern Mali averaged 6.5 tons per hectare per year with losses of up to 31 tons per hectare per year in some areas (Buursink 1990). Soil erosion promises to be a major problem for the fu-ture, even though a number of experimental programs to control it have begun (van Campen, Hijkoop, and van der Poel 1988).

Mali's physical environment constrains both national policy and individ-ual actions. Both governments and individuals tried to develop strategies that exploited favorable aspects, controlled some of the unfavorable ones, and adapted to environmental unpredictability. Yet these actions in themselves cre-ated effects that could change environmental characteristics, sometimes re-vealing conflicting objectives among different parties, as, for example, when governmental desire for the maintenance of forest cover opposed farmers' de-sire for more land. This meant that the effects of environmental constraints were neither obvious nor predictable.

*Engagement with International Markets*

Since one of the few ways Mali earned foreign exchange was through sales of primary commodities, a major constraint has been the international market for its main exports, especially in comparison to the cost of imports, primarily oil, but manufactured goods as well. This section looks at the export commodities on which Mali depended during the 1970s and 1980s, patterns of price variation, and the responses of the Malian government.

In the 1970s, cotton, peanuts, and animal products (livestock, skins, meat, and wool) were Mali's major exports. Perturbations in the peanut market led to decreasing exports in the 1980s. By 1988, 38.3 percent of export value was from raw cotton and cotton products and 29.5 percent from live animals; in 1990, cotton contributed 44.9 percent of value and live animals 24 percent (Encyclopedia Britannica *Book of the Year* 1992, 652; 1994, 664). Because cotton and peanuts were sold on world markets, it is possible to follow the effects of international supply and demand on their prices. Animal products were mostly exported regionally, and prices presumably followed regional patterns of supply and demand. Since these were not systematically recorded, we cannot trace their evolution. To the extent that regional commodity patterns of supply and demand diverged from international ones, the addition of a regional export stream may have stabilized Mali's trade income to some degree.

Mali's cotton was an extremely small part of world production, and the prices were mainly affected by the activities of the world's big three cotton producers, China, the United States, and the former Soviet Union, who together produced half or more of all cotton between 1960 and 1990 (Commodity Research Bureau 1970, 130; 1980, 132; 1990, 64).[2] During this period, China's production levels as well as its proportion of total world production grew substantially, while that of the United States decreased, both absolutely and proportionately. Disagreements between these two giants as each attempted to advantage its own producers affected producer prices in smaller countries, who had to adjust their prices to international trends.

Nevertheless, world market prices of West African cotton in 1980 were about triple those of 1970, peaking at a price almost four times as high a few years later (fig. 1). Although cotton prices fell somewhat by 1989, cotton has been the best and surest source of agricultural revenues since independence, both for the national treasury and for individual growers. Mali's production of cotton grew from 34,000 metric tons in 1965 to 151,000 metric tons in 1980 and 220,000 metric tons in 1987 (World Bank 1989, 233). Recent policies lib-

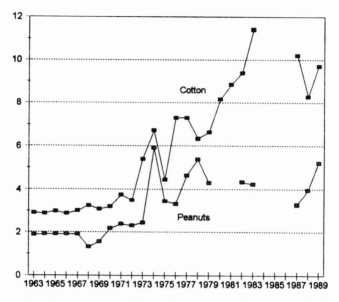

Fig. 1. World market prices of West African cotton and peanuts, 1963–89. No data are available for 1984–86 for cotton or peanuts, or for 1980–81 for peanuts. Prices are CAF in French francs, except for 1963–66, which are FOB for cotton. West African prices are used where available; when not, closest variety is used. (Data from *Marchés Tropicaux et Mediterranéens,* 1963–89.)

eralizing crop prices will make farmers more subject to international market fluctuations, but anecdotal evidence suggests that cotton farmers were net beneficiaries of the January 1994 currency devaluation. To maintain production, programs have attempted to decrease production costs as well as negative environmental effects, for example, through the increased use of integrated pest management techniques (Cauquil and Vaissayre 1994).

Mali's attempts at earning money from peanuts were less successful. For a very short period of time, when prices peaked in the mid-1970s, international peanut sales brought in funds to both the Malian treasury and farmers. Yet Malian peanuts had to complete not only with other peanut producers but also with other tropical oils, which are highly interchangeable. In response, prices fell in the 1980s, although they rose again slightly in the late 1980s and early 1990s (fig. 1). Yet they remained quite volatile. Rotterdam prices rose in October 1986 to U.S.$1,585 per ton, from a late 1985 price of U.S.$691 per ton; they rose again in late 1990 to U.S.$2,075 per ton but fell to U.S.$950 per ton in late 1991 (Commodity Research Bureau 1987, 177; 1992, 186).

In the late 1980s, the export market was dominated by the United States and Senegal, although the United States produced only 8.8 percent and Senegal only 3.6 percent of the world crop in 1989–90 (Commodity Research Bureau 1990, 176).[3] Again, Mali was one of the smallest producers and could do little to control prices. Peanut production levels varied considerably. In 1965, Mali produced 153,000 tons, and production decreased slightly (to 116,000–135,000 tons) by 1980, only to fall quite substantially in the early and mid-1980s, when annual production was around 45,000 to 60,000 tons. Production began to pick up somewhat in the late 1980s, with estimated production of 115,000 tons in 1988–89 (World Bank 1989, 232; Commodity Research Bureau 1990, 176). Since Malian peanuts had a substantial domestic market, people continued to cultivate and sell some even when the export market was fragile.

The prices of imports rose and terms of trade decreased through the 1980s (World Bank 1994a, 56). The most noteworthy increase was in the 1970s, due to two large oil-price hikes, first in 1973–74 and again in 1978–80. During the 1970s, the real world price of oil increased fivefold, and countries like Mali, which imported all their oil, felt a significant impact (World Bank 1981a). Malian governments did not face changing prices passively but attempted to diversify exports. They looked harder for exploitable mineral resources, entering into partnerships with foreign investors for the gold mines. They also encouraged the development of local resources that could substitute for imports; most notable was the use of Saharan rock phosphates to complement imported chemical fertilizers. They also encouraged diversification within primary products, beginning vegetable sales to Europe in the 1980s, for example. Although this is a very competitive market, it looks promising because fresh produce must move by air or risk spoilage; Mali suffers less from its landlocked location. Nonetheless, as a relatively small producer of any commodity, Mali is likely to remain at the mercy of world economic fluctuations.

*Dependence on Foreign Assistance*

Mali received a significant amount of national income from foreign assistance. In its early years, aid mostly came from socialist countries and was relatively low, U.S.$16.8 million in 1962 (Jones 1976, 363), U.S.$21 million in 1970. After the first Sahel drought, the amount of aid increased dramatically to U.S.$118 million in 1974 and U.S.$145 million in 1975, as did the range of donors (World Bank 1981a, 165). Amounts continued to increase thereafter; by 1980, aid receipts were U.S.$267 million and in 1987 U.S.$364 million (World Bank 1989,

251). Most aid was in the form of grants, 67 percent in 1980 and 71 percent in 1987 (World Bank 1989, 251).

Mali attempted to decrease the political dependence on a single aid source by diversifying donors and exploiting the different, sometimes contradictory, goals of each. Nevertheless both bilateral and multilateral donors have been able to express their priorities through the focus of their aid. Since the 1970s, three themes have been particularly important: recovery from the Sahelian drought, structural adjustment, and environmental conservation.

*Drought Aid*

The drought of the late 1960s and mid-1970s brought the Sahel to international attention and led to the creation of two organizations to meet the crisis more effectively. In 1973, the Sahelian countries formed the Comité Permanent Inter-Etats de Lutte contre la Sécheresse dans le Sahel (CILSS) to coordinate short-term relief and to formulate medium- and long-term development programs (Somerville 1986, 91, 92). In 1976, donor countries, led by the Organization for Economic Cooperation and Development (OECD), formed the Club du Sahel as a partner to CILSS. The two organizations developed and implemented projects together until 1985; since then, the focus has been on assessment and monitoring, leaving national project development to the member states (Somerville 1986, 233).

The effective lobbying activities of these two organizations led to a dramatic increase in aid to Sahelian countries, from U.S.$196.5 million in 1971 to U.S.$1.105 billion in 1978, and U.S.$1.513 billion in 1982 (Somerville 1986, 179). Recognizing that short-term relief would not solve long-term Sahelian problems, projects targeted rural growth and the least developed sectors of the economy. The United States Agency for International Development (USAID), for example, began to fund an integrated rural development organization in the Niger valley north and south of Bamako and provided significant aid to the livestock sector to improve pastoral production.

Although the increase in aid was partly a result of donors' short-term political objectives,[4] the impetus behind much of this assistance also grew from humanitarian concerns (Somerville 1986, 97–99). In the United States, aid to the Sahel was supported significantly by the Congressional Black Caucus. Overall, aid goals moved away from earlier attempts to develop industry and infrastructure toward food self-sufficiency (Somerville 1986, 92). Yet ten years after the founding of CILSS, the Sahel was no closer to feeding itself (Somerville 1986, xix). Aid was not always used effectively to promote development, and as the World Bank (1981a, 4) argued, it was diluted by inadequate domestic policies. Following the lead of the World Bank, most donors began to focus on structural adjustment in the 1980s.

*Structural Adjustment*

By the late 1970s, many donors had become concerned about the slow or declining growth of African economies. From 1980 through 1986, with GDP increasing at only 0.2 percent per year on average and populations growing at about 3.2 percent per year, African countries saw an average decrease in GDP per capita of approximately 3 percent per year (O'Brien 1991, 33). Donors attributed the stagnation to bloated administrative structures, inefficient domestic markets, overvalued exchange rates, and generally poor domestic macroeconomic management. They proposed the series of reforms meant to move African countries toward more "liberal" economies with more market-oriented policies, more efficient use of prices, and greater openness to international trade that came to be known as structural adjustment (O'Brien 1991). Credits from the International Monetary Fund were tied to adoption of structural-adjustment guidelines, essentially forcing national governments to adopt them.

A "complete reform package" included a variety of programs: (1) economic changes to let markets work; (2) getting the prices of commodities "right"; (3) privatization of state-controlled and public enterprises; (4) "rationalization" of national budgets; and (5) reform of government institutions to carry out new roles (Johnston 1991, 82). In practice, the particular changes varied from country to country. For example, currency devaluation, a key part of getting the prices "right," was only implemented in the African Financial Community[5] countries in January 1994. Even then the currency remained tied to the French franc, so that national currency values still did not directly reflect the economic circumstances of a single country. Structural-adjustment programs in Mali involved the privatization of the credit and commercialization roles of rural-development organizations and liberalization of market structures. By 1993, all export and most import monopolies were abolished. More than thirty state-owned enterprises were liquidated, restructured, or privatized (Cronje 1993, 109).

The World Bank (1981a, 1989) stressed the need for donors to continue, and more crucially, to augment, aid contributions during adjustment to encourage change. In Mali, aid receipts in 1987 were more than three times those of 1974. Yet donor targets changed. USAID, for example, put less emphasis on agriculture and livestock, moving money into policy reform (e.g., efforts to privatize cereal markets, reductions in the size of the civil service) and attempting to increase private-sector activity through support of nongovernmental organizations. In light of concerns that initial adjustment programs had deleterious impacts on investments in health and education (Cornia, Jolly, and Stewart 1987), USAID also funded significant initiatives in primary education and health.

### Environmental Conservation

Parallel to their focus on drought aid and structural adjustment, donors, often supported by well-organized national environmental constituencies, consistently expressed interest in combating problems of environmental degradation in the Sahel. They often moved from one environmental trend to another, especially as environmental organizations at home changed focus. During the drought years, the focus was desertification and deforestation. After the oil shocks in the 1970s, concern turned to renewable and alternative energy technologies that could simultaneously halt desertification and decrease oil import costs. Programs to develop improved wood stoves for cooking were popular, and USAID funded a large-scale project to support the Solar Energy Laboratory in Bamako in its search for high-technology solutions (e.g., photovoltaics and windmills). The German government funded a Regional Center for Solar Energy. In the 1980s, environmental concerns of donors turned more directly to conservation, including species conservation, biological diversity (Warshall 1989), and soil and water conservation (van Campen, Hijkoop, and van der Poel 1988). Building on donor interests in decentralization, programs to encourage local control of open bushlands and classified forests appeared (S. Traoré 1989).

In addition to funding projects consistent with their internal politics, both multilateral and bilateral donors preferred to finance projects easy to design and execute, with good benefit-cost projections, and in sectors where they had expertise (Somerville 1986, 205). The scope of this chapter does not allow an extended analysis of particular donors and their policies, but their varying politics and priorities meant that aid flows did not constrain the Malian government in a consistent fashion from 1960 to 1989. Malian governments attempted to use inconsistencies and contradictions among donor priorities to turn political constraints to their own ends. They were seriously limited in this strategy when a number of donors supported a single policy, as in the generalized support for structural adjustment during the 1980s. When donor interests varied, as they did in the 1970s, they were more successful, persuading socialist countries to fund one set of projects and capitalists another. The entire set of external constraints, physical environment, international market forces, and donor policies, rarely acted in a seamless fashion. While Malian governments had to make policy in a context limited by these constraints, they also attempted to manipulate and control them.

National Agricultural Policy since Independence

For Malians, independence meant the possibility of autonomous development. They consciously chose to alter radically the colonial economy that they had inherited by adopting a socialist government. Using centralized planning, the governments set targets and tried to mobilize the citizenry to meet them through public programs. Later regimes turned from an explicit commitment to socialist development but still attempted to use national agricultural policy to exert significant control over rural production systems to increase productivity, national food security, and foreign-exchange earnings.

Since independence in 1960, Mali has had four regimes. From 1960 to 1968, Modibo Keita, guided by orthodox Marxist socialism, hoped to collectivize agriculture while decolonizing the national economy. When Moussa Traoré came to power in a coup in 1968, he dropped some pieces of socialist ideology but retained a philosophy of centralization and command economy, which changed only after economic and natural crises and with prolonged international pressure. Under internal pressure for greater democratization, Moussa was overthrown in a second coup in March 1991. Ahmadou Toumany Touré led a transition government until he stepped down voluntarily after multiparty elections in 1992 when Alpha Oumar Konaré was elected. Under continued pressure from both the IMF and segments of the Malian population, Alpha's government moved toward greater economic liberalization, decentralization, and democratization. Since the data for this study were collected in 1989, before the 1991 coup, we concentrate on agricultural policy during Moussa's administration and its connections to Modibo's earlier policies.

*The Goal: Centralized Control*

Despite different philosophies, there were striking continuities in the approach of Mali's first two governments to agricultural development. Their common desire for centralized control of the economy—key to both Modibo's and Moussa's administrations—was crucial. This section looks at the general policy framework and then turns to particular initiatives affecting access to agricultural resources.

Mali became an independent nation on 22 September 1960, with Modibo

Keita as its first president, after a short, three-month attempt to exist as a federated union with Senegal.[6] Modibo faced the task of developing a very poor, undiversified economy with serious transport problems. Early government policies generated the themes that were to motivate agricultural policy for a long time: agricultural development for food self-sufficiency and to fund other investments, as well as a belief that foreign investment or assistance could solve budget deficits.

Food self-sufficiency became a critical priority in 1962 (Kébé 1981, 45) and has remained one ever since. Yet because agriculture was the only sector to generate much revenue, the government also expected it to contribute significantly to economic development. Rainfed agriculture and animal husbandry, for example, were expected to generate approximately half the growth envisaged by the first national plan (Jones 1976, 263). Yet all agriculture was to receive only 25 percent of planned investment, and, of that, some two-thirds was for irrigated, not rainfed agriculture, much for the Office du Niger (Jones 1976, 125). Funds were also used to create publicly owned enterprises in commerce, transport, and industry, many of which complemented agriculture (e.g., agricultural processing, rural transport) (M. Cissé 1981, 134–36).

To fund the planned investments, the government expected half the monies to come from foreign aid, mostly from Mali's former colonial power, France, and from sympathetic socialist countries (Jones 1976, 118). Much of this aid did materialize in the early years, but it did not always go into planned activities. More importantly, domestic investment funds fell short while costs increased more than expected (Jones 1976, 357, 362). Initial attempts to create development through centralized planning did not work. Farmers, pressured by government controls to produce more, resisted, and with few exceptions, agricultural production stagnated. By 1962, barely two years independent, Mali had severe balance-of-payment problems. Throughout the 1960s, economic conditions worsened, and by the mid-1960s, Modibo sought to strengthen ties with France.[7] Economic and political crises nevertheless continued, and on 19 November 1968, a military coup brought Moussa Traoré to power.

The new government dropped the rhetoric of socialism and removed a few of the policies that had negatively impacted small-scale farmers, yet remained a believer in central planning. It supported state enterprises, creating more, and continued market and price controls begun during the socialist era. It too looked to small-scale agriculture for internal budget support, and to foreign aid for help in balancing the national budget, which grew as the state attempted to implement its centralized policies. From U.S.$44.9 million in 1962, expenditures grew to U.S.$83.49 million in fiscal year 1967/8, U.S.$186.2 million in 1980, and U.S.$208.1 million in 1986. They jumped to U.S.$834.8 million in 1989.[8] Throughout, Mali was never able to generate sufficient domestic revenue to meet expenditures and fund development plans.

By the early 1980s, structural-adjustment pressures effected a move away from central control and toward economic liberalization. In 1981, approximately midway through Moussa's regime, Mali freed the market prices of millet, sorghum, and maize (CILSS/Club du Sahel 1983), and through the 1980s, more prices were liberalized and markets privatized. The state sold enterprises and reduced the size of the civil service. Nevertheless, the government remained committed to certain aspects of centralization. It retained formal ownership of most rural land areas, as discussed later in this chapter. Liberalization of the price of rice, the grain of choice for urban middle-class consumers, only occurred in 1984–85 and not until February 1986 in the Office du Niger (Dione and Dembelé 1987, 13). The government continued to generate centralized development plans.

While initial efforts toward reform focused on economic issues, they were soon followed by an interest in changing political structures to support economic growth and discourage corruption. This led to new donor initiatives, including democratization, strengthening legal frameworks, promoting effective civil society, and decentralization (USAID 1993). By the late 1980s, Malians were pressuring their government for greater democracy. In 1988, Moussa removed press controls (Hall et al. 1991, 10) but moved only hesitantly toward a multiparty system. After a series of demonstrations and protests, some violent, a coup overthrew and imprisoned him on 26 March 1991. Ahmadou Toumany Touré headed the transition government until Alpha Oumar Konaré was elected in 1992.

The fact that a military leader voluntarily stepped down for a freely elected government made Malians very optimistic about their future, but the new government remained under stringent economic constraints. Although Mali moved from its status as the world's ninth poorest country in 1980 up to the sixteenth poorest in 1991, it remained poor, with a per capita GDP below the mean for low-income countries and an average per capita growth rate from 1980 to 1991 that was negative (World Bank 1981b, 134; 1993, 238). It had few resources to invest in growth and development and no obvious way to generate them. As a post-structural-adjustment government, the new administration has had to continue economic reforms and political decentralization. The effects of continued reforms on rural producers are only beginning to be studied.

Despite the steady erosion of centralized control over the past 15 years, it remained an important theme of national agricultural policy. Since food security and self-sufficiency were consistently among the main government policy goals, governments attempted to control certain aspects of rural production systems, with an eye toward increasing their effectiveness. These included access to land, labor, and capital, as well as disposition of the final product.

## Access to Land

In theory, national control of land access was high. The land tenure code in force in 1989 made clear the government's ownership and rights over all lands, with the exception of those where private owners were registered, primarily urban house sites (GRM 1987). In fact, the state never attempted to assert its ownership rights everywhere, and the law recognized customary control, either collective or individual, as the major form of rural land tenure. The government asserted its ownership rights over agricultural land in limited instances, notably, in peri-urban areas and in infrastructure developments, including irrigation projects.

In peri-urban areas, farmland grew in value alongside cities' demands for food. The land tenure code included provisions for what it called a *concession rurale,* temporary recognition of private ownership that could lead to future title. A formal agreement between the state and the new proprietor to foster land development with a list of improvements was an intrinsic part of the *concession,* and title could be granted only after these were implemented (GRM 1987, 28–35). When a potential proprietor approached the state for a *concession rurale,* customary owners had a choice of abandoning the land or making a bid for it themselves. They did not, it appears, have the right to refuse the *concession,* although the state was to accord them an indemnity for any earlier improvements, and in certain circumstances, an additional indemnity to aid in resettlement (45). Using this legal instrument, elites dispossessed customary owners around major cities, but there was little impact elsewhere.

The state also exercised rights of eminent domain in areas where it carried out infrastructure projects, including roads, dams, bridges, and the like. It was legally obligated to provide the displaced with new lands and/or a financial settlement (GRM 1987, 46). In two recent cases of major infrastructure development, the construction of the Selingue and Manantali dams, resettled populations received more than the legal minimum. The state built new roads, drilled wells, assisted in housing construction, and aided the villagers find new farms. Land tenure in resettlement areas remained primarily customary tenure, as in the old sites.

The state did control access and use of land on irrigated perimeters, which it justified by the fact that national investments had improved them. The Office du Niger had originally planned to grant settlers occupation permits after ten years of cultivation, but nationalization of land in 1962 ended that policy. A settler's right to cultivate could be withdrawn even after many years if he did not follow regulations (DeWilde 1967, 254). The government also used other facets of land allocation to further national objectives. For example, to discourage absentee landlords, plot sizes were kept to a size that could be cultivated by a single household. Even though settlers could pass on parcels to heirs, land insecurity on Office du Niger perimeters negatively affected productivity and "stifled the *colons*' spirit of initiative for the past 60 years" (Djibo et al. 1991, 95). Tenure has been even more problematic at some newer perimeters.

When the government chose to exercise its rights, it could have significant impact on land ownership, but it did so in only limited geographic areas. Given its desire for control, it is not clear why it did not attempt more. To be sure, greater control would likely have led to greater rural resistance. Yet the fact that land access was not generally seen as problematic was almost surely also important. Mali's 1987 population density, 6.29/km$^2$, was much lower than that of its neighbors Burkina Faso (30.29/km$^2$) and Senegal (35.71/km$^2$) (World Bank 1989, 221). Only 2 percent of its land was cultivated, in contrast to 11 percent in Burkina and 27 percent in Senegal (World Bank 1989, 279). While national density figures were deflated by the large part of Mali in the Sahara desert, Mali cultivated only 2 percent of its land area; its neighbor Niger, with even more desert, cultivated 3 percent, despite lower rainfall (World Bank 1989, 279). In fact, there was sufficient arable rainfed land that areas cultivated in the 1970s could increase tenfold without major investments (Steedman et al. 1976, 1).

Although the state did not often exercise its potential control over rural land, it was always a possible interlocutor in any land dispute or transaction because of its legal ownership rights. Most commonly, it became involved when rural representatives of the state were called on to solve intervillage disputes over land, although in some circumstances state representatives played a greater role. Since disputes could be negotiated using customary regulations, the land tenure code, or a combination of the two, the solution to any rural land issue was always unpredictable.

## Access to Labor

National governments had no desire to re-create the massive labor requisitions of the French colonial administration, yet they did try through more subtle means to change patterns of labor use. Modibo's government attempted to change the unit of agricultural production from the household to the collectivity as a step on the road to agricultural collectivization. Other policies attempted to channel domestic and international migration.

As a step toward socialist agriculture and state farms, Modibo's government encouraged and later mandated the institution of village-level production and consumption cooperatives. In addition, each village had to cultivate a collective field, the produce meant for village development activities. Farmers resisted, as shown by extremely low production in these fields. One 1966 study found average yields on village collective fields of sorghum and millet to be only 308 kg/ha, while family fields averaged 900 kg/ha (Jones 1976, 294). In only a few cases, where villages decided to use these fields for local purposes (e.g., demonstration plots) were they even semisuccessful (DeWilde 1967, 312). Given the dismal results, Moussa's government dropped this policy, and labor remained primarily under family control.

The government has also been concerned about matching labor and resource availability with labor need throughout the country. Despite some desire to control internal migration, internal movement is not (and, to the best of our knowledge, has not been) formally regulated. Nevertheless, both Modibo's and Moussa's governments tried to limit internal migration by encouraging the development of each region based upon its unique mix of resources (DeWilde 1967, 270). Public-service advertisements on television tried to discourage rural-rural migration. Yet when crises led to greater-than-average internal migration, as when large numbers of people moved south to escape drought, the state did intervene to facilitate rural resettlement. However, Mali never developed any large-scale projects, like the Volta Valley Authority in neighboring Burkina Faso, to settle "underpopulated" lands. Nevertheless, people often moved to follow economic incentives, as our case studies will show. As in most developing countries, rural-urban migration was high, but so too was rural-rural migration.

Malians also sent family members outside the country, leading to high levels of international emigration. The number of emigrants abroad was recently estimated at 6.47 percent of the resident population. Although the government did little to control it, it viewed this level as significant and satisfactory (Russell, Jacobsen, and Stanley 1990, 2:80). Remittances from France by migrants from Senegal, Mali, and Mauritania were largely sufficient to offset trade deficits in the early 1980s (Russell, Jacobsen, and Stanley 1990, 2:81), a factor that surely played a part in government attitudes. Remittances also permitted various initiatives at the local level that might have otherwise been impossible.

For example, some people could purchase food with remittance funds when drought conditions decreased production (DNAS 1985).

Lacking any significant successful efforts by the national government to change patterns of land allocation or labor deployment, these remained structured by local practice. However, the state had other ways to influence farm production, by controlling access to capital or the disposition of produce. In these, they had much greater impact.

*Access to Capital*

To increase production, farmers needed not only land and labor but also new technical knowledge, access to inputs (fertilizers, selected seeds, pesticides, etc.), and equipment. Malian governments exerted significant control over these, primarily through the Opérations de Développement Rural (ODRs, or Rural Development Operations), vertically integrated organizations that focused on agricultural extension but incorporated other development programs, such as functional literacy, health, and rural roads as well. Each ODR was organized primarily around one major crop, a cash crop like cotton or peanuts in the south, but a food crop in the more northern, low-rainfall zones. In principle, each ODR covered a homogeneous agricultural zone, although political considerations often meant that several zones were included. The CFDT, which became the Compagnie Malienne de Développement des Textiles (CMDT) in 1964, provided the model for the ODRs.

The state controlled agricultural production through ODR monopolies on credit, input provision, and crop sales. Credit came centrally from the Société du Crédit Agricole et de l'Equipement Rural (SCAER), created in 1964 to replace an earlier institution. SCAER held a monopoly on the distribution of farm implements, fertilizer, and pesticides through the early 1980s and provided short- and medium-term credit through the ODRs. Yet the SCAER monopoly was criticized on many fronts. Extension agents considered SCAER a serious bottleneck because it was not able to deliver goods in a timely fashion. Outside analysts criticized SCAER for setting prices on equipment and inputs to include an indirect tax on farmers (Kébé 1981, 63). SCAER in turn complained of conditions that did not allow it to carry out its activities effectively. Farmers were slow to repay loans, and when they did, the ODRs often retained recuperated credit funds to finance crop buying rather than paying off SCAER. SCAER also suffered from delays on goods coming in via the Dakar-Bamako railroad, so had to place orders months in advance, before either farmers or ODRs had good estimates of need (Steedman et al. 1976, 87–89). These constraints meant that credit and inputs were only available in those ODRs deemed "successful" by SCAER. In the late 1970s, only two of them, the CMDT (cotton) and ODIPAC (peanuts), had significant access to either credit and imports (Steedman et al. 1976, 87; Kébé 1981, 62). SCAER also sold a small quantity of inputs through regional outlets for cash.

Since central control did not translate into broad-based access to new means of production, neither the ODRs nor farmers regretted the dissolution of SCAER by the privatization initiatives of the 1980s. Yet some centralized control remained over credit and input supply. The direct role of ODRs in credit supply began to break down in the mid-1980s with the development of villagewide farmer groups, known as Associations Villageoises (AVs), which got credit directly from private banks, based on joint liability. Although this became the standard way to get agricultural credit by the late 1980s, either the ODR itself or an embedded organization had to organize, certify, and support the AV. In this way, the ODRs continued to play an important role in credit provision.

After privatization, the ODRs also retained a practical monopoly on the provision of imported inputs, particularly fertilizers. In the mid-1980s, most private import firms dealt with ODRs, who then sold in turn to farmers. Wholesalers often preferred it that way, finding private distribution at the farmer level problematic. They claimed that there were insufficient alternative distribution networks and argued that the continued presence of government agencies in rural areas made for unfair market practices (Shea 1986, 41–44). Even in the early 1990s, most inputs continued to be funneled through the ODRs, and when they were not, farmer access was seriously compromised (T. Diarra et al. 1995).

The most truly privatized part of the agricultural-supply network was equipment, mostly ox-drawn plows or multipurpose tool frames. By 1974, a local factory produced farm implements on a large scale (Steedman et al. 1976, 88). Supplementary production was done by village-based blacksmiths, who learned to make farm implements through ODR training programs, adapted basic plow designs from elsewhere (Toulmin 1992, 159), and learned to produce spare parts. Locally made plows were distributed primarily through the private sector, as were draft animals, mostly oxen, but some horses and donkeys as well. Our case studies clearly showed two separate input streams in 1989. Equipment, small implements, and traction animals moved primarily through private-sector networks, while inputs, especially imports, were available in significant quantities only through ODRs.

Despite the liberalization and privatization initiatives of the 1980s, the ODRs retained some control over access to factors of production. Their personnel, dispersed throughout the country, usually retained the approach they had developed during the years of stronger control. They generally saw them-selves as authorities, directing farmers toward centrally specified objectives, or, as Steedman et al. (1976, xx) put it, farmers were too often seen as the objects and not the agents of agricultural development and extension. Nevertheless, many farmers developed close ties to ODR personnel. Extension agents usu-ally lived in one of their target villages and shared the living conditions of farm-ers. Because ODRs were the key government institution in rural areas, their per-sonnel often served as liaisons between farmers and other parts of the local administration (Steedman et al. 1976). ODRs served not only as a means of state penetration at the local level, but they also gave farmers access to the state. Farmers therefore developed complex patterns of resistance to, and collabora-tion with, ODRs.

## The Disposition of Agricultural Produce

ODR controls over credit and inputs most affected farmers who wanted to use new agricultural technologies; attempts to control product marketing affected many more. The state attempted to control three different levels: international markets, domestic markets for industrial commodities, and decentralized local markets. It was partially successful at controlling international and industrial domestic markets, especially when there were only a few buyers for large quan-tities. Crops such as cotton and peanuts were sold centrally, overseas through the Société Malienne d'Importation et d'Exportation (SOMIEX), the state-owned import-export concern, or to publicly owned domestic factories like the Société pour l'Exploitation des Produits Oléagineux du Mali (SEPOM), which made cooking oil, and the Compagnie Malienne des Textiles (COMATEX), which made cloth (Jones 1976, 235–37). ODRs used their control over com-mercialization to set standard producer prices that allowed them to recuperate credit, support their own activities, and tax agricultural production. There was much less control over livestock or fish exports, which went mostly to regional West African markets. An estimated 80 percent of cattle exports and half of fish exports went unrecorded and untaxed in the 1960s, in contrast to only one-third of peanut and one-fifth of cotton exports (Jones 1976, 341).

Alongside these two relatively centralized levels, decentralized local mar-ket systems continued to exist much has they had during precolonial and colo-nial eras. Wholesale and retail distribution of raw domestic produce, artisanal manufactures, animals, and consumer goods was carried out in daily and weekly markets throughout the country. Even the two major exports, cotton and peanuts, were actively traded locally. Peanut butter and domestic oils, important components of Malian cuisine, were processed in small quantities by women in their homes and bought and sold in local markets. Mali also continued to have an active artisanal textile industry similar that during the colonial period.[9]

The government also tried to control local distribution, most notably the grain market, because of the national emphasis on food security, yet was not successful. It used the same strategy as for industrial crops, setting up a state organization, the Office des Produits Agricoles du Mali (OPAM), to create a monopoly in domestic-cereals marketing that would buy and sell grains at set official producer and consumer prices (Steedman et al. 1976). Unlike industrial crops, where ODRs could control commercialization because they controlled access to credit, inputs, and large-scale domestic or overseas buyers, OPAM never was able to exert the same level of control on food crops since it had no incentives to offer farmers. Throughout the 1960s and 1970s, when it was technically illegal to sell in any other way, OPAM handled only 20 to 40 percent of the grain marketed domestically (Dione and Staatz 1987, 2). Weekly and daily markets remained active in most of the country even when state enterprises supposedly monopolized certain products, and a newcomer to Mali would have little way of knowing that certain sales in them were not legal. Farmers generally tried to sell to OPAM only when their prices were higher than those offered by private-sector traders (Steedman et al. 1976, 113).

Sometimes, OPAM coerced deliveries from farmers, the degree to which varied with market conditions (Dione and Staatz 1987). Then, villagers sometimes had to purchase grains to meet delivery quotas (Steedman et al. 1976, 114), since OPAM quotas and purchase prices were often set without regard to yield or consideration of factors affecting productivity, such as rainfall or input use (Sidibé 1978). In certain areas of the Dogon plateau in the late 1970s, grain was seized from farmers transporting millet from one village to another without authorization, forcing private grain transactions out of markets and underground (Sidibé 1978, 454). Yet the state was neither willing nor able to use high levels of coercion consistently to control grain markets. It preferred to meet its purchasing targets by buying from areas with cereal surpluses, as it did in the mid-1970s when it concentrated purchases in the south (Steedman et al. 1976, 112). Under the pressure of structural-adjustment programs, the government eventually gave up its attempts to control cereal production by controlling product distribution. Outside donors financed the Programme de Restructuration du Marché Céréalier (PRMC) to facilitate privatization (Kante 1993), and by the late 1980s, the grain market was completely privatized.

Analysts strongly criticized state commercialization channels in the years of strong control, on grounds of both equity and flexibility. Many suggested that rural producers received only a small part of the value of their crop and contributed more to the government budget than they got in return (Steedman et al. 1976; Kébé 1981; Hall et al. 1991). Others criticized the lack of flexibility within OPAM, which was legally required to buy at specific times and places, and in standard amounts. Consumers preferred the practices of private traders, who charged different prices for varying qualities of grain and sold in small quantities, in contrast to OPAM, which sold only in 50 and 100 kg sacks of unknown quality (Steedman et al. 1976). Private traders sometimes could even pay lower prices than OPAM since they went directly to farmers to purchase and appeared at times when farmers were likely to need money (Steedman et al. 1976, 115).

Yet the value of privatization is not unambiguous. No matter the distribution network, farmers the world over often receive only a small percentage of the final consumer price. Crop prices have become more volatile in recent years, sometimes falling below the levels of the old official prices. Moreover, the ODRs had indeed increased the availability of inputs (Steedman et al. 1976), and their departure has decreased access in many areas. Parallel private distribution networks have developed in some areas but remain expensive because of poor transport. Private distributors have also been criticized for not being able to deliver in a timely fashion, just as were the ODRs (Bingen, Simpson, and Berthé 1993, 24). Finally, few organizations other than ODRs have been able to offer complementary services like farm-to-market roads or literacy programs.

While the Malian government was able to control agricultural production in some commodities at some periods, they generally failed to achieve the degree of control that they sought. In part, this was due to constraints imposed upon them by external pressures. Yet it was also due to their desire to maintain popular support, which would have been impossible if they imposed too much change. Nevertheless, the state did penetrate rural areas with a variety of national institutions, most notably the ODRs, which in turn constrained some farmer choices and facilitated others.

Local Traditions

Unwilling to invest large amounts of political capital and energy to create radical change, the Malian government generally tried to build development on existing custom. Hence, local constraints, often termed "tradition," affected population responses to various initiatives. Cultural rules for access to land and labor formed a context for the social construction of farm enterprises.

## Modes of Access to Land

As in much of Africa, access to land in Mali was still regulated by indigenous systems of land tenure (Bruce 1988). Modes of access to land have, to be sure, come under pressure from larger political and economic contexts, but unlike many other areas, commercialization has not led to a "fundamental reorientation" of people's relationship to their land (Reyna and Downs 1988, 2). The move toward more continuous cultivation meant that families tended to use the same land for long periods, and certain pieces were identified as belonging to them, but communities retained tenure over large areas with farmland, fallowed fields, pasture, and unused bush. Overlapping and multiple rights remained common. This section looks first at some general Malian cultural principles that structured access to land within the household, and then turns to community control.

Most societies in Mali were patrilineal, and family land was managed by a male household head. On his death, the management role passed to his male heir, usually either a younger brother or a son. The family head typically divided the land, by order of priority, into areas for collective fields and women's individual fields, and sometimes men's individual fields. Collective fields were managed by the household head for the benefit of the entire household, while individual fields (either women's or men's) were usually managed by a single owner who retained rights to distribute the produce.

Collective fields usually occupied the largest land area and produced the greatest quantity of crops. The collective area was typically divided into several discrete fields with different crops or crop mixes. These usually included one or more fields in different grains, often varieties of millet and sorghum, and sometimes rice and maize. The objective was to provide sufficient food grains for the entire household for a season. A major cash crop, for example, peanuts or cotton, was often grown on another collective field, and the cash earned was used for household needs such as taxes, school fees, bridewealth, and capital investment.

The second priority was usually individual fields for women. Women rarely inherited land, and their land rights remained derivative since they were allotted land by the head of the household, but most Malian traditions honored women's rights to land. This was linked to the ideal gender division of responsibility where women provided meal ingredients other than food grains. They also grew supplementary grains, should collective production be inadequate. Some of their produce was consumed, and they sold some in local markets to purchase what they did not grow. If a woman did not have fields, her husband had to provide her with money to buy complementary ingredients and fulfill her family responsibilities. In a few Malian cultural traditions, for example some Soninke, men preferred to give women money rather than fields, but more echoed the Malinke of the Bafing, who strongly preferred to provide women with land. While women had the right to use produce from their fields as they chose, their families often depended on their production, especially during the hungry season and if collective production was insufficient. Women also provided household necessities like clothing and shoes from their crop sales. Unlike many parts of Africa (Reyna and Downs 1988, 13; Bassett 1993a, 4), women's land rights have not seriously eroded with commercialization and modernization in most of Mali.

While most households had collective fields and granted individual fields to women, the question of whether a head would grant land to other male members, commonly called "dependent men" in the literature, was more problematic. Many households had no individual men's fields, and men worked only on the collective fields. When men did cultivate individual fields, they were sometimes given a piece of household land, but other times they had to clear their own. The variability in land allocation among men appeared to depend heavily on individual negotiation, and may be linked to the tensions between fathers and sons that began with the abolition of slavery discussed in the previous chapter (Berry 1988). It also depended on the household's resources and the size and composition of the family. When men had individual fields, they used the produce to help feed their nuclear families if they were already married, and if not, for a part of their bridewealth or to purchase consumer goods.

The household farm, with several field owners and many fields, was embedded within a larger community, usually a village, which controlled a large, varied territory. As in many savanna societies, the territory was managed by village leaders who had ritual as well as political status (Raynaut 1988; Saul 1988). This could be the village chief and his council of elders, or a separate land chief with specific responsibility for land. In general, the chief was considered to be the senior member of the founding lineage and was obliged to work in consultation with senior representatives of major lineages. This cultural model masked much variation and even contradictions. In the past, the chieftainship was often taken by families that conquered autochthonous populations (cf. W. Murphy and Bledsoe 1987). If there were power differences among the original settlers, the chieftainship would presumably fall in the family of the more powerful, for example, in the lineage of a captain rather than a lieutenant. Rival families could each mount claims, provoking the creation of village factions. In the colonial period, the French chose certain chiefs. Some villages decided to elect chiefs or instituted rotating chieftaincies.

Within this context, village chiefs or councils usually maintained control over the allocation of noncultivated lands to new users. Despite ambiguities over boundaries between different village areas, one or another virtually always claimed rights over any given piece of uncultivated land. A settler risked severe problems if he (and the settler was virtually always a man) did not address the appropriate local authorities. Moreover, demographic growth increased claims on lands. As households grew, their members often needed to clear additional lands, while population growth in one area often pushed villagers out of their own lands to clear new farms.

Although village leaders were concerned lest their own community members have insufficient fallow to maintain a sustainable agricultural system, they generally welcomed new settlers. These aspects of the land tenure system were clearly consistent with precolonial state and settlement patterns. In the past, new settlers would have increased the manpower to defend the village in time of war (Kopytoff 1987). Today, larger, more prominent villages appear to be more likely to receive development initiatives, including schools, health clinics, extension agents, markets, and so forth. As elsewhere in Africa, contemporary traditions continued to envision village settlement primarily in political rather than economic terms (Bassett 1993a). A "successful" village would attract more members who owed deference and allegiance to the chief and elders, increasing their political influence and prominence. Rarely was payment asked from new settlers. Nor did sharecropping exist in the study areas. Rather, people gave symbolic payments, mostly 10 kola nuts or 10 kola nuts and a chicken, for the right to cultivate.

Villages grew with natural population growth and new settlers. The original village (in local parlance, the mother village) often ran out of land in its center and so created new agglomerations, called hamlets, for the growing population, either autochthonous or migrant. Depending on land availability, newcomers could settle within an existing village; adjacent to the village in their own area, referred to as either a neighborhood or a hamlet; or in a new permanent hamlet at some distance from the mother village. Hamlets were of two types. In one, common when the hamlet had no year-round water sources, individuals resided there during the rainy season only, returning to the mother village during the dry season. In the second, people lived in the hamlet year round, creating a new dependent agglomeration. Areas of recent migration could have many permanent hamlets, indistinguishable from villages except for their authority structure. In one of our study sites, more than 50 percent of the population agglomerations were hamlets (Y. Cissé et al. 1989).

New settlers received similar rights in different areas. They almost always got usufructuary rights only and could not sell the land or alienate it permanently. They virtually always had the right to do what they chose with its produce and could pass on cultivation rights to an heir. However, someone needed to keep the land under (more or less) continual cultivation or else rights would be lost. As in most of Africa, owners were usually hesitant to permit settlers to plant trees, as this symbolized permanent residence and ownership (Bruce 1988, 41; Saul 1988, 272).

Although most land transactions took place within the framework of customary tenure, national land policies added to the possibilities for overlapping claims. Moreover, the government would intervene in land issues where it saw an interest in doing so (cf. Saul 1988, 271; Goheen 1988). It tried, for example, to convince villagers in some areas to welcome new settlers from drought-prone areas. It also refused to recognize village ownership of uncultivated woods or pastureland during the period of the study. For example, the central government retained its right to give wood-cutting permits in any area it chose, despite village complaints.[10]

Nevertheless, since independence, governments mostly attempted to promote agricultural development within the context of customary land control. Community-based land control was more consistent with early socialist ideals than private land tenure would have been. Even when more capitalist forms of agricultural change were promoted, the relative abundance of land has meant that lack of land registration has not been seen as a major brake on agricultural change, as it has elsewhere (Bassett 1993a, 4). Governments saw no reason to institute a change that would bring neither economic nor political rewards, but would have almost surely brought local resistance.

*Local Forms of Access to Labor*

Since most farm labor was unwaged household labor, family structure and composition were essential factors in determining the farm labor force. The ideal model of the Sahelian farm family—extended, polygynous, and multigenerational—provided a framework for action. The senior male of the household organized the labor of its other men and women on the collective fields, where all household members were expected to work. Dependent men formed the primary labor force, and they often were expected to work four or five days out of seven. In contrast, women's duties varied from group to group. In some they worked only on the harvest, while in others, they planted and weeded as well. Villagers tended to devalue women's work as "helping," while counting men's as "essential," and both villagers and researchers often underestimated the efforts of women on collective fields (Koenig 1987, 18).

When they were not working on the collective fields, household members could tend their individual fields, where the male or female owner's labor was most important. The distribution of labor reflected the allocation of land, since an individual could not work a field if s/he did not have one. Among men, negotiations over labor use reflected the same issues as did negotiation over land. Household heads usually tried to keep control while younger men weighed autonomy versus security. They lost some autonomy by working for a father or older brother, but they gained material benefits and long-term security if the household head was a successful farmer with access to many resources. Many rural Malians and researchers (Steedman et al. 1976, 30, 31) believed that dependent men were more often choosing autonomy and their own households because of colonialism and modernization. However, the struggle between elders and juniors was ongoing and not resolved, as lineage heads sometimes revived "traditional" controls of land to increase control over migrant sons (Berry 1988, 65). In parts of Mali, individual fields disappeared in the 1960s, while collective fields increased in importance, as villagers came to see the cultivation of individual fields as too divisive (Toulmin 1992, 32–33).

Households made different accommodations to these tensions. In some, dependent men worked only on collective fields. In others, extended families continued to reside and eat together, but each nuclear family head had his own individual fields. When a household had many individual fields, men sometimes collaborated, working first on one man's fields, then another's.

For women, production levels depended on access to their own labor, as well as on access to labor of other household members. Women's obligation to cook (and associated tasks of food processing and procuring fuelwood and water) impacted on access to their own labor. Domestic tasks were typically rotated among all women of child-bearing age, so women in polygynous households and/or extended families cooked less often. Hence, rural women often encouraged their husbands to marry multiple wives. When a woman had a daughter-in-law, she was no longer required to cook and she had greater access to her own labor. Older women in good health often were productive farmers and valued household members. More affluent households often had a higher proportion of "extra" women (e.g., widows, divorcees) as well as more married women (Koenig 1986). Few female-headed households existed in rural Mali, since unattached women, including those with husbands on wage labor migration, were usually absorbed into existing male-headed households.

Women's productivity was also enhanced if they had access to the labor of other household members. Sometimes their children or other younger family members would work on their fields, and men of the household commonly cleared and prepared them. When the household had agricultural equipment, women could sometimes use it.

The ability to use household labor flexibly depended in part on household size; large households could profit from economies of scale. Household size in turn depended on regional resource availability and ideals about appropriate size, usually framed in ethnic terms. In some areas, households were extremely large, for example, an average 18.2 members in Bambara households north of Segou (Toulmin 1992, 31) and 22.7 members in some Malinke villages near Kita (Koenig 1986, 37). Other areas had small households. Average size of Dogon households ranged from 4.3 and 5.3 on the plateau to 8.0 on the plains, where there were somewhat greater resources (S. Cohen 1981, 93, 104; Eskelinen 1977, 324).

Even larger households needed extra labor at times of peak labor need such as weeding or harvesting. Strategies for getting extrahousehold labor remained phrased primarily in customary terms. Much extrahousehold labor was provided by one form or another of the *ton,* the villagewide group for collective agricultural work discussed in chapter 1.[11] In addition to a young men's *ton,* some villages had a *musoton,* or women's *ton,* for women married into the village. Individuals also formed smaller groups (sometimes called *grupu* in local languages, clearly an adaptation of the French, *groupe*) that worked for a lower fee because they included fewer people. Sometimes, work groups were paid immediately; at other times, payment was deferred until after the harvest. All the groups mobilized a number of people to work for a very short period of time (usually a half to a full day), allowing important agricultural tasks to be done in a timely fashion. The managers of both collective and individual fields made use of these groups. Small groups of men and women working individual fields could also form rotating mutual-aid groups.

If a farmer needed labor more regularly over the entire agricultural season, he could hire a *navetane,* usually a single man who left his own village to work in another during the agricultural season. Conditions of employment resembled those of the household's dependent males. He worked on the collective fields when dependent men did, and in return received an individual field to cultivate on off days. He was fed and lodged by the host family, and his remuneration was essentially the produce of his individual field. *Navetanes* tended to come from poorer areas, although sometimes young men were pushed into this work by a desire to earn their own money. *Navetanes* were usually engaged only by household heads.

Alongside these two major forms of extrahousehold labor, individuals with their own farms but short of cash sometimes worked for neighbors for a daily wage during the farming season. Few household heads were landless because the relative abundance of land and the flexible tenure system meant that an individual who could form his own household could usually clear a farm. However, some had farms or labor forces insufficient to produce what they needed. They found themselves torn between working for others for immediate income or working in their own fields to ensure next year's food. Individuals in this position often had a choice between off-farm jobs and farm labor to generate needed income, with the former often more attractive (Berry 1993).

People tended to talk about local forms of land and labor access as if they were unchanging and invariable tradition, yet the evidence suggests changes over time and variation among individuals. Nevertheless, cultural models of land and labor access formed a third level of constraint on individual choice about farm organization.

## Agricultural Development and the ODRs

Farmers made agricultural choices in a context where international structures, national policies, and local cultural traditions constrained choice, but by no means did the different levels work in a coordinated way to provide a seamless context for action. At best, the different levels sometimes had convergent or overlapping interests and provided a framework for economic growth. At least as often, interests were in conflict, but rarely was the level with the greatest political or economic power able to assert its interests without resistance, negotiation, or manipulation. The final section of this chapter looks at the ODRs, the organizations through which farmers experienced national policies. After a brief introduction, we turn to the three ODRs important in the study zone, with a focus on the way that international constraints, national policy, and local tradition played out.

Even at the height of his policy of collective agricultural development, Modibo Keita let the CFDT continue to work with small-scale family farms in the southeast, because the cotton they grew earned Mali needed foreign exchange. CFDT earnings allowed cotton farmers greater access to consumer goods, stimulating production. Although production elsewhere in Mali stagnated, cotton harvests more than doubled, from an estimated 16,000 metric tons in 1960–61 to 33,000 metric tons in 1966–67 (Jones 1976, 365). Modibo's government looked to the CFDT as a model for the new rural development organization that would become the ODRs. When Moussa Traoré came to power, efforts at collective agriculture were dropped, and ODRs became the focus of agricultural development and extension.

The ODRs were structured as parastatal organizations, each with administrative and financial autonomy (SATEC 1984–85). None was financially self-sufficient, so each depended on one or more international donors, and hence donor priorities. Virtually all agricultural zones of the country were touched by one or another ODR (map 3), yet funding levels were variable between and within ODRs, and among different activity sectors and geographic zones. There were also regional and class biases in activities; better-off farmers near ODR centers tended to get the most attention.

In the mid-1970s, following the rhetoric of donors, most ODRs became "integrated rural development" organizations, offering a mix of activities alongside agricultural extension. These included feeder road construction, functional-literacy programs, agricultural credit and commercialization programs, community development efforts, and so forth. ODR personnel increased as activities expanded, linked to the efforts to increase production after the first Sahelian drought. The structural-adjustment programs of the 1980s led to efforts to rationalize and privatize ODR activities, and make them financially self-sustaining (SATEC 1984–85). As already discussed, credit and commercialization were privatized. ODRs reduced their personnel and scope of activities, as they became once again primarily extension agencies, although this focus made problematic the goal of generating income to finance their activities.

Despite these changes, the ODRs remained significant rural institutions throughout the 1980s. They were still the major point of contact between farmers and the Malian administration. Farmers had grown to depend on the formal and informal services they offered. Where there was a strong cash crop, particularly cotton, ODRs even grew. In contrast, smaller operations, in areas marginal to cultivation, for example, the millet ODR in the north, ceased to exist. The strengths and weaknesses of each reflected the interplay of the different constraints acting upon it.

*CMDT*

If the ODRs are judged by average farmer income in their zones of intervention, clearly the CMDT was the most successful. Created as a cotton organiza-

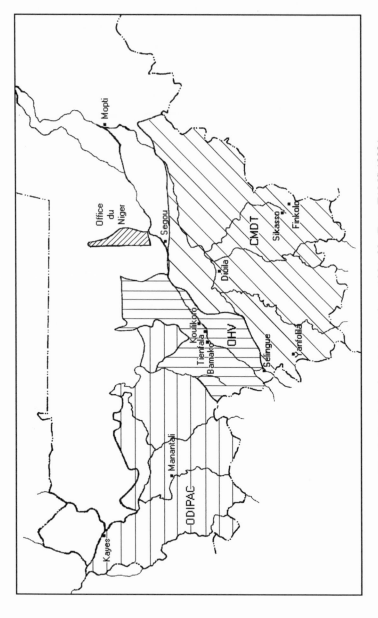

Map 3. Rural development operations, 1981–82. (From TAMS 1983.)

tion, it added other crops, including food grains, to its endeavors in the late 1960s and early 1970s. It began blacksmith programs in 1970 and a training and community development component in 1971. It started its own AV movement in 1974 on the initiative of farmers who wanted to organize and take a hand in their own affairs, well before this became central government policy (CILSS/Club du Sahel 1983, 72). CILSS and the Club du Sahel (1983, 75) attributed the CMDT's success to the "prudent and progressive" way it began new activities. More recently, it began experimental programs in land and soil conservation and was considered in the mid-1980s to be one of the few ODRs with the possibility of self-financing (SATEC 1984–85).

In the 1970s, some were concerned that the concentration on cotton was leading farmers to move out of food-crop farming, with an adverse impact on nutrition (R. Brain 1975, 16). More recent studies have suggested, however, that the CMDT zone is also Mali's granary, since increased production of cotton has been accompanied by increased food grain production. The CMDT produced more grain than an adjacent ODR, the OHV, and equipped farmers who produced much cotton were also likely to have large grain surpluses (Dione 1987).

To be sure, not all farmers were able to benefit from CMDT actions, since it did not work with farmers too poor to grow any cotton at all. Its geographic coverage was also uneven. The northern and eastern parts of the CMDT (the *cercles* of Koutiala, Sikasso, and Dioïla) were best covered, and the southwest, although technically a part, was not well served. In 1989, however, plans were under way to develop the three previously underserved CMDT *cercles* of Bougouni, Yanfolila, and Kolondieba (Buursink 1990).

The CMDT has been funded by the French, the Dutch, the European Community, and the World Bank. The French used their expertise in cotton research to improve its cultivation in their former colonies, including Mali (Cauquil and Vaissayre 1994). The Dutch were particularly interested in soil conservation and farming-systems research and funded experimental antierosion technology as well as a farming-systems research center. The World Bank, among other goals, was anxious to invest in a project with a good rate of return.

The CMDT has been a success because the interests of donors, national government, and farmers all coincided. Located in the most fertile and well-watered region of Mali, close to the roads to Côte d'Ivoire and Burkina Faso, CMDT has had relatively good management, which enabled added investment to increase farmer and national income. It also benefited from stability and growth in world market prices of cotton. Farmers saw that they could make money from cotton and responded early on to the incentives of the CMDT and have continued to do so. The very success of the CMDT allowed farmers in collaboration with either donors or the national government to ignore some external or national constraints. During Modibo's regime when farmers were required to cultivate village-level collective fields, they sometimes worked with the CFDT to turn them into demonstration plots (DeWilde 1967, 312). Although structural-adjustment initiatives encouraged privatization since the early 1980s, the CMDT retained a countrywide monopoly for cotton processing and sales as of 1992 (Bingen, Simpson, and Berthé 1993, 25).

*ODIMO/ODIPAC*

ODIMO began as Opération Arachide (OA) in 1967 and became Opération Arachide et Cultures Vivrières (OACV) in 1974, as the concern for food self-sufficiency grew. In 1981, identifying itself as an integrated rural-development project, it became Opération de Développement Intégré des Productions Arachidières et Céréalières (ODIPAC). It changed its name to Opération de Développement Intégré du Mali Ouest (ODIMO) sometime after our study in 1989.[12] Since our study was done during the ODIPAC period, we will refer to it as such.

The names indicate ODIPAC's emphasis on peanut cultivation, but the changes reflect its fragility and dependence on donor funding and priorities. In the mid-1970s, when peanut prices were good and ODIPAC (then OACV) relatively well funded by the World Bank and French, it appeared to be a vibrant ODR. In addition to offering standard agricultural programs, it upgraded rural feeder roads and had an extensive functional-literacy program (DNAFLA 1978). Both average and well-equipped farmers who grew peanuts could earn good incomes for rural Mali, and the level of equipment use increased markedly (Koenig 1986). With German collaboration, a factory was built in Kita, one of ODIPAC's most productive zones, to process oil for export.

Yet by the mid-1970s, the international peanut market was growing uncertain (Steedman et al. 1976, 158), and by the early 1980s ODIPAC's future looked problematic. Not only had the world price of peanut fallen, but peanut oil had to compete with cheaper cottonseed oil within Mali (FAO/World Bank 1986). Although ODIPAC looked for alternative crops, its options were limited because of the serious constraints posed by the physical environment. Although rainfall was good, ODIPAC, located primarily in Mali's isolated First Region, had great transport problems, since evacuation of products to Bamako or the exterior depended on the railroad (FAO/World Bank 1986). Only crops with a long conservation period offered viable export opportunities.

During this period, ODIPAC lost much of its external funding. The oil factory closed and ODIPAC agents were laid off. Remaining agents had to cover more farmers but had fewer resources to do so. ODIPAC nevertheless began to implement many of the complementary activities fashionable in the 1980s, most notably the creation of AVs. Farmers continued to grow peanuts for sale because domestic demand was important and they saw few alternative cash crops, but they had to sell through private merchants and complained of price volatility.

In contrast to the CMDT, where national policy and donor interest worked together to form an environment conducive to agricultural dynamism, the constraints on remunerative production led to agricultural stagnation in southwestern Mali. Natural conditions were good enough to make subsistence farming sufficiently viable that rates of emigration were only slightly above average (BCR 1987), but rural immigration into the zone for agricultural purposes was minimal. Farmers were quite dependent on national structures to provide services, yet the ODRs were vulnerable to donor requirements.

*OHV*

The Opération de la Haute Vallée du Niger (OHV or OHVN) began in 1965 as an integrated rural-development project (CILSS/Club du Sahel 1983) but by 1968 gained a cash crop focus as the European Development Fund financed Action Tabac (Steedman et al. 1976, 217). Receiving additional funding from USAID since 1978, the OHV has undertaken many of the same complementary activities as the other ODRs, including AV formation, literacy programs, farming-systems research, and rural road construction (Bingen, Simpson, and Berthé 1993). The growing interest of USAID in women's issues encouraged OHV to increase outreach to women farmers. Most sectors had at least one female extension agent, and women formed over 20 percent of new literates and 10 percent of literacy teachers (Bingen, Simpson, and Berthé 1993, 30). More recently OHV has entered small-enterprise development.

While USAID interests led to innovative programs for women and small enterprises, it also provided more constraints than other donors. Unlike France, the United States was a major producer of both cotton and tobacco, and the 1988 OHV redesign avoided financing activities on these crops, concentrating instead on complementary activities such as credit, roads, and livestock development. Project documents explicitly stated that the OHV had to segregate funds used for the production and sale of tobacco from USAID monies (USAID 1988, exhibit 6, 55).

OHV also covered a very heterogeneous geographic zone. In the northern part, annual rainfall was less than 600 mm, while in the south, it was over 1,000 mm. Since OHV's zone included the capital, Bamako, it had at its center an extremely specialized market that offered unique opportunities and constraints. No one mix of crops was appropriate for all these ecological and marketing zones. Unlike the other two ODRs, OHV had no single cash crop that gave it identity and focused its programs. Although in theory, support of diverse crops should be better for national development, the level of expertise of the agricultural-extension staff was such that they could not reasonably support a wide range of crops.

The end result was that farmer participation in activities was very spotty. Sometimes they had strong agricultural support, and sometimes they did not. Sometimes they had significant complementary programs and sometimes not. In the north, there were few opportunities for cash earning through agriculture because of the difficulty in finding crops remunerative at low rainfall levels. Many farmers did not even produce sufficient grains to feed themselves (Dione 1987). The OHV researched experimental crops like sesame and henna, but none were ready for large-scale extension in 1989. Some farmers, in a zone that was earlier part of ODIPAC, cultivated peanuts and sold them through the private sector. Poor farmers also made ends meet by entering nonagricultural activities, while wealthier farmers invested in livestock raising (SARSA/USAID 1994).

In the south, in contrast, cash-earning opportunities proliferated. Tobacco continued to be grown and sold in the zone of the original Action Tabac. In the southeast, the OHV gained an area that had previously been part of the CMDT; farmers here continued to grow cotton, and the OHV received inputs and sold produce through the CMDT. Some farmers responded to the possibilities of the urban Bamako market, while others began to grow vegetables for organizations that arranged export to Europe, an activity facilitated by easy access to the Bamako airport.

The ability to profit from these opportunities depended on the extent to which farmer initiative could build on the activities of other organizations apart from the OHV. Some producers for big markets got aid from the CMDT for cotton or private contract growers for exported vegetables. Those exploring small niches could not count on support. For example, urban market-gardeners within Bamako seem to have received no assistance from any public or private technical-assistance organization (Bingen, Simpson, and Berthé 1993, 7). Even village-based farmers serving domestic markets were often cut off from OHV support. Well-organized yam growers, for example, could not receive support for their AVs (McCorkle 1986).

While all the ODRs worked with the same basic pieces (some agricultural extension, at least one "cash crop," complementary activities, donor funding), these pieces fit together differently in each of the zones. Donor constraints interacted with government policies and locational advantages and disadvantages to provide varied levels of incentives for farmers to grow specific crops. When the interests of donors, nation, and farmers overlapped, as in the CMDT, the result was agricultural dynamism. In the other sites, farmers found the actions of ODRs of variable utility, and although there were patches of opportunity, they were less widespread.

Sectoral investment patterns also showed the varying interplay of donor, national, and farmer priorities. Malian governments consistently placed a priority on the expansion of irrigated agriculture, which coincided with donor priorities, particularly after the drought.[13] This meant that Mali could invest significant funds in irrigated agriculture, despite continuing technical and management problems that often made irrigation schemes more attractive to the national administration and international donors than to the farmers who actually cultivated there (Bingen 1985; Steedman et al. 1976). When rainfall was relatively good, farmers avoided these schemes, especially the Office du Niger, where they rarely able to earn good incomes by farming alone (DeWilde 1967; Kamuanga 1982). Yet drought years made farmers as well as administrators skeptical of rainfed agriculture, and localized land shortages in some parts of the country and among some groups of people encouraged voluntary migration to irrigated perimeters in the 1980s. In the 1990s, the World Bank and others financed a U.S.$80 million renovation of the Office (World Bank 1994b).

At first glance, it might appear that donors and the national government held similar priorities in terms of environmental conservation as well, but although they both claimed to support the idea, this did not translate into a consistent program. As noted above, donor interests changed over the years, partly in response to environmental lobbies in their own countries. It appears that the Malian government was content to let donor priorities take precedence, since these programs offered substantial funding and did not conflict directly with their own priorities. At the local level, the result was confusion, as different institutions and sometimes even recommendations within a single one contradicted each other. The Forest Service was trying to do participatory local forestry while the population still saw it as the police. Agro-forestry projects recommended keeping trees in fields even though agricultural-extension services had told people for years to remove them all to facilitate plowing. This confusion only increased the population's skepticism toward forestry initiatives. One common sight in rural compounds was women cooking on their traditional three-stone fire, next to the obligatory improved woodstove, unused.

Conclusion

Rural Malians farmed in a context affected by physical resource constraints, national policies, international activities, and their own cultural traditions. The different levels did not act uniformly to create a seamless structure of constraint, nor were there consistent lines of conflict among them. Rather, activities at each level interacted to create complex contexts that varied over time and across space, creating conditions favoring negotiation of outcomes, individual choices, and innovation.

As Malian farmers faced a mixture of constraints and opportunities created by the inconsistencies and contradictions of their environment, their response was generally to try to use those conditions they found advantageous, and to ignore, manipulate, or resist those they perceived as detrimental. Whether they found a particular aspect to be an opportunity or a constraint was not always predictable since individual sets of resources were quite variable. The succeeding chapters will show how one subset of farmers, those who have carried out rural-to-rural migration and resettlement, responded to the situations presented to them by the contemporary context of rural production.

Chapter 4

# *The Study Population*

Intervening variables, including local ecology, history, and the characteristics of migrating households, mediated the ways that larger constraints affected household production choices. This chapter provides an overview of the study sites, the diverse reasons for migration, and the varying contexts for economic and social choice, as a prelude to analysis of production activities. The first section of the chapter looks at the reasons for rural migration in 1980s Mali, factors that pushed people to leave home and pulled them to other areas. The second section turns to the study data. We begin with an overview of the study sample in comparison to other rural residents and then discuss the major characteristics of each study site. In each, a particular economic and environmental context attracted specific kinds of migrants. Each site description ends with information on its sample.

## Contemporary Population Movements

Chapter 2 showed that population movement was important for the formation of precolonial states and remained common during the colonial period. Economic conditions since independence have also influenced Malians to move in order to better their chances to make a decent living. Movement allowed them to respond to both the normal problems of living in a resource-scarce environment and specific environmental and political crises. Rural-to-rural migration had two distinct phases: deciding to move and then choosing a place with sufficient resources for settlement.

### *Leaving Home*

Temporary wage labor migration has long been local cultural practice for many young men and has more recently become a standard rite of passage for single women as well (Grosz-Ngaté 1988). In addition, the gerontocratic structure of most rural households pushed some young men to migrate more permanently. Setting up single-family homesteads in the bush or moving to other villages has long been an alternative for individuals disaffected from their larger communities. Population growth induced village fission or the creation of agricultural hamlets.

Migrants tried to move to regions they considered economically more dynamic than where they were. Many moved to other countries, since the Malian economy has consistently been poorer and more isolated than its coastal neighbors, such as Côte d'Ivoire. Some even moved to other Sahelian countries perceived as wealthier, such as Senegal or Burkina Faso. Some went overseas. Best known are the Soninke, who migrated to France and other countries, including the United States. Only old people, women, and children inhabited some Soninke villages because virtually all economically active men were elsewhere. The lack of remunerative economic opportunities at home coupled with strong networks in Soninke centers overseas facilitated migration over long distances. Other migrants remained within Mali. While the inhabitants of southern Mali were moving southward to coastal countries, northerners were migrating not only internationally but to the south as well. For them, economic possibilities in the south seemed substantially better because of the differential development of southern and northern Mali.

Specific crises augmented migration streams. The first drought, in 1972–74, made survival in the north more difficult, and the second, in 1983–84, increased uncertainty. In 1985, the Malian government estimated that some 30,000 to 50,000 people had fled the northeast and moved south toward the Third Region (Sikasso) (Brett-Smith 1985, 1).[1] Many returned home when the rainfall improved again in 1986–88, but others remained in the Third Region because they saw a better chance to earn a living there. Total numbers are impossible to estimate, but a significant number appear to have stayed.

Political crises as well as ecological ones affected movement. Migration was especially marked during the stagnation in agricultural production that characterized Modibo Keita's regime (see examples in Jones 1976, 305). More recently, some international migrants have begun to return home, voluntarily or involuntarily, as receiving countries have sought to oust nonnationals as a way of dealing with their own economic crises. In 1984, for example, Malian citizens were repatriated from countries as diverse as Saudi Arabia, Algeria, Libya, Niger, and Nigeria (DNAS 1985, annex, 11). In the late 1980s, transhumant FulBe were sent back from Côte d'Ivoire. Our sample included people expelled from Saudi Arabia and two farming cooperatives (CAMUKO and CAMSEL) that took advantage of programs encouraging voluntary repatriation of migrant workers in France. When repatriated people returned to Mali, they did not necessarily return to their regions of origin. They often settled in other places that they believed to have greater potential for growth.

All these factors—the relative poverty of the Malian economy in contrast to its neighbors, the structure of the traditional family, repatriations, and especially the drought—pushed people to look for areas of greater development potential. While many went to the cities, others looked for rural areas where they could farm.

*Finding a New Farm*

Rural migrants tended to look for areas that had the resources they believed necessary to create remunerative economic strategies. This study looked at two different strategies: primary reliance on farming and a mixed strategy that combined farming with other income-earning activities. In both cases, migrants needed access to arable land and often undertook some nonagricultural activities. The difference lay in where they put their primary effort.

For people who intended to be farmers, the primary need was good farmland. They tried to avoid areas with high population densities or with limitations on cultivation due to rocky, mountainous, or lateritic terrain. But good land was not enough; they also wanted areas where they could increase sales as well as subsistence cultivation. They looked for an extension service that facilitated access to inputs and commercialization of a readily marketable crop, markets, roads, and other infrastructure. Since it was often difficult to make a living by farming alone during the first years of settlement, possibilities for off-farm occupations, particularly during the dry season, were also important.

One of the most attractive areas was the Third Region (see map 1 in chapter 1), the most favored in terms of rainfall as well as the most agriculturally developed because of CMDT activities. It had good infrastructure and its roads were among the best in Mali. Yet population density was still relatively low, 15.3/km$^2$ overall. Recent migrants avoided a few areas such as Koutiala, where earlier migration had pushed population density to 22.9/km$^2$ and where less land was available (TAMS 1983).

Specific CMDT infrastructure attracted migrants to particular zones. Their initial zone of activity was around Koutiala, in the northeast corner of the Third Region, and early waves of migrants moved there. They also built cotton gins in the towns of Fana and Dioïla, in the Second Region adjoining the northwest part of the Third Region. This attracted the first wave of migrants in our study, who began to settle in the late 1960s. People continued to move in throughout the study period, but other areas began to prove more attractive as the CMDT expanded. Through the 1960s and 1970s, the southwest part of the Third Region (Bougouni, Yanfolila) saw little immigration because of its isolation. Yet in the 1980s, the government rehabilitated the national road from Bamako to Bougouni and upgraded the secondary road from Bougouni, through Yanfolila, to the gold mine further south at Kalana. There were plans to bring electricity from the Selingue dam into Yanfolila town. The CMDT was planning a major new initiative, yet the population density remained extremely low. The zones of Bougouni and Yanfolila became much more attractive in the late 1980s than they were ten or fifteen years earlier.

After the droughts, irrigated perimeters also became more attractive to farmers. Although the monetary returns remained uncertain, the promise of food security became more important. Beginning in the 1970s, the Office du Niger saw a growth that Kamuanga (1982, 43) attributed in large part to the drought. Within our study, people were attracted by the irrigated perimeter created in conjunction with the Selingue dam.

In contrast, other well-watered rural areas (e.g., the southern part of the First Region and the southwestern part of the Second) remained less attractive to migrants because they remained relatively isolated and their ODRs were less dynamic. There were also limitations on arable areas because this zone contained the rocky, mountainous, and lateritic Manding Plateau (PIRT 1986). These areas did not see the same level of farm immigration as found in the CMDT zones. However, they sometimes were attractive to those who wanted to combine farming with nonfarm activities.

As Bamako grew, the peri-urban zone around it consistently attracted new migrants who hoped to combine agriculture with nonagricultural activities. Growing population densities meant that migrants could not get very large farms, but they often could get some land, and nonagricultural options were much more abundant than in more rural areas. In other cases, specific rural infrastructure provided occupational alternatives that could be combined with agriculture. This study includes migrants to the area around Finkolo, in the southeast Third Region, where people came for salaried work on a tea plantation. Later, the construction of the Selingue and Manantali dams also attracted people for salaried work. Selingue in particular aimed to become a center of development. A town grew around a resident civil-servant population running the dam and the market for lake fish. A tarred road from Ouellessebougou (on the Bamako-to-Bougouni road) to Selingue facilitated transport. Industries situated in rural zones attracted workers, but the standard of living of the migrants and their families often improved if the migrants were able to farm small plots to complement wages.[2]

Economic dynamism sometimes resulted in very quick growth of localized areas, leading to land shortages in previously underpopulated zones. Areas that appeared to be poles of attraction could quickly become problematic. In general, early migrants had the best access to resources and significant advantages over people who came in later. The potential for unbalanced growth was one factor leading the government to discourage internal migration and to encourage investment in all areas of the country. Planning agencies simply did not have adequate resources to do the long-term local planning necessary to encourage balanced growth. Nevertheless, migration did not stop to areas considered attractive by migrants. While state activities encouraged or discouraged rural settlement at particular places and times, people continued to make their own decisions about their options and to act on them.

Study Sites

The study was based on information from six sites with different contexts for rural settlement. In sites with dam construction, some relocation was involuntary, but in the others, movement was at least quasi-voluntary. In some areas, people emphasized the negative factors that pushed them to move, while in others, they stressed they opportunities that they perceived in new areas. Looking simultaneously at six different sites enabled us to understand better the variation in ways that national processes and policies were interpreted and implemented locally. As already noted, five of the six sites (most named after the major town center)[3] were studied within the framework of the OCP land resettlement project. The sixth site, Manantali, was studied within the context of a USAID-funded resettlement project.

In each OCP site, the goal was to sample up to 30 households randomly selected from three villages. A core of quantitative information was gathered on each household via three formal questionnaires. First, a *household* level survey collected demographic data as well as general information on recent agricultural-production levels and ownership of equipment and draft animals. Second, a *farm* level questionnaire collected production information once again, as well as data on animals and goods ownership, crop sales, and use of agricultural inputs and water conservation technology. Because each farm potentially had multiple fields and field owners, a third *field* level questionnaire got information on a sample of fields, including field histories and estimates of household and extrahousehold labor used. This questionnaire looked once again at production, input, equipment, and water conservation technology use, but at the individual-field level. In addition, a sample of fields was measured. Gathering data at several levels allowed for cross-checks.

Although all researchers followed the same core strategy, there were differences in the final database at each site, since each team had to respond to different contingencies. Thus, not all samples had precisely 30 households. A few sites included samples of indigenous residents, while others could not. In some sites, the study covered virtually all the household's fields, because the households had mostly collective fields. In one site, Yanfolila, the researcher included more fields than required by the sample, while in others, the sampling design was followed exactly.

All researchers also collected qualitative data, but this was less formalized and the content varied more widely. All collected migration histories of household heads, but some histories were more elaborate than others. Information on women was better in those sites where a woman was on the team. Supplementary qualitative information was gathered according to the interests of the research team as well. The Manantali site had more qualitative data because ISH had worked there over a three-year period and Koenig over five.

The section on each site specifies the size and nature of its particular sample. Unique pieces of information will be raised as they become relevant. We used our long-term knowledge about Malian farming to check these data, and each specific database from this study checked the others. As we proceed with our discussion, we also raise a few areas where the data did not seem reliable and the reasons for it. This overview turns first to commonalities among the sites, and then looks at each in terms of its distinctive characteristics.

*Characteristics of the Sample*

The people who chose to leave their homes and start farms in other rural areas did not appear noticeably different from rural Malians who remained in the villages of their birth. This section looks at the demographic, educational, religious, and ethnic characteristics of the study population. In the sites where we had both indigenous and immigrant groups, they have been broken into separate samples. We looked simultaneously at differences and similarities among the study sites, between indigenous and immigrant populations in the two sites where we have information on both, and between study sites and the Malian population as a whole. Further information on each specific site is in the section following this one.

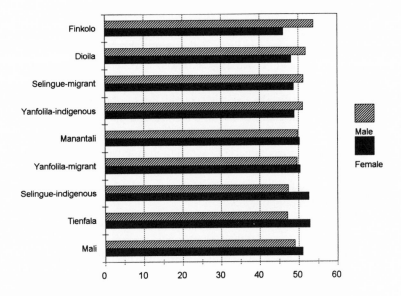

Fig. 2. Sex ratios in the study sites. (Data for all Mali from BCR 1987, 1.)

## Demographic Structures

Permanent settlement and balanced economic development would suggest relatively balanced sex ratios (Momsen 1991), although ratios in small samples like ours would be more skewed than larger ones. Since young men were the most mobile part of the rural population, areas with substantially more women suggested a high degree of male out-migration, while an excess of males suggested perceived economic opportunity for men, who may either migrate in or remain in these areas rather than moving elsewhere. Overall, the Malian population had 51 females to every 49 males (BCR 1987, 1). Sex ratios in the study sites ranged from about 53 women to 47 men (in two samples, one immigrant and one indigenous) to 46 women to 54 men in one migrant sample (fig. 2). Three of the five samples of voluntary migrants showed at least a slight excess of men, an expected reflection of the attraction of these areas to immigrants. In contrast, one migrant sample, the peri-urban site of Tienfala, had the largest surplus of women. Here people suggested that the young men in sample households had themselves migrated again to take advantage of full-time urban wage-earning possibilities. However, none of the ratios was enormously skewed, as might be expected if migration streams were composed of large numbers of un-married individuals. An individual man rarely migrated with the intention of starting his own farm unless he was already married, or planned to marry soon.[4]

A farm household needed at least one man to manage and work the col-lective fields and at least one woman to manage domestic tasks; these two were usually, but not universally, a married couple. But most families hoped to move beyond this minimum and create an extended and polygynous household, in part as a way to increase the domestic farm labor force. The 1987 census showed that the average household size nationwide was 9.6 persons, only 58 percent of whom were nuclear family members (i.e., husband, wife or wives, and their unmarried children) (BCR 1987, 1). Affluent rural households were usually larger than poor ones.

In four of the five sites with voluntary migrants, average household size on the family farms was smaller than the national average, ranging from 5.7 to 9.2 (table 1). These sample averages were also lower than the average household size in the relevant arrondissement (BCR 1987). In contrast, the two indigenous samples were larger than the country average, 9.7 and 34.3. In Manantali, com-pulsory relocation made for an average household size, 21.3, more reflective of an indigenous rather than a voluntary migrant group. Only in Dioïla was the av-erage household size in a family-farm sample of voluntary migrants (9.8) larger than the country or arrondissement average, due, it seems, to lengthy settlement in an affluent zone. The households making up the two cooperative farms, CAMUKO and CAMSEL, also tended to be larger than the mean.

The relatively small size of migrant households appears to be linked to their relatively recent establishment. In settled areas, household heads tended to be older, since younger men did not usually found new households at marriage, but rather remained with a father or older brother. The smaller households of migrants tended to be headed by younger men, although they were not very young, since a man needed resources to make it through the first few years and to have paid bridewealth for the wife that accompanied him (cf. Saul 1988, 256). In the three sites with recent migration (Tienfala, Selingue, and Yanfo-lila), the average age of household heads was around 40. In contrast, in Dioïla, with larger households and migration since the late 1960s, the average head was in his midfifties, similar to the indigenous household heads. In Finkolo, the site where people were drawn to work on the tea plantation in the 1960s, settlement was long-term, and household heads were older, with an average age of 48, but households remained quite small. This was linked to their distinctive produc-tion strategy based on wage labor.

Other demographic figures also suggested that the ability to establish

**TABLE 1.   Household Characteristics**

| Site | Mean HH Size | Mean Age Head | Mean Age Wives | Proportion Nuclear | Wives per Head |
|---|---|---|---|---|---|
| Tienfala | 5.7 | 39 | 30 | 94% | 1.1 |
| Selingue-migrant | 6.6 | 41 | 26 | 86% | 1.4 |
| Finkolo | 7.2 | 48 | 34 | 94% | 1.3 |
| Yanfolila-migrant | 9.2 | 41 | 30 | 65% | 1.3 |
| Selingue-indigenous | 9.7 | 48 | 37 | 76% | 1.5 |
| Dioïla | 9.8 | 55 | 36 | 72% | 1.5 |
| CAMUKO | 10.9 | — | — | — | — |
| CAMSEL | 15.2 | — | — | — | — |
| Manantali | 21.3 | — | — | — | — |
| Yanfolila-indigenous | 34.3 | 55 | 30 | 26% | 1.8 |
| All Mali | 9.6 | — | — | 58% | — |

*Source:* For all Mali, the source is BCR (1987, 1).

polygynous, extended households depended both on length of residence and lo-cality. Although all migrant groups relied more on their core nuclear families than did their indigenous counterparts, those who were most nuclear were the two peri-urban sites (Tienfala, Finkolo). In those sites, polygynous marriage was rarer as well. In all sites, the average age difference between the head and his wives remained substantial, suggesting a continuation of the gerontocratic ideal.

A final demographic indicator, the percentage of older people, reflects both the length of migrant settlement and their ability to reach economic viability. The highest proportions of older people were found among the two indigenous samples and at Dioïla and Manantali. In the two indigenous samples 3.6 per-cent (5/137) at Yanfolila and 4.1 percent (4/97) at Selingue were over the age of 60; at Dioïla 5.1 percent (15/293) of the population was older. At Manantali, 7.9 percent (84/1058) were over the age of 55 (T. Diarra et al. 1990). In marked contrast were the migrants to Selingue, Finkolo, or Tienfala, where each sam-ple had at most only 1 individual over the age of 60. The Yanfolila migrants had a few more (6/240 or 2.5 percent), but fewer than the indigenous population. Although people had migrated for many years to both Dioïla and Finkolo, it was only at Dioïla that they were able to create a secure production base that allowed them to retire gracefully. In contrast, many at Finkolo preferred to re-turn to natal villages upon retirement.

Most migrants set up households based upon the ideal described in chap-ter 3, with overlap between family, household, and production unit. Only in the two cooperatives did members make a conscious decision to create a new type of farm structure. Yet most migrant households were not as able as some in Mali to actualize their ideals. In part this was because many were still young and had had insufficient time. In other sites, as we will discuss in the following chapters, this was because economic conditions did not allow them to do so. Nevertheless, these households formed a recognizable subset of the range of recognized possibilities for farm households. Their lack of distinctiveness is even more evident when we look at other background characteristics.

*Education*

Mali has had quite low literacy rates. In 1990, 68 percent of adults were illiterate, while only 23 percent of the population of primary-school age and 6 percent of those of secondary-school age were enrolled in school in 1989 (World Bank 1992, 218, 274). Urban populations were more educated than rural ones. Farming was considered an occupation for those who did not have qualifications to undertake more remunerative or skilled jobs.

The samples showed the expected relatively low level of education (table 2). Only Finkolo and Tienfala showed somewhat higher educational levels, and informants made it clear that one of the attractions of semiurban situations such as these was the accessibility of schools. Some migrants and their children also pursued alternatives to formal education. Some in Yanfolila, Finkolo, and Dioïla learned to read and write in local languages through ODR literacy programs, while in Selingue, both migrants and indigenous inhabitants frequented Koranic schools. Clearly rural dwellers wanted more educational opportunities for themselves and their children, but these remained quite limited.

**TABLE 2.   Educational Levels**

| Site | N | Illiterate | Functional Literacy | Koranic School | Primary Only | Secondary And Higher |
|------|-----|-----------|--------------------|----------------|--------------|---------------------|
| Finkolo | 217 | 68% | 0.9% | 3.7% | 27.0% | 2.8% |
| Tienfala | 51 | 78% | 2.0% | 4.0% | 13.7% | 2.0% |
| Yanfolila-migrant | 240 | 84% | 7.5% | 0.0% | 7.5% | 1.3% |
| Selingue-indigenous | 97 | 86% | 0.0% | 7.2% | 7.2% | 0.0% |
| Manantali | 10,459 | 88% | 0.3% | 3.5% | 7.8% | 0.4% |
| Selingue-migrant | 125 | 91% | 0.8% | 4.0% | 4.0% | 0.0% |
| Dioïla | 293 | 91% | 1.4% | 1.4% | 5.1% | 1.4% |
| Yanfolila-indigenous | 137 | 93% | 0.0% | 0.0% | 6.6% | 0.0% |

*Source:* For Manantali, the source is IER (1984, 28).

*Ethnicity and Religion*

Much African conflict has been carried out through the idiom of ethnic differ-ence, and ethnicity has been a major focus of much contemporary analysis. Yet the historical material in chapter 2 suggested that ethnic identity has been fluid during much of Malian history and interethnic mixing common. Ethnic groups have lived alongside one another for centuries, and even though this often re-flected power differences, the level of ethnic conflict in Mali has been low.[5]

To be sure, contemporary Malians can report an ethnic identification, al-though they might report another in a different situation. They do use ethnic stereotypes in general conversation, but these are only one of a range of stereo-types. Overall, the utility of ethnicity as a category of analysis in this study was extremely limited. Only in localized cases, for example, where migrants were all one ethnicity and autochthonous populations mostly another, did ethnicity become part of the local discussion of difference. But even then, it was rarely the major way of allocating farming resources.

Overall, the indigenous populations were more ethnically homogeneous than the migrant ones, with the most isolated, Manantali, the most homoge-neous. In contrast, the ethnic composition in some of the migrant areas (Dioïla, Finkolo, and Tienfala) was strikingly heterogeneous. Individual villages did tend to be less ethnically heterogeneous than were sites as a whole. This was especially true in Finkolo, where almost all the Bobos lived in one village, most of the Bambara in another, and the Senufo in a third. At Dioïla, in contrast, at least two of the sample villages were very ethnically mixed, a pattern that was reproduced on an individual level. Of the 28 household heads with living wives, 12 (43 percent) had at least one wife of an ethnic group different from their own. Moreover, 6 of the 12 had no wives from their own ethnic group.[6]

Like Mali, most of the study sample considered itself Muslim, more than 90 percent of most samples. Exceptions were found in Finkolo (69 percent Mus-lim) and among the migrants to Yanfolila (79 percent Muslim). Most of the non-Muslims were either Catholics or Protestants, although parts of the sample at Finkolo and Dioïla still followed traditional religions rather than either Islam or Christianity. The substantial representation of Catholics in the Yanfolila sample can be linked to the role of a Catholic nongovernmental organization (NGO), Secours Catholique du Mali (SECAMA), in settlement activities there. Only at Finkolo did people discuss religious differences, which overlapped eth-nic ones.

On the whole, people tended to claim the ethnicity of their ancestors and to adopt the dominant religion of their area of origin. Among those who claimed a certain ethnicity or followed a particular religion, the meaning attached to it was quite variable. On the one hand, the Muslim Malinke of the Bafing had only rudimentary mosques and combined Islam with traditional religions; on the other, some Dogon were Wahabiyya who secluded their women. In any event, we found no evidence that either ethnicity or religion affected farmers' production strategies in any substantial way.

Overall the sample characteristics suggested a rather ordinary group of Malians. They represented a diverse cross-section of the population who were similar only in their decision to move from home areas to others seen as economically advantageous. Those who had once worked in France were more affluent than other rural Malians, but the others were not noticeably so. Diversity in the sample echoed the diversity of the national population and showed a range of ethnic identification and family size and composition. Shared characteristics, the vision of ideal family structure and lack of education, reflected the larger population as well. The characteristics of the specific sites proved more useful in understanding possibilities for agricultural success than did the characteristics of the migrants. The following section introduces each of these sites, beginning with those settled longest.

### Dioïla

Migrants initially began to come to this area of sparse population, approximately 15–20 km west of Dioïla town, about 25 years ago, drawn by an abundance of fertile land and the possibility of cultivating cotton within the CMDT. The sparse population in the 1960s was a consequence of its previous history. As noted in a 1954 report: "All this region, 60 years ago (i.e., in the 1890s), was highly populated and cultivated. Samory passed through. Very few inhabitants were able to escape the *razzia;* few were those who returned to their country" (cited in Y. Cissé et al. 1989, 138). In principle, some remembered the natural fertility of the zone, and when economic and political conditions were attractive, they returned.

Natural resources were good in this *cercle* in the Second Region (map 4). Rainfall in 1968 was at the 1,000 mm isohyet, although during the 1980s, it diminished considerably as in most of Mali, and figures from 1981 to 1987 showed a mean yearly rainfall of 678 mm. Some 53 percent of the zone's soils were arable, located largely on the plains (PIRT 1986). These were deep, sandy alluvial soils at the surface, and alluvial clay soils at greater depth, with a medium level of natural fertility. In addition, the forage potential in forests and savanna was very high. Natural vegetation included trees and shrubs such as shea *(Butyrospermum parkii), nere (Parkia biglobosa),* tamarind *(Tamarindus*

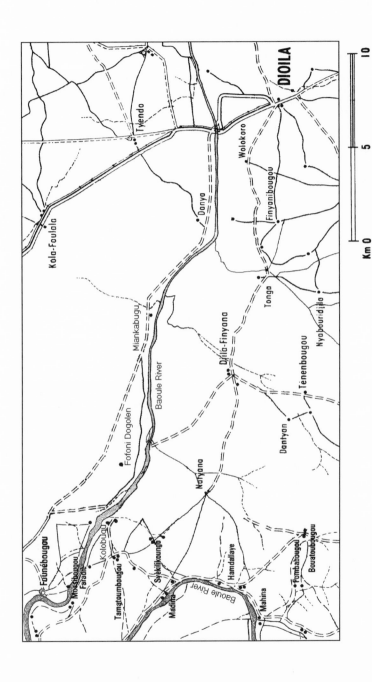

Map 4. Dioïla villages. (From IGN Mali ND-29-V [1986] and ND-29-VI [1961].Copyright IGN, Paris and DNCT, Bamako.)

*indica),* baobab *(Adansonia digitata),* and kapok *(Bombas costatum).* Virtually all provided useful products, but women especially valued the shea trees for their fruits that could be processed into butter and soap. In the 1950s, game was abundant, including hyenas, hippos, lions, and even a herd of elephants (Y. Cissé et al. 1989, annex 1). The Baoule River and other small watercourses crossed the zone.

As the CMDT developed its programs, people moved in spontaneously, creating agricultural hamlets with the agreement of existing proprietor villages. These hamlets grew slowly, and most seemed to be permanent, although ownership rights were not transferred and they were not considered independent. It was impossible to get exact figures about the scale of immigration, although it clearly was significant, as shown by a study of the nearby Sounsan forest. The average age of the villages and hamlets there was only 17 years (Y. Cissé et al. 1989, 13), and hamlets clearly outnumbered established villages. Among 91 villages and hamlets were 11 villages, 20 units that included both village and hamlet, 45 hamlets, and 15 units of unknown status (Y. Cissé et al. 1989). Immigration was so significant that by 1985, internal World Bank documents for a forestry project characterized the Dioïla zone as overpopulated.[7]

Increased population led to degradation of nonagricultural natural resources. For example, locals claimed that hunting was no longer possible in the Sounsan classified forest because game had disappeared. Some 60,000 head of livestock passed through the forest each year, leading to deforestation (Y. Cissé et al. 1989, 26, 84). Many wanted to cut the forest to expand cropland (Y. Cissé et al. 1989), although the government was trying to encourage local forest management for environmental conservation. Dioïla and the Sounsan region showed the kind of negative ecological changes that made the government worry about the impacts of future migration and development of hitherto isolated areas of southern Mali.

Immigrants came as individuals and families, arriving from throughout the country, although most were from nearby *cercles.* Some of the migrants became quite successful economically, although their hamlets tended to lack infrastructure such as wells or schools. Migration into the three survey villages began in the 1960s and continued until at least the late 1980s.

The first study village, Fofoni Dogolen, was situated some 800 meters from the left bank of the Baoule River, spread out in a narrow space between the river and a small hill. It took its name from this physical feature; in Bambara, *fofoni* means limited space and *dogolen* means hidden or unseen. A group of five Marka (also known as Soninke) from two villages in the *cercle* of Baraouéli (Fourth Region), pushed out of their natal villages by land problems, discovered the area and settled there in 1968, having received permission from Kola-Foulala, the mother village, some 15 km distant. The settlement grew little by little over the years, and by 1989, Fofoni had grown to 15 households, the last having settled in 1988. This village had become quite ethnically diverse, including Bambara, FulBe, Hausa, and Malinke as well as the original Marka. Fofoni retained its identity as a hamlet, dependent on Kola, which had never cultivated the site.

The second village, Kolobugu, was situated on the right bank of the Baoule River in a vast plain. An old agricultural hamlet of its mother village, Natyana, about 5 km to its southeast, it was surrounded by larger villages. Kolobugu was an important transport point, the only place in the area where canoes could cross the Baoule when the river was high and the current strong. Despite its attractive location, Natyana had abandoned its hamlet more than 50 years earlier because flies carrying onchocerciasis had appeared.

Two different men came prospecting for farmland in the late 1960s and received permission almost simultaneously to settle there. A Bambara from some 25 km away discovered the spot in the course of a hunting trip and founded the neighborhood of Kolobugu I in 1968.[8] Another group of Bambara, looking for cotton fields, founded and settled Kolobugu II the same year. These two neighborhoods, separated by some 600 meters, grew over the years, with the last migrant arriving in 1984. In 1989, there were 13 compounds in Kolobugu I and 15 in Kolobugu II. Although Bambara continued to predominate, the village also included FulBe and Bobo residents, as well as Bozo and Somono fisherfolk who settled along the river. The road from Kolobugu to Dioïla and Fana was often inaccessible during the rainy season, but Kolobugu had a weekly market on Sundays. Kolobugu also retained the political status of hamlet.

The third village, Miankabugu, was barely 15 km west of Dioïla, on the left bank of the Baoule, approximately 200–300 meters from the river. Situated on a vast plain with rich black soils, it too was owned by Kola-Foulala, from whom the original settlers received permission to settle. In 1973, two men, a Marka from Baraouéli and a Mianka from Koutiala, were prospecting for land and discovered the spot. The village was called Miankabugu after the Mianka, whose family provided its chief. New migrants were accepted into this village only until 1983. In 1989, there were eight compounds, and Bambara had come to predominate. This village, more than the other two, looked like a "traditional" village, with a central plaza and a collective livestock pen for village animals. Houses were situated in the center of its agricultural lands. The model for the village layout appeared to be the Mianka village, despite the predominance of Bambara inhabitants. This village also retained the status of hamlet.

The sample for Dioïla included 30 households in three migrant hamlets: 8 in Miankabugu (all of its households); 12 in Fofoni Dogolen; and 10 in Kolobugu I and II.

*Finkolo*

A large-scale tea plantation was begun with Chinese technical assistance in 1967 in Finkolo, in the Third Region, about 25 km east of Sikasso town. The site (map 5) was presumably chosen in light of its good natural resources, including rainfall at a long-term isohyet of 1,250 mm/yr, dropping to a mean of 968 mm/yr in the mid-1980s. There were also abundant surface waters in temporary streams, the most important of which was the Farako, on which the plantation was located. In the plains draining the watercourses were deep soils with medium natural fertility that offered few limits to agricultural production. Only 55 percent of the zone was considered arable, due to slopes, susceptibility to soil erosion, shallow soils on rocks, or the lateritic crust (PIRT 1986).

Workers came to the plantation from 1965, when two experimental farms were started, until the mid-1980s, with recruitment peaking during the 1970s. At first, workers were housed either in the existing village of Finkolo or were bused in daily from Sikasso town. Neither of these alternatives was sustainable with a full labor force, hence the construction of two official worker towns, Camps I and II, on the 402 ha of the tea farm. In time, with a growing labor force, these structures became inadequate as well, so two other worker villages were founded in the mid-1970s. These were Tominian on land given to workers by the plantation, and Sokurani on land contributed by local owners outside. People who came to work on the tea farm often expected to combine salaried work with supplementary farming on their own fields.

The study included the three main worker villages, but not Camp II, which lodged technicians and management. Camp I was a true worker town. The main criteria for receiving housing were simply its availability and being a worker; whether a worker was permanent or temporary made little difference. Married persons were given priority over single ones, although if housing was available, single people got it as well, typically in a shared house with other workers. Retired workers often continued to live in the camp, either because they then became temporary workers or because another family member was employed by the farm. Initially, responsibility for housing workers was given to a designated Camp I chief, who gave keys to workers needing housing and informed the management later. Later, the management administered housing directly.

In the mid-1970s, when the plantation had grown considerably and the

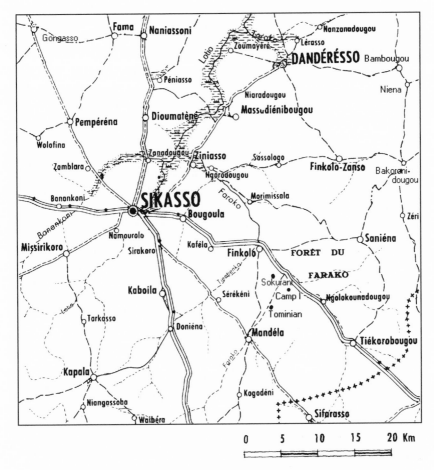

Map 5. Finkolo villages. (From IGN Mali ND-30-NO [1967]. Copyright IGN, Paris.)

Camp I lodgings were insufficient, some inhabitants were asked to cede their places to newcomers. These voluntary expellees each got a site on which they were authorized to build. In this way, in 1976, the village of Tominian was created on a parcel of tea farm land.

Simultaneously, the village of Sokurani was founded by other plantation workers. The principal reason evoked by them was a dispute over rentals claimed by management, which the workers found excessive. The workers tell the following story of its founding.

For three years, we lived in the camps without paying any money for rent. In the fourth year, the farm demanded a monthly fee of 400 FM, then 450 FM, this at a time when our salaries were on the order of 4,100 FM/month. This was considered a contribution to the costs of finishing the work on our apartments. In effect, when we moved into these houses, they were not yet plastered, and it was to finish this task that fees were required. For three years, these contributions were retained from our salaries. Once this work was finished, monthly rental fees for the apartments were fixed at 2,250 FM.

Taking account of the size of our salaries as well as the families we had to support, it was impossible to pay this sum while also meeting our other obligations. After negotiations between worker and management representatives had failed, three of us decided to leave the camp to build our own houses. We began to look for a site, and when we found one, we undertook to find the owner. Knowing that we were within the domain of Finkolo village, we went to see its chief, who took the responsibility of finding the landowner. Discussions were successful, and the owner delimited a place where we could build our houses. One day after beginning our work, more than 20 other workers came to ask for permission to build. The village has not ceased growing. Today [i.e., 1989], it has 62 compounds, only 4 of which do not belong to tea farm workers. The first condition necessary to get a housing site here is to be Muslim.

Although economic reasons were cited as the impetus for creating Sokurani, inhabitants of Tominian maintained that the other village was mainly peopled by those who refused to live with them there. The populations of the two villages were ethnically and religiously distinct. Tominian, named after a major Bobo village, had a population primarily Bobo and Christian, with some Senufo Christians. Sokurani, also known as Dar-es-Salaam, was peopled primarily by Muslim Senufo, Mianka, and Bambara. Once settled in their own villages, people did not remark upon other problems between ethnic groups.

The indigenous population of the zone was primarily Senufo, mixed with Bobo and Samogo. Agriculturalists like their Bambara neighbors, Senufo had more Christians among them than in most other Malian ethnic groups. Given the focus of this case study on plantation workers, the indigenous population was not studied. The Finkolo sample included 30 households, 10 in each of the three worker villages: Tominian, Sokurani, and Camp 1. The sample, like the villages, was quite ethnically diverse.

*Tienfala*

Tienfala (map 6) was located along the main road from Bamako to Koulikoro, approximately 20 km from Bamako, in the administrative Second Region. Parallel to this road lay the railroad between the two cities and the Niger River. The confluence of transportation possibilities had attracted settlers for some time. In the late nineteenth century, the zone was the final leg of the grain route from Banamba to Bamako, and many traders moved through. Modern migration to the zone began with railroad construction; Tienfala-gare was founded by retired railroad workers between 1910 and 1915. The zone continued to draw people after independence, when much of the land along the river was turned into large commercial plantations, mostly owned by elite Malians.

The expropriation of prime riverbank land for the plantations, presumably through use of the *concession rurale,* constrained farming opportunities for small farmers, but migrants still saw the possibility to combine agriculture and other activities in this peri-urban zone. Rainfall was good, as Tienfala was in the long-term 1,000 mm isohyet, although it fell in the late 1980s: to 895 mm in 1985, 667 mm in 1986, and 630 mm in 1987. Some 74 percent of the land in this agro-ecological zone was arable, although in the immediate region of Tienfala, hills leading to the rocky plateaus north of the Niger banks limited farming. However, these hills, covered with treed savanna, had great forage potential (PIRT 1986). The relatively good resources complemented access to roads, markets, and the urban centers of Bamako and Koulikoro. People came from many different places, and many had migrated elsewhere before settling here.

Some migrants came from relatively great distances, while others moved to the study villages from other areas within the arrondissement, pushed toward the river and road by the drought, onchocerciasis, and lack of drinking water on the hills and plateaus. Many wanted better access to health care centers and better possibilities for work. Market possibilities also increased near the road. For example, Tienfala served as an important charcoal center because of Bamako's high demand for cooking fuel. The three study villages had a total of 28 immigrant families; nearly half (13) had come from other villages within the arrondissement. Those moving within the arrondissement most often came to Tienfala itself, the arrondissement center.

Immigrants to the Tienfala zone often moved onto farms abandoned because of the simultaneous emigration of indigenous residents. The zone's population and activity had boomed prior to independence when railroad work was complemented by a rice-hulling factory that was part of the Office du Niger complex. After inde-

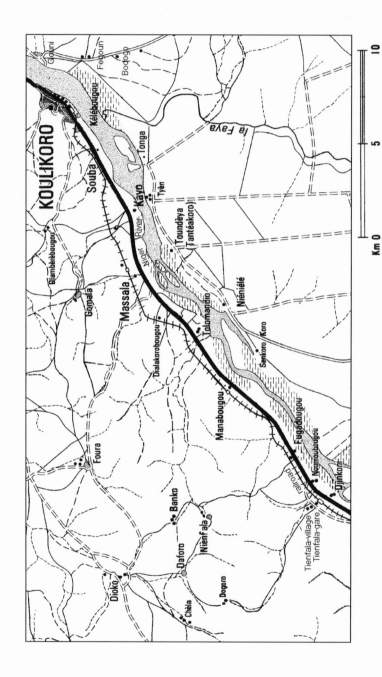

Map 6. Tienfala villages. (From IGN Mali ND-29-V [1986]. Copyright IGN, Paris, and DNCT, Bamako.)

pendence, when the government decided to concentrate all Office infrastructure near the main perimeters in the Segou Region, the factory closed. The economy stagnated, and most local families sent youth to Bamako to look for work. Many remained there, leading to a slight decline in population during a period when most of Mali grew. The village of Tienfala had approximately 700 inhabitants according to the 1976 census, but 680 in 1989 according to arrondissement figures. New migrants were able to take advantage of indigenous emigration to get land.

Three village neighborhoods were chosen for study, but sample sizes were smaller since Tienfala was less intensively studied. They were chosen to illustrate two different economic strategies. In Tienfala-gare and Tienfala-village, two distinct neighborhoods of the village of Tienfala, most inhabitants practiced a conscious strategy of multiple activities, combining agriculture with commercial, artisanal, or wage work. The settlement of Tienfala-village predated that of Tienfala-gare, and, according to its chief, it was one of the oldest villages in the *cercle* and continued to be "traditionally" organized. Tienfala-gare, in contrast, was formed by the railroad workers and later migrants and, as the site of the arrondissement, was less traditional in orientation. There were a total of 7 migrant families in Tienfala-gare and 9 in Tienfala-village, even though the latter had only 200 inhabitants.

In some more rural villages (e.g., Manabougou and Fugadougou) migrants adopted more agricultural lifestyles, although they still were more likely to emphasize nonfarm activities than in completely rural sites. In the third study village, Fugadougou, about 3 km from Tienfala, between the road and the river, people were consciously trying to redynamize agriculture. Having worked in close collaboration with technical services and the administration to undertake new activities, Fugadougou was the first village in the arrondissement to have had its AV become the higher-level *ton villageois* (in 1988). It had a successful functional-literacy program, groups working on fruit and vegetable farming, and had built a warehouse and literacy center. The village had approximately 150 inhabitants with 12 migrant families.

The sample from this site included only 9 families, 3 from each of the 3 villages. The sample was ethnically diverse, including Bambara, Dogon, Bobo, and Malinke. In the five sample households where migration histories were done, duration of settlement ranged from 3 to 20 years.

*Selingue*

During the 1970s, the Malian government built the Selingue dam on the Sankarani, a tributary of the Niger, to provide electricity for Bamako, the cap-

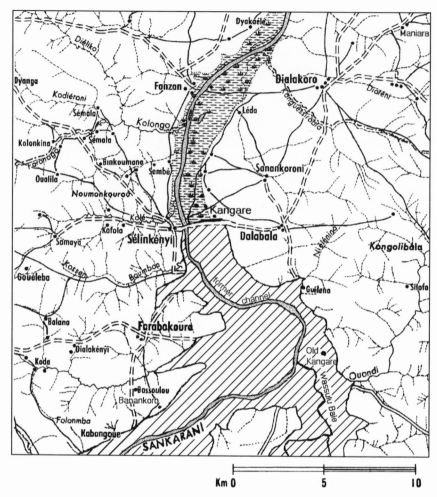

Map 7. Selingue villages. (From IGN Mali NC-29-XXII [1964]. Copyright
IGN, Paris. Reservoir boundary adapted from 1973 Carlo Lotti plan.)

ital, some 135 km to the north (map 7). Dam construction first attracted people,
and complementary activities kept them coming. Given the policy of national
food self-sufficiency, planned infrastructure included an irrigated perimeter of
2,000 ha on the right bank just downstream from the dam. By 1986, 1,200 ha
had been improved (Sissoko et al. 1986, 97). The reservoir, covering 40,900 ha,
had many fish. A paved road, built in conjunction with the Selingue project, facilitated transport to and from Bamako. These resources drew many migrants.

In addition, migrants often expected the new opportunities around the dam to be complemented by relatively abundant natural resources. The Sankarani had gallery forests on its banks, with irregular woodlands in the zone as well. Agricultural soils varied from marginal to good, depending on their location. Those on the plateaus were generally quite shallow and interrupted by out-croppings of laterite, but the depressions had a combination of alluvial and col-luvial soils, many quite fertile. The zone had good annual rains, varying from 1,000 to 1,400 mm. Its 1968 isohyet was 1,300 mm (Sissoko et al. 1986, 9), al-though rainfall diminished in the 1980s. Figures from its *cercle,* Yanfolila, showed an average rainfall of 1,038 mm from 1979 to 1988 (PIRT 1989, 3:38).

Yet the natural resources were less than they appeared, also due to dam con-struction. The reservoir covered many of the gallery forests and necessitated the involuntary resettlement of some 12,500 persons from 30 villages (Sissoko et al. 1986, 4). The Selingue project (1971–81) relocated and rebuilt villages, mostly on the plateaus around the reservoir perimeter. Although the project re-placed house sites, it did not pay sufficient attention to fields. Moreover, non-resettled villages near the dam also lost significant amounts of farmland to flooding, even though studies prior to construction had indicated that sufficient land would remain. By 1990, the need for rainfed fields, even among indige-nous inhabitants, had outstripped their availability (Sissoko et al. 1986, 39).

The indigenous inhabitants of the study zone, mostly Malinke who traced their ancestry back to the medieval Mali empire, claimed ownership of the rain-fed farmland and bush areas around the dam. They were reluctant to lend rain-fed farmland, already perceived to be in short supply, to migrants. While other zones welcomed drought migrants in the mid-1980s, the Selingue population resisted their settlement (Brett-Smith 1985, 61). Yet other resources drew mi-grants, and they continued to come. Between 1976 and 1987, annual growth in the arrondissement of Kangare, Selingue's zone, was 6.04 percent in contrast to 2.18 percent for the Yanfolila *cercle* as a whole, and 1.70 percent for the coun-try (BCR 1987, 27).[9] The administration thought that the development of the irrigated perimeter would help solve the land problems.

Diverse streams of immigrants were attracted by the dam. Among the first to exploit Selingue's perceived potential were former construction workers, a certain proportion of whom decided that they could combine agriculture with either permanent or short-term wage work if they remained in the old worker camp of Kibaru. Among the possibilities was working for the Office de l'Ex-ploitation des Ressources de Haut Niger (OERHN), which developed the irri-gated perimeter and ran the hydroelectric plant. In addition, the arrondissement with its governmental services offered some employment, and a part of the town originally built to house dam workers became a tourist and conference center, where Bamako residents came to pass weekends on the lake. This worker population was ethnically very diverse, with Bambara, FulBe, Bobo, Senufo, and Dogon.

Bozo and Somono fisher families came after the lake filled. Filling coincided with the mid-1980s drought, and an estimated 4,681 fisherfolk arrived in Selingue between 1981 and 1985 (Brett-Smith 1985, 9). Their numbers have remained substantial since then, and by 1986, OERHN considered overfishing to be a problem and wanted some to leave (Sissoko et al. 1986, 86). Yet many fishermen stayed, since the market in Bamako, where virtually all Selingue fish were sold, was very large (Sissoko et al. 1986, 106). Traders, mostly women, arrived daily with ice chests to purchase and transport fresh fish. In 1985, estimated fish production from Lake Selingue was 1,258 tons with an estimated value of 202,734,000 FCFA (U.S.$504,313)[10] (Sissoko et al. 1986, 105, 175).

After the irrigated perimeter had been improved, the government used it as a recruiting device to lure agricultural migrants. A number of groups came with the expressed purpose of cultivating there. Among these were some 35 Dogon families expelled from Saudi Arabia in the late 1980s. Members of the Wahabiyya sect of Islam, they modeled their lifestyle after the Saudis. The women, especially, lived like Arab women, wearing veils and often remaining secluded within their quarters. The husbands took responsibility for all their financial and other needs, in stark contrast to most of the rest of rural Mali, where women were usually mobile and economically active, despite adherence to Islam.

A second group recruited to the perimeter were high school and college graduates who, in the wake of structural-adjustment programs, were no longer guaranteed civil-service jobs. In an effort to encourage them to devote themselves to national goals such as food self-sufficiency, they were encouraged to cultivate rice at Selingue. Arriving there, they were assisted by an NGO, Céssiri-So, which gave them 22,500 FCFA (U.S.$68) per month for eight months. When their produce was sold and the production loan from OERHN repaid, they were to reimburse Céssiri-So. In the dry season of 1988, 45 graduates cultivated tobacco and rice; approximately 100 were expected for the 1989–90 agricultural season.

In addition to these groups, others, mostly Dogon, came spontaneously because they had heard about the possibilities of the Selingue perimeter. In 1989, Kangare and Dalabala villages counted 104 Dogon households, of which only a third were returnees from Saudi Arabia. These Dogon came because of drought conditions in their home areas and were attracted by the generally better rainfall of southern Mali as well as the irrigation scheme.

Not all who came to Selingue came to cultivate on the perimeter. Selingue also hosted a cooperative formed by repatriated Soninke workers from France who benefited from training programs for Africans wanting to return home run by a French NGO, the Association pour la Formation et la Réinsertion des Africains Migrants (AFRAM). Their cooperative, the Coopérative Agricole Multifonctionelle de Selingue (CAMSEL) arrived in 1987 and had 24 members and their families, including seven indigenous villagers. Due to the programs for returnees, they were able to return with significant resources. They continued to receive salaries for one year after their return, which they used to build housing. With the help of local political and administrative authorities, they received 200 ha downstream from the dam, approximately 4 km from the village of Selinkenyi.

Given the diversity of the groups at Selingue, the study could not include them all. The team chose to concentrate on three villages, but to include both indigenous and migrant farmers. One of the study villages, Kangare, the site of the arrondissement, was displaced by the reservoir to a new site next to the dam, alongside the town built for management and workers. Although the core of Kangare remained the indigenous village, it had grown to include an administrative zone, the old management and worker camps, and several neighborhoods made up of old and new migrants. The Kangare study sample included people from Kibaru, the old worker camp, and others living in the neighborhood of Lafiabougou.

The two other villages, Selinkenyi[11] and Dalabala, were indigenous villages that did not resettle, although they served as host villages to migrants attracted by the dam and its infrastructure. Dalabala, a Malinke village, hosted Wahabiyya Dogon. Selinkenyi, also Malinke, and founded some 270 years ago, hosted the Soninke cooperative and other migrants. Its sample included only indigenous inhabitants, some of whom had joined the Soninke cooperative.

The total Selingue sample included 29 households, distributed as follows: in Kangare, 7 Dogon households from Kibaru and 3 from Lafiabougou; in the village of Dalabala, 9 households, all Dogon migrants; and in the village of Selinkenyi, 10 indigenous Malinke households. The Soninke cooperative was interviewed separately.

*Yanfolila*

Farmers were drawn to Yanfolila (map 8) by its abundant open land, good for agriculture. The zone was one of the least populated in southern Mali, with a population density of 11 persons/km$^2$ in 1976 (TAMS 1983). Some 70 percent of the soils were estimated to be arable. The alluvial soils in particular were

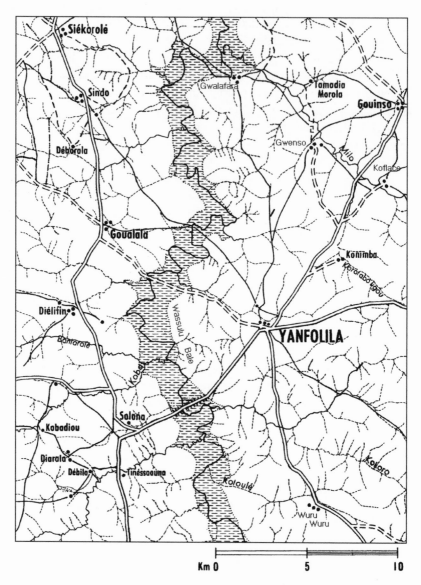

Map 8. Yanfolila villages. (From IGN Mali NC-29-XXII [1964]. Copyright IGN, Paris.)

very fertile; there were many plains with good water retention, which could be used for recession cultivation of rice. The area had medium agricultural fertility and very high forage potential (PIRT 1986). Good rainfall meant that it was relatively easy to use land resources productively. Rainfall in Yanfolila *cercle* ranged from 787 to 1,217 mm annually between 1981 and 1987, with a mean of 940 mm/year for this period. Surface water in a number of major rivers (the Niger, Sankarani, Wassulu Bale, and Baoule) and many intermittent water sources could also be used for small-scale irrigation.

Farming could be supplemented by the use of wild natural resources, particularly the plentiful forest, including thirteen classified forests with almost 185,000 ha. Game was still abundant, although many of the larger species had disappeared or become rare. An FAO study estimated that 90 percent of adult men hunted, with 94 percent of the game for family consumption (cited in Warshall 1989, 34). Wild fruit trees provided good harvests, and other species were used for tools, furniture, and housing.

The first and largest migrant stream to Yanfolila was composed of spontaneous migrants, drawn by land availability. They began to come in small but significant numbers in about 1976 and have continued to dribble in since then. Until the road from a nearby *cercle,* Bougouni, 80 km to the northeast, was improved in recent years, Yanfolila was too isolated to attract people in large numbers. More recently, improving infrastructure and new CMDT activities appear to have spurred migration, making for increased growth. Among the Dogon, our sample group, the first migrant arrived in 1977. By 1989, he had become the head of a small Dogon community.

The second major migrant stream included organized groups who came after the drought. In 1985, then-president Moussa Traoré asked Yanfolila residents to host drought refugees looking for more productive agricultural land. Local political authorities worked closely with several NGOs to coordinate settlement. In 1985, a Canadian NGO, Centre Canadien d'Etudes et de Coopération Internationale (CECI), brought 66 families, primarily Dogon, from Sikasso, where they had sought initial refuge, to Yanfolila. In December 1987, SECAMA brought another 12 families from Bandiagara in the north to Yanfolila.

Local authorities decided that settlement would be most amicable if the Dogon were assimilated by residing in existing villages. After discussions with village councils, Dogon migrants moved into Yanfolila town and five surrounding villages: Sodala (11 families); Gwalafara (20 families); Gwenso (13 families); Koflacè (13 families); and Wuru Wuru (12 families). The NGOs helped alleviate the difficulties of resettlement among these migrants, who were mostly very poor and had few resources. CECI, for example, provided agricultural equipment. In addition, the United Nations World Food Programme (WFP) provided food aid for the first year.

Many had difficulties establishing themselves, but most decided to stay in the area (Dandenault 1987). Migrants did move from village to village, however. By March 1989, only 4 of the original 12 families settled in Wuru Wuru were still there, although 2 new families had come. In contrast, 17 of the 20 original families remained in Gwalafara. It appears that movement inside the zone was from poorer villages to ones with better or more land, or from outer villages to Yanfolila town, where migrants could combine agriculture with temporary wage work. For example, five of the eight who left Wuru Wuru went to Yanfolila town. In June 1989, half of the zone's 1,200 Dogon resided there.

The third set of migrants to Yanfolila was another group of Soninke workers, who had returned to Mali after spending between 8 and 23 years in France. In contrast to the Dogon, they arrived with substantial means and heavy equipment, thanks to AFRAM programs. This group of 11 immigrants had learned agriculture, mechanics, and management before returning and had been given equipment by a French organization, Agriculteurs Français et Développement International—Haut Rhin. AFRAM (1988) also helped them to create a development plan, which they could use to solicit funding for specific projects. The Soninke organized themselves into a cooperative farming unit, the Coopérative Agricole Multifonctionelle de Kokolon (CAMUKO), and received 300 ha of land adjacent to the village of Wuru Wuru, where they had begun to farm. In 1988, they had a population of 120 of whom 37 were economically active; they expected to grow to 370 (AFRAM 1988, 9). In 1989, they had begun to build housing in the village but continued to live in Yanfolila town. They commuted to their fields every day, in a truck they had brought from France.

The indigenous inhabitants, hosts to the migrants, were primarily Wassulunke. According to N'Diayé (1970, 90), they were sedentarized FulBe who had been enslaved by Samory and became independent after his fall. A certain proportion may have been descendants of the freed slaves who returned from Banamba (chap. 2). All our sample villages claimed settlement before Samory, however, and regarded themselves as the autochthonous inhabitants of the zone. They had typically FulBe patronyms (e.g., Diallo, Diakité, Sidibé, and Sangaré) but spoke a language similar to Bambara. They farmed like their Bambara neighbors but also made much use of forest areas, having reputations as hunters, sorcerers, and smugglers.

Why the Wassulunke accepted the migrants was not clear, although it appears to have been due partly to administrative coercion and partly to a desire on their part to benefit more from development activities. Because of Yanfolila's low population and relative isolation, it had been cut off from the beneficial effects of development projects, although it sometimes felt negative effects. The village of Gwalafara, for example, had been affected by the construction of the Selingue dam, many kilometers upstream, when dam closure raised the level of the Wassulu Bale River, flooding some of its houses. The village had to move only a minimal distance, one-half to four kilometers (Sissoko et al. 1986, 35), but the villagers felt traumatized. They recalled that they had barely moved into their new houses when water began to enter their old ones, and regretfully talked of drowned trees and destroyed wells. They also had numerous complaints, impossible to evaluate in 1989, against the organization that had facilitated their resettlement. However, it was evident that the villagers felt that the government owed them for their pains. Many thought that hosting the Dogon in their village would be an occasion to get benefits they saw as their right.

By 1989, there clearly was tension between the political and economic advantages that might come from increased settlement of the zone, on the one hand, and the potential negative effects on the abundant wild resources due to changing land use patterns, on the other. At particular risk were the gallery forests along the rivers, also prime land for recession rice cultivation. This tension was expressed by villagers, government personnel, and development project experts (e.g., Buursink 1990).

The Yanfolila sample included three villages to illustrate the variety of migration into the zone. Yanfolila town was chosen because it was the first host area and had the greatest number of Dogon migrants. Settled in the seventeenth century by a FulBe from a village of the Futa Djallon (present-day Guinea), the town remained very rural, although, as the site of a *cercle,* it received the accompanying administrative, technical, and social infrastructure. In 1986, it had some 3,400 inhabitants, by Malian standards still a village, although by 1989 it had grown because of continuing migration.[12] It was more ethnically diverse than its surrounding villages and clearly had a more urban atmosphere, with an active market and many artisans. The possibilities to earn incomes supplementary to agriculture attracted migrants.

The second village, Gwalafara, was chosen because it hosted the greatest number of migrant families. Approximately 15 km north of Yanfolila, it was also settled by FulBe from the Futa Djallon approximately 360 years ago, according to the village chief and his council. Gwalafara had 355 inhabitants in 1986, according to the administrative census. By 1989, the village had 17 Dogon households in addition to the 23 indigenous families. Because of its proximity to the Wassulu Bale River, fishing groups had also settled at the edge of the village. Both Dogon and fisherfolk had their own neighborhoods.

Wuru Wuru, the third village, was chosen because it hosted the Soninke cooperative as well as Dogon migrants. Located 13 km south of Yanfolila, it had a population of 401 inhabitants in 17 families in 1986. Its founders also came from the Futa Djallon, again well before the Samorian wars. The village had a dispersed habitat, and the indigenous population included Bambara, who had lived there for many years, alongside the dominant Wassulunke. Located at some distance from the Wassulu Bale River and not affected by the Selingue dam, this village had a serious water problem. Many dug wells dried up at the end of the rains, and the village had only one drilled well with permanent water to serve well over 400 people by the late 1980s.

The total sample at Yanfolila included 30 households: 10 Dogon households from Yanfolila town; 10 Dogon households from Gwalafara; and in Wuru Wuru, 6 Dogon migrant households along with four indigenous households, of whom three were Wassulunke and one Bambara. In addition, the Soninke cooperative was interviewed. The only group from which we got consistently unreliable data was that of the indigenous people of Yanfolila. Data they provided were regularly different from what we expected and from other studies in the area. Since this was also the site with the most overt tension between migrants and autochthonous people (see chap. 7), we believe that our explicit interest in migrants led locals to be less open with us.

*Manantali*

Manantali (map 9), in the administrative pour First Region, was one of the most isolated areas in Mali until the Organisation la Mise en Valeur du Fleuve Sénégal (OMVS), a multicountry river basin authority, built a dam on the Bafing River to provide electricity for member states and irrigation in the Senegal River valley. When dam construction began in 1981, the village of Manantali, near the dam site, had seven households. By the end of construction in 1987, the town had grown to approximately 15,000 people. Between 1976 and 1987, the arrondissement of Bamafele (the site of Manantali) grew at a rate of 10.51 percent per year, far above the country's annual growth rate of 1.7 percent (BCR 1987, 5).

The partial disenclavement of Manantali began in the early 1980s with the construction by the Entreprise pour la Construction du Barrage de Manantali (ECBM) of an all-season road from the rail station at Mahina (on the Dakar-

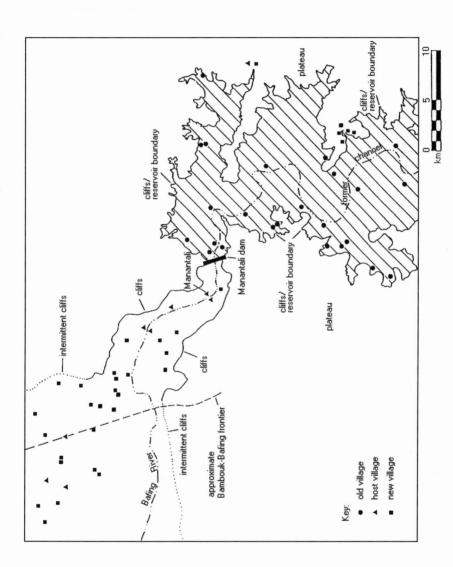

Map 9. Manantali villages. (From Horowitz et al. 1993. Copyright Westview Press.)

Bamako railroad) to Manantali, some 80 km south. ECBM also built much other infrastructure, including two housing developments for management and workers, a generator, water and sewage treatment facilities, and associated offices and construction facilities. As at Selingue, this activity encouraged the temporary migration of workers for dam construction and associated activities, as well as others who provided public and private services for them. For a short period, existing villages just downstream of the dam grew substantially as village chiefs began to rent or sell house sites and fields to these migrants. Yet because Manantali remained relatively isolated even after construction, it did not retain many of the temporary immigrants. Only a small core of service providers remained, to support the few civil servants who ran the dam, giving Manantali somewhat the air of a ghost town in 1989. A few laborers also stayed, awaiting the construction of the hydroelectric plant, which had not yet begun even in 1994.

Nor did postdam activity prove very attractive to new settlers. Marketing remained relatively difficult, in contrast to Selingue, which had easy access by paved road to Bamako. There was no irrigation, although a small perimeter was planned.[13] The only new group attracted to the zone were fishermen, but even they were disappointed. In June 1988, an estimated 6,000 had arrived, but by June 1989, the number had diminished to less than 1,000. The lake was too deep to be fished easily with existing equipment, since fish simply swam under the long, narrow nets. Due to the distance from major markets, it was virtually impossible to sell fresh fish. All had to be either dried or smoked.

The major settlement activity in the zone was the involuntary relocation to new villages of approximately 10,000 people from the dam reservoir area that stretched some 70 km southward. These people were resettled in 1986 and 1987 by the USAID-financed Projet pour la Réinstallation des Populations de Manantali (PRM), run by the Direction Nationale de l'Hydraulique et de l'Energie (DNHE) of the Ministry of Industry, Water, and Power. The goal was to allow the indigenous population, almost exclusively Malinke, to continue their major subsistence strategy, farming, in this area of relatively good rainfall. Long-term rainfall at Manantali was 1,100 mm annually (M. Traoré 1980), with significant variability: 754 mm in 1983, 1,091 mm in 1988 and 1,266 mm in 1989. The farming area was somewhat restricted because only 55 percent of land was arable in this zone filled with small hills. Scattered among areas of lateritic outcrop, arable zones usually had soils of medium or great depth and average natural fertility (PIRT 1986).

While the PRM organized the selection of sites for new villages, it tried to encourage relocatees to work with host populations to make viable long-term choices. Most villages chose to move downstream from the dam to lands they had previously used as agricultural hamlets. Site choice was facilitated because the resettlement zone was very sparsely populated, and kinship links existed between host and resettling villages. After a series of meetings organized by the PRM, chiefs of host villages gave formal approval to resettlement village choices. Representatives of resettlement villages gave appropriate gifts to host village chiefs and elders, although, unlike the other sites, resettlement villages maintained their status as independent villages.

Once sites were chosen, PRM organized field clearing by local workers and house construction by professional builders. They drilled wells and built access roads to villages. People built complementary structures, such as mosques, livestock pens, and granaries.

The resettlement led to some concentration of population, as 44 villages and hamlets became 34 new ones. Most villages moved as units, although hamlets sometimes combined with mother villages or other hamlets. Some villages split, with the new piece either establishing a new hamlet or joining another village. The lake covered both fields and forests, pushing both people and animals into more constricted areas. Although the zone's forage potential was high (PIRT 1986), the lake also led to loss of grazing areas. These changes rendered somewhat problematic the project goal of allowing people to re-create the pre-resettlement production strategy, which had rested on abundant use of naturally occurring resources.

Data on Manantali came from two sources. One was the qualitative studies done by Koenig and other members of the IDA technical-assistance team. The second was a sample of 50 households in several villages followed from 1986 to 1989 by an ISH team, including some of the present authors. This study, on the changes in domestic economy following resettlement, was also funded by USAID.[14]

Conclusion

The situations that led rural Malians to leave their home villages and seek other places to cultivate were quite diverse. The factors included those that have plagued the country for centuries (e.g. drought) as well as those that reflected the latest perturbations of the world economy (e.g., repatriations of guest workers). Yet, except for the cooperatives, the farms they established were structurally not very different from those in existing villages. The family usually became the unit of production and the basic labor force and drew on its core resources in relatively predictable ways.

Yet people were willing to experiment and try new things, and they acted in ways not necessarily predictable from cultural background or household structure. The remaining chapters turn to an examination of the production systems created by the migrants. We use a framework focusing on the interaction of larger structures and human action to understand the creation of family production strategies. In the next chapter, we address one of the key activities, agriculture.

Chapter 5

# Access to Agricultural Resources

Agriculture was part of the economic strategies of almost all the study house-holds, yet they entered it with a variety of objectives. It could be the key to economic survival or a complement to nonagricultural income. Its purpose could be to provide food for the household, or both food and cash; no households in our study had purely commercial farms.

The ability to realize agricultural goals was a function of available resources, at household and zone levels. Chapter 3 outlined the salient national constraints and cultural traditions that conditioned people's access to resources, while chapter 4 discussed each site's specific resources and configurations of access. Here, we turn first to the patterned ways that people in the different sites got access to the key agricultural resources: land, labor, and technology. The second half of this chapter turns to results—the ability of groups and individuals to meet their objectives. We look at the varying roles of basic cereal grains and complementary crops in agricultural strategies.

Fertile Cropland

Land was the key agricultural resource, for without it, a farmer could not farm. Strategies of land access varied substantially among the sites, depending on land availability and who (locals, private outsiders, and/or the government) actively claimed the rights to it. Results can be evaluated in part by the sizes of farms that migrants could procure. Once a parcel was obtained, ideas about local custom were important in allocating parts of it among different family members.

*Getting Land*

At only one site, Dioïla, did land control remain primarily local. At the two peri-urban sites, local control was restricted by the actions of large-scale plantation owners, either private individuals, as at Tienfala, or organizations, as in the parastatal tea plantation at Finkolo. At the other three sites, the state asserted its right to play a part in land allocation, officially at Manantali and Selingue in conjunction with dam relocation, and informally at Yanfolila and in other areas of Selingue. Varying interlocutors influenced the potential ability of settlers to get substantial farms.

In Dioïla, the process of land transfer most closely resembled what informants and chapter 3 described as the "traditional" ideal. Migrants, invariably male because this was considered a political task, undertook negotiations with the chief and elders of the mother village that claimed ownership over the uncultivated land. A symbolic payment, usually 10 kola nuts and a chicken, transferred use rights to a new migrant. In return, settlers were allowed to plant fields containing annual crops, but not perennials or trees. Access was secure as long as the land was cultivated by a family member, and they could and did pass land on to heirs. If the land were ever completely abandoned, it would revert to the mother village.

Once settled, the core of migrants set up its own governance structure in its hamlet and became responsible for allocating further fields. New migrants addressed themselves first to the hamlet chief and council, who then would introduce them to the mother village. Over time, the hamlets gained a sense of permanency. By 1989, some immigrants had already passed land to heirs, and villagers said that they could now plant trees if they wished. The settlements remained hamlets, however, politically dependent on mother villages.

The success of land-access procedures can be measured in a rough sense by looking at average farm size, including individual and collective fields, among the different groups (table 3). Compared to the other migrant family farms in the study, Dioïla farms were the largest, and their size was second only to the indigenous population of Selingue. In terms of land per person, the two cooperatives were larger, but these measures were not directly comparable, since cooperative figures reflected the entire land base, including that not yet put into cultivation. For the family farms, only cultivated area was measured. We have no figures with which to compare farm size among neighboring indigenous farmers, although Dioïla farms were also substantially larger than average farm size in the very heterogeneous Third Region as a whole. There, the average farm had only 5.2 ha, even though its total family size was larger, 12 persons in contrast to Dioïla's 9.8 (TAMS 1983, D57).

Yet many Dioïla farmers wanted even more land than they had. They had the oldest fields, 9.7 years, in the sample (table 4), suggesting that fallowing possibilities were more limited. They were able to cultivate their fields over long periods because they had access to fertilizers and other inputs, but they also were obliged to do so.[1] Both government policies encouraging sedentar-

**TABLE 3.  Farm Sizes**

| Site | Total Hectares | Number Households | Hectares/ Household | Number Persons | Hectares/ Person |
|------|------|------|------|------|------|
| Dioïla | 132.1 | 15 | 11.07 | 166 | 0.80 |
| Finkolo | 15.75 | 15 | 1.05 | 132 | 0.12 |
| Yanfolila-indigenous | 15.64 | 2 | 7.82 | 93 | 0.17 |
| Yanfolila-migrant | 48.77 | 13 | 3.75 | 133 | 0.37 |
| CAMUKO | 300 | — | — | 370 | 0.81 |
| CAMSEL | 200 | — | — | 200 | 1.00 |
| Manantali | 63.25 | 7 | 9.04 | 194 | 0.33 |
| Selingue-indigenous | 72.79 | 5 | 14.16 | 64 | 1.13 |
| Selingue-migrant | 6.68 | 13 | 0.51 | 88 | 0.08 |

*Source:* For Manantali, the source is T. Diarra et al. (1990).

*Note:* Table includes only households where fields were measured; one Selingue farm with 113 hectares deleted; CAMUKO population based on maximum future size.

ization and rising population densities made it more difficult to clear land than it had been 25 years earlier. The very success of their agricultural strategies (as we will discuss later in this chapter) meant that when farmers could get more land, they often preferred to expand cultivation rather than to let existing fields fallow. Local control of land remained effective at Dioïla because it was relatively abundant until recently, local political organization remained strong, and there were no substantive claims by either the Malian government or elite Malians. Saul (1988, 1993) found a very similar situation in western Burkina Faso.

In the two peri-urban sites, Tienfala and Finkolo, national-level actors had complicated land access by taking some of the prime agricultural land away from local control. In Tienfala, land under local control was limited because of the presence of the *concessions rurales* and plantations belonging to affluent Malians, while at Finkolo, the tea plantation had taken much of the best land. Yet the migrants in our samples were neither affluent nor well connected; they had to address customary owners.

The land pressure created by the tea farm at Finkolo was relatively stable. The farm had come into existence over 20 years earlier, got its land, and had not substantially expanded since then. Growing pressure on rural land would have come from natural population growth in surrounding villages or urban spread from Sikasso. Even though the plantation had earlier intervened to help villagers get house sites, it did not become involved in their efforts to get farmland. That remained a local-level transaction between those wanting land and the customary owners.

TABLE 4.   Average Age of Fields

| Site | Years | Number of fields |
|------|-------|------------------|
| Dioïla | 9.7 | 40 |
| Finkolo | 5.6 | 34 |
| Tienfala | 4.3 | 17 |
| Yanfolila-indigenous | 1.4 | 34 |
| Yanfolila-migrant | 1.5 | 92 |
| Selingue-indigenous | 5.1 | 15 |
| Selingue-migrant | 1.5 | 18 |

The nearby Senufo villages where workers found fields distinguished between temporary and permanent use rights. The lineages who settled first received permanent rights from the village founder; later migrants could also get permanent rights if the whole area claimed by a village was not yet exploited. Once the entire area had come under cultivation, further claimants were given only temporary use rights, a loan from the person with permanent rights. Tea plantation workers were able to get temporary rights only and had to return land to the lender if it was needed. Workers did not mention paying for this land, even a symbolic gift, but there were strong restrictions against symbols of permanent use such as tree planting.

Since nobody mentioned that they had had to return their parcels, tenure seemed relatively secure, but people usually received only very small farms. The average farm size of 1.05 ha in Finkolo was the second smallest among the sample groups, as was the area per person (0.12 ha). Average farm size in a nearby area of full-time farmers was much larger, 5.81 ha (Whitney 1981). The length of field use, 5.6 years, the second longest in the sample, also suggested that Finkolo farmers had a difficult time expanding field areas. Like the other farmers, they would have liked easier access to more land, although because farming was a secondary occupation for them, lack of land did not necessarily compromise economic survival. Locals and workers seemed to have reached an agreement that workers could receive small amounts of land, if they accepted the temporary nature of their access. This suggests that local owners were conscious of increasing land pressures coming from sources outside the plantation. Temporary loans to tea workers could help them resist more permanent claims from neighbors or kin.

The effects that rapidly growing land pressure could have in peri-urban areas were more apparent at Tienfala, where the national government was actively trying to expand its authority over land allocation. The *chef d'arrondissement* presided over a domanial commission to attribute building lots in areas already formally divided, and had requested further division in other parts of the arrondissement. This would allow him to build political influence by allocating them. There were also demands to the administration for *concessions rurales*. Yet, village chiefs continued to distribute land to new arrivals. This appeared to have been a conscious attempt to preempt state authority and keep land allocation in local hands, but the elders seem to have been divided about how best to implement this strategy.

Some continued "traditional" land lending against symbolic payments. Given the competition for land, this only makes sense if viewed as a way to maintain local control. Because of the high level of youth out-migration, locals risked losing control over lands declared vacant,[2] given the desire of large landowners and the state to make land claims. Hence it was in the interest of villages to welcome temporary users of their farmland, particularly relatively poor migrants who would have a sense of obligation toward village chiefs. This was similar to the situation in western Burkina Faso, where villagers freely lent land to those they knew would respect local norms but refused to lend to migrants whom they suspected would try to use national laws to undermine local control (Saul 1988). Thus chiefs of both Tienfala-gare and Tienfala-village were giving lands to new arrivals under conditions virtually the same as at Dioïla, 10 kola nuts and 500 FCFA (U.S.$1.52, roughly the price of a chicken). Virtually all our sample households got their land in this way.

Other chiefs tried to maintain local control but in a new form. The chief of Djinkoni village, the original mother village of both Tienfala-gare and Tienfala-village, had evidently begun to sell uncultivated bushlands to new arrivals. The exact terms were unclear, but prices were rumored to be very high since he was selling to Bamako residents for tree plantations. At Fugadougou, the payment until just prior to the study had been 3 kola nuts and 500 FCFA if the migrant was sponsored by a village resident. But the village felt under pressure to grant *concessions rurales* to city dwellers, and the village council decided to charge each new migrant 50,000 FCFA (U.S.$152) for a field. The chief did not agree. He moved out of the village proper and began personally to sell its uncultivated bushlands to individuals, again at prices rumored to be very high. At the time of the study, at least one migrant had paid the 50,000 FCFA to the village council. These villages or their chiefs had apparently decided that if the village would be unable to keep its land through customary lending, the village rather than the government should get the money for the land. These processes were common in many parts of Africa since indigenous tenure was often vulnerable to land grabbing in similar situations. "Traditional" leaders could easily abuse their rights to allocate land (Bruce 1988).

The team was unable to measure any farms at Tienfala, but they appear not to have been very large, and it was not always easy to increase land areas. Moreover, because of their concerns that vacant land might be claimed by others, people at Tienfala had the most conscious concern about losing land rights if they fallowed. The average age of the sample fields, 4.3 years, was relatively high, although less than at either Finkolo or Dioïla. Moreover, we heard of no cases where migrants' farms had been expropriated, once they had begun to cultivate. As in Finkolo, people also earned from nonagricultural occupations so that they did not have a pressing need for large farms for economic survival. Migrants were able to get land by allying with local elders against the claims of government and elite Malians, at least over the short term.[3]

The possibilities for land access changed substantially when the government decided to assert its claims over land allocation, since national land law granted precedence to its interests. Sometimes administrators took an "unofficial" role, acting as liaison among local groups, as when they helped settle drought refugees in Yanfolila and when they assisted the Soninke cooperatives in finding farmland. Since Malian land law formally recognized village ownership of cultivated fields and some fallow, administration and political party representatives were able to claim that they were respecting village custom, while urging villages to grant uncultivated land to migrants. Formally, the transactions remained between village chiefs and councils on the one hand, and migrants on the other. Yet because land law did not recognize village claims over pasture or uncultivated bush, the mere presence of government representatives in the discussions devalued village ownership of these lands. Because of the power differences between the actors, it was difficult for villagers to refuse "to help" unless they had very severe land shortages.

In Yanfolila, the settlement of drought refugees in family farms was part of a national call to assist those who had sustained losses. Party militants from the UDPM, at that time the sole political party, decided on the policy they called *cohabitation,* settling migrants in existing villages rather than in their own hamlets, and they organized local villages to accept migrants. Although land was abundant, locals were not necessarily keen to accept migrants that they themselves had not chosen. They appear to have consciously considered the costs and benefits of playing hosts. In Gwalafara, the village displaced by the Selingue dam, the hope of future project benefits played a major role in their decision to accept newcomers. Locals also laid down a few conditions, most notably, a refusal to accept herders. They also demanded that all farmers divest themselves of any livestock before settling.

There were indications that refugees were not welcomed with entirely open arms. In one village, migrants were given house plots subject to flooding. Land conflicts between migrant and indigenous villagers occurred, resulting in the repossession of land from at least one migrant household. The relatively high number of Dogon who left outlying villages for Yanfolila town suggests that they were not always able to get sufficient resources. Yet, once again, the customary form of land transfer remained intact; rights were passed for a symbolic gift of 10 kola nuts to show respect.

The farms received by Yanfolila migrants were relatively small, averaging only 3.75 ha (table 3). This was clearly smaller than the average farm size in the Third Region as a whole, 5.2 ha. Yet because Dogon households were smaller than average, the average land area per person, 0.37 ha was only slightly smaller than the regional average of 0.43 ha/person (TAMS 1983, D57). Their farms also appeared to be smaller than those of most indigenous farmers in the zone. Our tiny sample of indigenous Yanfolila farmers showed smaller farms than the migrants on a per person basis (0.17 ha/person vs. 0.37 ha/person for migrants), but this data set was the most unreliable. Comparative data suggest that although reported indigenous farm size (7.82 ha) was about average for the zone, reported average household size in the sample (34.3) was much greater. A baseline study for CMDT expansion found average family size to be about 20 persons, while households with some equipment had farms averaging from 7.17 to 15.5 ha. Only those with no equipment had average farms as small as those of the Dogon migrants, averaging 3.26 ha (I. Cissé, Coulibaly, and Sow 1989, 81). Even if migrant farms were not that much smaller than those of indigenous counterparts, they wanted more land. In part, this was because they also perceived their farms to be smaller than they might have been at home. One study found that farms on the Dogon plateau averaged 4.27 ha, while those on the plain were 8.3 ha on average (S. Cohen 1981, 89, 90). Even though land was more productive in Yanfolila because of higher rainfall, migrants were comparing areas to those at home.

It was not yet clear whether the Dogon households would be able to fallow their existing fields and get new ones in turn. The average age of their fields, only 1.5 years, in part reflected their recent migration. In contrast, the similar young age of the fields held by the indigenous Wassulunke, 1.4 years, suggested that sufficient land was available to continue bush fallowing. Migrant tenure rights over the long term were unclear, however. If migrants were to show appropriate respect for their hosts and if their presence and/or increased settlement density were rewarded by greater infrastructure, it is likely that hosts and migrants would work out their differences and land rights become more secure. If, however, the migrants were to emphasize their links to nonlocals, either administration or NGOs, locals would be likely to be wary of their intentions and land conflicts likely to increase (cf. Saul 1988).

Government representatives also helped the Soninke cooperatives find land. Their goal of large-scale rice farming was bound to be attractive to a Malian administration continually concerned about national rice production. Moreover, the Soninke were literate in French and backed by an international NGO. Hosts came out a poor third to a combined force of migrants and administrators, and villages handed over hundreds of hectares of ambiguous status because it was considered vacant. In Selinkenyi, the 200 ha given to the cooperative was village pasture, the loss of which caused problems for herds. In Wuru Wuru at Yanfolila, the local village thought that it had only given temporary usufructuary rights to the cooperative, while CAMUKO maintained that it had received permanent ownership. In both cases, the only payment was the customary 10 kola nuts. Since the villages were not using this land at the time of the loan, there was no immediate conflict, but the potential for future problems was there. The cooperatives did not find their actions problematic since they knew that Malian law gave ultimate land ownership to the government, and they considered their high-technology farming superior to the small farms of villagers.

The large size of the two cooperatives was not out of line with the size of the population they were meant to support. Since they included uncultivated areas that other farms did not, they were not much larger than many family farms on a per inhabitant basis. They seemed larger since they were unfragmented parcels with clear borders, unlike family farms where cultivated areas were divided among multiple distinct parcels. These single large tracts had the potential to benefit from economies of scale.

In cases of infrastructure development such as dams or irrigated perimeters, the government took a more formal role. At both dam sites, the administration expropriated land for the dam area and its associated infrastructure but also created organizations to oversee the resettlement of people living in reservoir areas and secure land rights for them. The process of land allocation at Selingue was not well documented, but at Manantali, the PRM organized the transfer of "traditional" land rights from hosts to relocatees in resettlement areas. After a series of preliminary meetings, the PRM held a general meeting in July 1983 with representatives of host villages, resettlement villages, the Malian government, and the donor (USAID) to determine general areas of resettlement. Then hosts and relocated villages chose specific areas, formally recognized by the PRM. After villages moved, ceremonies were performed to pass ownership rights from hosts to new villages, the only case in which settlers were immediately given more than use rights over the lands on which they settled. The relocating villages generally kept their old names, and their old social and political organizations.

In this case, the resettlement authority decided to use the framework of customary tenure rather than to create a new tenure system. Agreement between hosts and relocatees was relatively easy because they were kin and because the host area was very sparsely settled. The promise of new infrastructure such as drilled wells also helped convince hosts to accept the situation. Yet, if there had been any serious resistance on the part of hosts, the government would surely have exerted more authority.

Manantali households got reasonably sized farms, averaging 9.04 ha in a small sample (table 3). On a per person basis, land areas were about average for the country as a whole. Yet the PRM ignored the amount of fallow needed to maintain the existing bush fallow system and paid insufficient attention to pasture access, which led to land competition both between host and resettlement villages and among different resettlement villages after several years.

In the irrigated perimeters, the government asserted its right to change tenure rules, directly controlling the terms under which farmland was exploited. On established perimeters like the Office du Niger, families tended to have relatively secure tenure on specific parcels. At Selingue, the situation was quite different, in large part because the OERHN was under considerable pressure to make the perimeter "successful" to justify continued investment and expansion of the perimeter from 1,200 ha to the full 2,000. Success was measured primarily by the quantity and yields of rice produced.

When the Selingue perimeter began to function in 1985–86, initial guidelines gave priority for tenancies to those relocated by dam construction (Sissoko et al. 1986, 171). This policy led to lower-than-projected production, so the OERHN administration began to look for "better" farmers. They were particularly impressed by one Dogon farmer who had had a spectacular harvest, and they began to think in ethnic terms and to encourage Dogon to come, in light of their reputation as hardworking farmers. They also recruited individuals to the perimeter from among Dogon drought refugees and repatriated workers.

The OERHN believed that intensive cultivation of small plots (as opposed to extensive cultivation of large ones) would lead to the highest yields. As it recruited more people, it decreased the parcel size. In 1984–85, a farmer received from 0.5 to 1.2 ha, depending on the size of his family (Sissoko et al. 1986,

101). By 1988–89, a family with 1 to 8 active members received only 0.25 ha; one with 9 to 16 active members, 0.5 ha; and only if a household had more than 16 workers would it get a whole hectare. Average plot size decreased from 0.81 ha in 1987–88 to 0.64 ha in 1988–89. Moreover, tenants often received different parcels from year to year. Just as a farmer learned to appreciate the unique agricultural qualities of his land, he was moved elsewhere.

From OERHN's perspective, productivity was improving, but from the point of view of farmers, land access was inadequate. It was relatively easy for a new migrant to get a single irrigated plot, but average farm sizes at Selingue were by far the smallest overall and per person (table 3). Because few farmers could feed their families using only irrigated parcels, most wanted to pursue rainfed agriculture alongside irrigation. To do so, they had to address the indigenous villagers under customary rules. Yet local villages, pressured by land shortages due to dam resettlement and new migrants, responded by refusing to lend land to newcomers. The 19 migrant households in our sample had only three rainfed fields, two of which were smaller than 0.1 ha. In contrast to the help given by the state to the cooperatives or to drought refugees at Yanfolila, the administration did not see the need to help these migrants negotiate with village groups for rainfed land because the OERHN was already giving them irrigated land.

In contrast, the indigenous inhabitants of Selingue appeared to have relatively large farms, the largest per household and per person among the study groups (table 3). In fact, the average farm size among indigenous Selingue farmers would have been even larger, but we omitted one farm of 113 ha, so enormously large for a household farm that we believe it was mismeasured. Fields were 5.1 years old on average, among the older fields in the study (table 4). We suspect that these data indicate another strategy used by indigenous people to retain land under their control in light of population pressure. They kept large areas under extremely extensive cultivation, even with relatively low yields, as a way to illustrate land ownership and keep land from being declared vacant. This meant that migrants to Selingue found it virtually impossible to get land outside the perimeter, and they had a very difficult making a living from agriculture.

In comparison to indigenous inhabitants, migrants everywhere had fewer rights to clear new land, less land, and often less fertile land, since the very first inhabitants of a zone had usually moved onto the best land. Yet, most farmers, indigenous and immigrant, harkened back to an ideal era where land was freely available. Chapter 2 suggested that insofar as this era existed, it was the result of violence rather than an idyllic past. Contemporary land access has also been affected by dramatic population growth in the last 100 years, due to both natural increase and immigration.

However, most farmers expected to undertake extensive, bush fallow cropping despite perceived land shortages. To do so, they needed rights to fallow lands as well as those under cultivation. Yet human actions affected the ability to continue extensive agriculture. At most sites, the potential for field loss to other new or old villagers led people to shorten fallow periods so that there could be no confusion between unclaimed bush and fallow fields. Government policy also had an impact, since the Malian policy of sedentarization introduced fees for clearing new lands and fines if the fees were not paid. Yet continuous cultivation without adequate practices to conserve soil fertility can lead to serious soil degradation. In some areas, intensity of land use was high enough to jeopardize continued soil fertility. So virtually all the migrant groups wanted more land as well as more secure tenure. While farmers knew a number of practices to conserve or improve soil fertility, all required some investment of either labor or capital. As we shall see later in this chapter, there were limits on their capacity to carry out these practices, so farmers continued to try to get more land and more secure tenure for what they had.

The experiences in the different sites show that in all land transactions there were three potential actors: the host village with its claims, the Malian government, and the settlers. As in many African countries, legal tenure rights did not so much replace customary rules as add another negotiating tool (Reyna and Downs 1988, 11; Shipton and Goheen 1992, 316). There was not always much of a power difference between host and settler, but the Malian government always had significantly more power than the other two. Nevertheless, the government became involved only where it saw an interest. The lone migrant household who tried to involve the local administration usually did not find much help. Moreover, when the government got involved, it was rarely willing to revolutionize local land tenure. Thus it had to recognize formally the validity of local claims, primarily by involving local chiefs and councils in discussion, even while asserting the priority of its own claims. Only in the relatively rare cases of infrastructure-related expropriations did it change tenure rules.

Because they continued to see potential benefits to larger population groupings, villages were often willing to allocate lands to others if there were still unused bushlands within their territories. But when villagers saw their own ability to survive decrease through increasing land pressure, they resisted allocating land to new migrants even when subject to government or elite pressure. However, they sometimes collaborated with migrants that they could control (ordinary farmers like themselves) better to resist that pressure. Cropland was rarely bought and sold, except around Bamako, nor were rents collected. People either agreed to let others have farmland for relatively symbolic payments, or simply refused. Yet access to land was by no means "traditional."

Rather, the ideology of "traditional" land tenure provided a framework within which government, host, and settler interacted, and covered many different possibilities in terms of rights transferred, permanency of settlement, and the actual role of each party. It is clear that attempts to create "modern" land tenure systems in countries like Mali cannot work if they begin from an idealized version of "traditional" land tenure or local customs, but rather must recognize the formal and informal roles of the many actors involved. In particular, the informal and potential role of the state in many transactions needs to be more formally recognized, as does the existence of multiple forms of tenure within one area (Berry 1993; Reyna and Downs 1988).

*Allocating Fields*

After household heads negotiated with landowners for land, they allocated land within the household, between collective and individual fields, and between men and women. Although each family followed cultural traditions to some extent, different patterns of land and labor availability led to distinctive choices at the different sites (table 5). Since fields varied widely in size, figures showing allocation of fields among household heads (virtually always collective fields), women, other men, and unknown household members are more useful for illustrating which categories of farmers received land rather than for making precise estimates of land areas.

Clearly collective fields were a priority. Most sites showed at least one collective parcel for the household. Yet there were exceptions. Among the Selingue migrants, a few had arrived too recently to have yet received even an irrigated parcel. They expected to cultivate a collective field the following year. In Finkolo, a few (four) households in the sample had no collective field, a more conscious choice than in Selingue. These households included two headed by specialized workers (mechanic, driver) who made higher salaries and one headed by an ill older retiree who could not farm. Among the indigenous farmers of Selingue, a few had decided to join the Soninke cooperative, CAMSEL, using their share in the cooperative's production to replace what they might have gotten from their own collective fields. This appears to have been another way that the indigenous population of Selingue tried to cope with their own land shortages, as well as a way to get access to new technology, as we will discuss later in this chapter.

**TABLE 5.   Number of Fields by Owners**

| Site | N | Household Heads | Women | Other Men | Unknown | Number of Households |
|------|---|-----------------|-------|-----------|---------|----------------------|
| Manantali | 70 | 31.0% | 0.0% | 0.0% | 69.0% | 7 |
| Selingue-indigenous | 15 | 47.0% | 33.0% | 6.7% | 13.0% | 10 |
| Yanfolila-indigenous | 30 | 53.0% | 0.0% | 37.0% | 10.0% | 4 |
| Tienfala | 17 | 59.0% | 35.0% | 0.0% | 5.9% | 9 |
| Dioïla | 40 | 75.0% | 25.0% | 0.0% | 0.0% | 30 |
| Selingue-migrant | 18 | 78.0% | 5.6% | 11.0% | 5.6% | 19 |
| Yanfolila-migrant | 92 | 91.0% | 2.2% | 2.2% | 4.4% | 26 |
| Finkolo | 34 | 100.0% | 0.0% | 0.0% | 0.0% | 30 |

*Source:* For Manantali, the source is T. Diarra et al. (1990).

Yet migrant households did not grant land as easily to other members of the household as did indigenous ones, a common pattern when land is perceived to be short. Women were slightly more likely than other men to get fields, yet indigenous women were more likely than migrant women to have their own fields. Group interviews with the autochthonous women of Yanfolila suggested that many had fields and information gathered from individual interviews (table 5) was simply wrong. In Selingue many of the indigenous women had fields as well; the number included some whose family heads had gone to work for CAMSEL. In Manantali, women were a large number of the "unknown" owners of individual fields. The situation among voluntary migrants was more variable. At Tienfala, many women had fields, while in Dioïla, only a minority did. In the other three migrant groups, few women had fields.

The decision to allocate fields to women or not appeared to have been based on several factors: land and labor availability, whether women had alternative ways to meet their family responsibilities, and whether other family members, usually men, were willing to take over some of women's familial responsibilities. Women's responses to this change were varied. In general, if they had alternative sources of income, as in Dioïla and Finkolo, women did not perceive lack of fields as problematic. However, when they had neither fields nor alternative sources of income, as among migrants to Yanfolila and Selingue, they were vocal in their complaints.

Dependent men were even less likely to get their own fields. Only among the indigenous Yanfolila residents and the Manantali relocatees, trying to reproduce preresettlement households, were there many individual male fields. Migrants usually moved as nuclear households, without many extra male members. Where there were additional men, there was apparently some pressure on them to work on the collective fields as the surest route to economic survival and success. The Soninke returnees even called upon kin still at home to join them on their collective enterprises. Among the Selingue indigenous population as well, there were few male individual fields, again probably a response to perceived land pressure.

Although it is not clear from the figures alone, interviews with Selingue migrants suggested that they were a major exception to the pattern of encouraging dependent men to work on collective fields. This was clearly a response to the rules for access to irrigated land. Since a household would need nine active members before it received more than the minimum allocation of 0.25 ha, there was no incentive for maintaining a single household labor force. If two brothers farmed together, they would usually receive only 0.25 ha, but if their households split, they would receive 0.5 ha, two minimum allocations. Farmers responded by "officially" splitting households that included several adult men and receiving multiple fields. They could continue to farm together if they chose, working first on one parcel, then the other.

When they migrated, households did not simply reproduce preexisting forms of household production but allocated land in ways they thought would be most propitious for future growth. Household heads did not make decisions without consulting other family members, although their desires usually did take priority. When resources were short, households usually concentrated on collective production. When the government controlled the environment, people were willing to change family organization to increase access to resources.

Access to Labor

Land without labor to put it into production was useless. Yet it has not always been easy to get agricultural labor in Africa. Where land has remained relatively abundant, farmers often preferred to begin their own farms rather than work for someone else (Saul 1988, 1993). If they needed to supplement their incomes, it was often more remunerative to do so through nonagricultural employment (Berry 1993). Since it was difficult to get labor from outside the household, most farmers had to rely on family members. Conditions were no different in our sample, where the vast majority of households depended mostly on their own members for labor. Yet, as discussed in chapter 2, members, especially young men, would go elsewhere to work if labor conditions were too exploitative.

Access to labor was evaluated by the reported quantity of labor furnished on the fields included in the field-level survey.[4] This information, furnished by recall, did not reliably provide absolute quantities of labor and so could not be used to determine economic returns to it. Nevertheless, it is useful for showing the relative distribution of labor input. Each individual's labor was counted in terms of days and half-days, and the labor of men, women, and children was valued equally, since our concern was to understand how households allocated labor across alternative activities.

*Household Labor*

Virtually all farmers relied primarily on the labor of their own households. All sites except one reported that 96 percent or more of labor-days came from household members. The exception was Tienfala, where 32 percent of recorded labor came from extrahousehold sources. Collective fields had the most land area and hence received the most labor, 60 percent or more of all recorded labor except among the indigenous residents of Selingue. However, when other household members had access to fields, they also had access to labor. Among the indigenous inhabitants of Selingue, where women had 33 percent of the fields, they received 38 percent of recorded labor; in Tienfala, where they had 35 percent of the recorded fields, they received 21 percent of the recorded labor. Among the indigenous group at Yanfolila, dependent men had 37 percent of the recorded fields and received 32 percent of the labor. Although our data were not sufficiently detailed to verify if men and women had equal access to others' labor, women had more ability to command labor than in other cases, for example, in northeastern Ghana (Moore 1988, 57–59). Dependent men and women with individual fields often had access not only to their own labor, but also that of other household members. And in Dioïla, the only site with high equipment use, all women field owners except one had the use of the household's equipment on their fields for strategic tasks such as field preparation.

Whether labor was concentrated on collective fields or spread across women's and other men's fields as well, households called on all adult family members, and in most cases, children, to work. Women provided from 20 percent to 38 percent of all recorded work, except among the migrants of Selingue, where they provided only 6 percent. Children provided from 25 percent to 33 percent of recorded work in Yanfolila (among both migrants and indigenous groups), Dioïla, and Finkolo. It is not clear whether they really did not work at Selingue and Tienfala or whether interviewers did not pay sufficient attention to their work. The low level of women's work among the Selingue migrants is likely due partly to their adherence to Wahabiyya Islam and partly to the lack of rainfed fields, where women generally did more work than on irrigated parcels. Unless there were more remunerative activities, all adult household members were expected to make a labor contribution to agriculture, on either collective or individual fields, but often on a mix—except in the rare cases, for example, Selingue, where extremely limited land availability meant that the household had surplus labor.

The only alternative to reliance on household labor was found in the two cooperatives, where members worked collectively and, in return, received shares of the produce. These formal organizations, composed of male members, held regular meetings to discuss cooperative activities. Although each cooperative began with a core of returned migrants, their labor was insufficient. Each group requested that relatives from home areas join them and also opened membership to local villagers. In 1988, four men in Selinkenyi's 10-household indigenous sample had joined CAMSEL. In Yanfolila, only two locals had joined CAMUKO; one was a single man from Yanfolila town and the other the son of the village chief of Wuru Wuru, reportedly sent to keep an eye on the cooperative.

The patterns of adherence reflected different attitudes toward the cooperatives in the two sites. In Selingue, CAMSEL had reached satisfactory production levels at a time when villagers felt land pressure. The cooperative also offered the only access to "modern" technology off the perimeter. Giving their village lands to other family members to cultivate, the household heads joined the cooperative as a way to increase economic alternatives. In contrast, in Wuru Wuru, the village did not perceive a land shortage, and indigenous inhabitants could participate in CMDT activities. Moreover, CAMUKO had still not established satisfactory production levels. Locals claimed that the cooperative members worked too hard; several had joined but quit, and the two who remained were clearly special cases.

*Extrahousehold Labor*

Extrahousehold labor was provided in a variety of different forms: through village-level work groups of young men or women (the *tonw* as well as smaller groups), by laborers who joined the household for an agricultural season *(navetanes),* and through wage labor paid daily or by the task. Only two sites, Tienfala and Dioïla, reported more than minimal use of extrahousehold labor. Distinctive uses reflected their different orientations toward agriculture.

With their emphasis on cotton production, the Dioïla farmers had some of the most commercialized farms in the sample. Hired labor was most used by affluent farmers at times of peak labor need to meet pressing cultivation requirements. Some 89 percent of the reported extrahousehold labor was used by only four households, of whom three were clearly among the sample's most affluent. Sometimes, they would recruit 50 people or more to work on a single task, suggesting use of the villagewide *ton*. Virtually all this labor was paid in cash, and laborers received an average of 510 FCFA per day (U.S.$1.55). It was not clear who furnished the labor, although some may have come from poorer families, as well as collective work groups. The qualitative part of the study suggested that some of the wealthier farmers had also brought *navetanes* into their households.

In Tienfala, use of extrahousehold labor was much more egalitarian. All five households where field-level data were collected used extrahousehold labor, and it was used on both men's and women's fields. Among the workers, men and women each furnished approximately half the days. The labor was usually paid in kind, rather than in cash. Yet there was a clear distinction in daily rate by the type of crop. On crops more commonly grown to sell (e.g., peanuts and rice), workers earned an equivalent of 500–600 FCFA (U.S.$1.52–1.82) per person-day, while workers on rainfed cereals, the main food crop, earned less, approximately 100 FCFA (U.S.$.30) per person-day.

In most sites, however, the qualitative data suggested that use of hired labor, especially in group form, was somewhat more common than the quantitative data indicated, especially among autochthonous populations. The indigenous women of Yanfolila claimed to have groups that did agricultural work for money. In Manantali, where we only had qualitative information, agricultural work groups also existed, and most were reconstituted after the villages moved. Later data from the early 1990s also suggested that use of work groups was relatively common. Indigenous farmers may have been better able to use putative lines of kinship and village solidarity to get access to village-level agricultural work groups, and more of them may have had the resources necessary to hire labor. In contrast, most of the migrants could not rely on extrahousehold labor and had to use family labor to sustain production.

As Berry (1993) found elsewhere, there was less variety in labor deployment than in patterns of access to land, or, as we will discuss later in this chapter, in input use or crop selection. The supply of people willing to do agricultural labor was low. A large-scale enterprise like the Finkolo tea plantation was able to get a labor force, but this was in part because the workers received formal benefits. The commercial plantations run by wealthy Malians near Bamako paid their laborers around 12,500 FCFA (U.S.$38) per month, barely more than the daily rate for workers on small farms at either Tienfala or Dioïla, and they had a very difficult time finding laborers, especially from neighboring villages.

The ability of small farmers to find extra labor when they needed it (but only then) remained quite limited. The only real alternative to household labor found in this study was the cooperatives, where no one was employer or employee, but where all were seen as equal members and participants. In most cases, migrants preferred to earn extra funds by off-farm or dry-season activities that did not conflict with farming. Enough of those existed to depress the supply of farm laborers. Although it was risky, people did stay in rural areas on their own farms because this gave them more autonomy. They turned to customary ways of increasing family size—marriage and reproduction—to increase household labor.

Access to Technology

Given the difficulties in increasing human labor power, farmers looked to agricultural equipment and inputs to increase production without increasing labor. To get these, they needed capital, either directly by earning cash, or indirectly through credit. This section looks first at access to agricultural equipment, then at inputs.

*Equipment*

Plows, multipurpose tool frames, and draft animals were used to increase the area under cultivation, or more rarely, to intensify. Equipment proved very popular, as farmers quickly grasped its value. As of 1972, Mali was already considered to be "probably the most mechanized farming population in West Africa" (cited in Steedman et al. 1976, 93). However, access to cash to purchase equipment and draft animals constrained access, even though both agricultural equipment and draft animals were widely available in the rural private sector. Although ODRs had often introduced equipment initially, private-sector sellers had become important even before ODRs were forced to pull out of equipment and draft animal sales by structural adjustment. Plows, multipurpose tool frames, and spare parts entered markets alongside handheld hoes and other tools. Some came from urban factories, and others were made by rural artisans. Although many farmers preferred to repair and keep their equipment as long as possible, there also appeared to be an active market in used agricultural equipment. Draft oxen sales were an adjunct to existing cattle markets. Once a few people had learned to castrate and train local Malian cattle, the process could be carried out locally.

In this study, the rate of equipment ownership was high among all the established groups who considered farming their primary activity, whether or not

**TABLE 6. Equipment Ownership**

| Site | Number of Households | Plows | Multi-cultivators | Seeders | Carts | Other Equipment | Oxen | Donkeys |
|---|---|---|---|---|---|---|---|---|
| Yanfolila-indigenous | 4 | 3 | 0 | 0 | 1 | 0 | 6 | 0 |
| Selingue-indigenous | 10 | 9 | 3 | 4 | 3 | 3 | 12 | 4 |
| Dioïla | 30 | 27 | 17 | 10 | 12 | 6 | 55 | 8 |
| Manantali | 50 | 25 | 28 | 36 | 9 | 0 | 68 | — |
| Yanfolila-migrant | 26 | 4 | 0 | 0 | 0 | 1 | 8 | 1 |
| Selingue-migrant | 19 | 0 | 0 | 0 | 0 | 0 | 1 | 3 |
| Finkolo | 30 | 2 | 0 | 0 | 0 | 0 | 4 | 0 |
| Tienfala | 9 | 1 | 0 | 0 | 2 | 0 | 2 | 2 |

*Source:* For Manantali, the source is T. Diarra et al. (1990).

they had access to ODRs, and whether or not they were subject to land pressure (table 6). This included the indigenous populations of Selingue and Yanfolila, the relocatees of Manantali, and the migrants to Dioïla. In our samples, equipment and animals were bought mostly through the private sector and for cash. Fewer than a third of purchases had been made through ODRs. Because ODRs sold at fixed prices, people often thought they could do better in the private sector, which sold equipment and animals of varying quality and price, including used equipment. Credit of any type was used for less than a quarter of the purchases; people were willing to pay cash up front.

In the sites where people viewed farming as a secondary activity (Tienfala, Finkolo) and where they were not yet well established (migrants to Yanfolila and Selingue), equipment and animal ownership was low. The small farms of Tienfala and Finkolo may have made the use of equipment and draft animals uneconomic, but in Yanfolila and Selingue, the relative poverty of the migrants made it difficult for them to afford equipment. In Yanfolila, the requirement that migrants divest themselves of livestock before arriving also made it more difficult for them to use animal-drawn machines. These groups clearly had less access to capital resources than did the other groups.

Where there were relatively high levels of equipment, people reaped secondary advantages. For example, once people had substantial herds, they could select draft oxen from among their own animals. In Dioïla, where the rate of ox ownership was highest, 24 of 55 draft oxen were born into the owners' herds. In Selingue too, 7 of the 12 oxen belonging to the autochthonous population were born in their own herds. Obviously, draft oxen did not themselves reproduce, but as long as farmers had other cattle, familiarity with draft oxen allowed them to select and train their own animals.

Rentals also allowed people without equipment to use it, but the data suggested that a relatively high level of equipment ownership was necessary for a rental market to develop. As long as equipment was limited, the prime time for rentals was when people needed to use it themselves. With more equipment, demand for any one piece was less. Until expertise in handling animals was widespread enough that owners had confidence that renters knew what they were doing, they usually accompanied the rented team (cf. Toulmin 1992). In that case, rentals impacted on the time that they could spend on their own fields. Thus, the only site with any significant degree of equipment rental was Dioïla, where 22 of the 30 sample households had rented equipment at some time, for a total of 26 rentals. Farmers rented equipment for many tasks: plowing, threshing, seeding, and even weeding. In all, Dioïla farmers spent 518,750 FCFA (U.S.$1,572) on equipment rental, equal to 17,292 FCFA (U.S.$52) per household. Since rental information came from the field study, where only a quarter of all fields were included, actual use rates of rented equipment were probably higher. Despite the fact that a critical mass of equipment appeared necessary for a rental market to appear, once it did, those with least equipment could rent. Half the Dioïla rentals were in the village with the least equipment, Fofoni Dogolen.

Rental markets not only made equipment available to more people, but they also encouraged owners to make more innovative purchases, since they could rent out equipment as well as use it themselves. One Dioïla man with a minitractor rented it out to help amortize his cost, since cotton sales figures suggested that the credit could not have been repaid on the basis of his cotton harvest alone. Another farmer had hired a Land Rover from an unknown person to do his threshing for him. Obviously the access to expensive machinery carried with it the potential for greater rural differentiation. The cost of the tractor, 4 million FCFA (over U.S.$12,000), was approximately 20 times the cost of a high-end plow and two draft animals. This was an impossible investment for most people in a country where GNP per capita was only U.S.$270 in 1990 (World Bank 1992, 218). It is not clear where this man found the resources for this investment. He was the founder of his hamlet, which gave him a privileged position. He had obviously courted the agricultural-extension agent who helped facilitate his purchase. Yet he claimed to earn his money from work in agriculture and further investment in livestock. He had no obvious kinship connections and was no more educated than his neighbors. While the developing rental market did suggest differentiation between owners and nonowners, private rentals were the only successful means by which equipment was made regularly available to nonowners.

The only other motorized equipment was found in the two Soninke coop-

eratives, who owned a great deal of it. For example, CAMUKO had two tractors, two plows, threshers, and a maize seeder, all brought from France as a part
of the repatriation package, some a gift from French agricultural organizations.
In each cooperative, two members had been trained as mechanics to keep the
machinery in good repair. Nevertheless, in 1989, much of it did not work. Most
was older used equipment, and it was difficult to get appropriate spare parts.
Hence the cooperatives were not able to use it to increase productivity in the
way they had hoped.

In contrast to locally generated innovations, for example, the growth of the
local rental market in Dioïla and new uses for equipment, attempts by outside
organizations to introduce innovative forms of equipment ownership were not
successful, as shown by CECI's attempt to establish equipment cooperatives in
the Yanfolila villages. Some 52 plows and 26 pairs of oxen were given to the
five villages where CECI had aided Dogon settlement; among sample villages,
Gwalafara received 6 and Wuru Wuru 5 pairs of oxen. The animals were given
to the village as a whole, to be used by both migrants and the indigenous population. In each village, a bi-ethnic management committee was chosen and the
village chief named president. The treasurer was to be a Dogon and his assis-
tant an autochthone. A Dogon was chosen to care for the animals. In principle,
use was to be rotated among Dogon and indigenous households, and user fees
were to provide care for the oxen. The experiment failed. Community management was problematic; villagers let the oxen wander, and they often were
lost or died (Dandenault 1987). In several cases, including Gwalafara, the village chief confiscated the equipment and refused to let anyone else use it.
Clearly the different parties involved did not trust one another sufficiently to
cooperate on this initiative.

Overall, agricultural equipment was available to a broad base of Malian
farmers through local markets. At various times, this had been aided by ODR
activities, which assisted equipment ownership among those they thought
would be the most productive. However, the poorest, in this study, those who
used farming as a secondary occupation or recent migrants, without animals or
sufficient cash to pay for equipment, did not have it. The demise of ODR programs meant that they no longer provided alternative access to equipment.
Farmers clearly appreciated the growth of sales and rental markets for agricultural equipment but wanted access possibilities to increase beyond them.

*Inputs*

Farmers needed commercial inputs, especially fertilizers, to help sustain continuous cultivation without degrading lands (Gladwin 1991b; Reardon et al.

**TABLE 7.   Input Purchases**

| Site | Total Spent | Total Households | Amount per Household | Total Users | Amount per User | Manure Users |
|---|---|---|---|---|---|---|
| Dioïla | 2,095,245 | 30 | 69,842 | 30 | 69,842 | 18 |
| Yanfolila-indigenous | 60,000 | 4 | 15,000 | 2 | 30,000 | 1 |
| Selingue-migrant | 163,000 | 19 | 8,579 | 8 | 20,375 | 0 |
| Yanfolila-migrant | 207,500 | 26 | 7,981 | 6 | 34,583 | 0 |
| CAMUKO | 130,500 | — | — | — | — | — |
| Finkolo | 84,200 | 30 | 2,807 | 6 | 14,033 | 12 |
| Tienfala | 0 | 9 | 0 | 0 | 0 | ≥3 |
| Selingue-indigenous | 0 | 10 | 0 | 0 | 0 | 2 |

*Note:* Data from farm-level questionnaires.

1995). While access to equipment depended primarily on access to the funds to buy it, access to commercial inputs (seed dressings, improved seeds, pesticides, and herbicides, as well as fertilizers) still depended directly on an active ODR. When the ODR was sure that credit would be reimbursed because it had had a hand in crop sales, farmers had greater access to inputs on credit. In this study, there was a clear correlation between ODR activity and use of inputs; access to an active ODR was more important than access to cash.

Dioïla had by far the highest use of inputs, both in terms of number of users and quantity used (table 7). Following the CMDT increase in activity in Yanfolila, half the indigenous population had begun to use commercial inputs. The migrants to Selingue, land and cash poor, but farming on the perimeter managed by the OERHN, also had significant use of inputs. Two-thirds of the inputs bought in Selingue and virtually all bought by Dioïla and Yanfolila small farmers were purchased through the ODRs.

In contrast, use among other family farm groups was low. Some Yanfolila migrants had begun to work with the CMDT, but they still had less access than the indigenous population; presumably their numbers would increase as the CMDT became more active and farmers more established. In Manantali, the stagnation of ODIPAC had significantly cut farmer access to inputs. Finkolo, although in the CMDT zone, received few services from them because the CMDT preferred to work with full-time commercial cotton farmers. Tienfala farmers, in the OHV, but far from either the tobacco or cotton zones, had little access as well. Those with the least possibilities for access were the indigenous farmers of Selingue, who lived in the only area of southern Mali not even technically covered by an ODR (see map 3 in chapter 3). This was a major sore point for them, and they had made formal requests to both CMDT and OHV to make them part of their area of intervention. These organizations evidently hesitated to enter an area where the OERHN was already active, even though they worked only on the irrigated perimeter. The indigenous people saw themselves first pushed off their land because of the dam and associated population growth, then pushed off the perimeter because they did not produce enough, yet unable to have access to inputs through the ODRs that their neighbors did.

Although a few more affluent or well-connected farmers got access to inputs in a few sites with little ODR activity, the only major exception was the two cooperatives, CAMUKO and CAMSEL. Use of inputs was essential for their planned high-technology farming, and they bought and used them, although we did not have information how much CAMSEL spent. These men, educated and with vehicles, could go to Bamako to buy inputs not locally available. Presumably, CAMSEL's access to inputs was one of the points that encouraged indigenous farmers to join.

Farmers used manure as well, although use was high only in Dioïla, Finkolo, and Tienfala. In Dioïla, use of manure complemented purchased fertilizers, a process aided by the high numbers of animals owned. Some households kept animals in pens to facilitate access to their dung, and one person even mentioned paying for some, the only time this occurred. In the other two sites, manure served more as a substitute for fertilizers. Many migrants found it difficult to get manure because they lacked animals (see chap. 6), but Finkolo was able to make judicious use of what its animals produced because most fields were small. Tienfala found itself well placed to get manure because commercial herders pastured their animals in nearby bush before taking them into Bamako for slaughter. Local farmers were able to collect this for their fields, and three of the nine sample households had even dug silage pits to improve animal nutrition and year-round access to their own animals' manure.

The use of fertilizers and manure was particularly important as a way to maintain soil fertility because the use of other techniques, including crop rotations, intercropping, planting in mounds, or agroforestry techniques was low. Many of the techniques, especially rotations and intercropping, were known. One farmer in Finkolo, for example, described an ideal sequence of fields in a crop rotation:

When I begin a new bush field, I make mounds using a local hoe during the first year. In these mounds, I plant sweet potatoes and Bambara groundnuts [*Voandzeia subterranea*]. In the second and third years, I plant intercropped maize and finger millet. In the fourth and fifth years I plant sorghum with peanut added during the fifth year. In the sixth year, there is fonio, and then it's time to fallow.

This ideal sequence was not followed in any of the sample fields of Finkolo. Only 6 of 34 showed any rotation; farmers said that since their fields were all small and close to their homes, they received enough manure and other household refuse that they did not need to rotate to improve fertility. At Tienfala, farmers maintained that their two major crops, white sorghum and rice, required different types of soil and hence could not be rotated. In Yanfolila, the fields were so young (88 of 122 were in their first year of cultivation) that questions of rotation were premature. And in Selingue, rice was grown continuously on the perimeter, and even the indigenous farmers rarely practiced crop rotations.

Only in Dioïla, which had the oldest fields on average, were rotations regularly practiced. There, the most common rotation alternated two crops: cotton and a food grain, usually a year of cotton followed by a year of food grain or multiple years of grain to one of cotton. In general, rotations only began once the field was five years of age or older; before that, farmers tended to use fields for a single crop. This rotation was a direct response to ODR recommendations. Dioïla farmers (like many CMDT farmers) used fertilizers on cotton fields only, and the grain planted the following year benefited from residual fertilizer effects. Yet farmers did not follow these recommendations precisely; they often added more years of grain to the standard recommendation. ODIPAC had tried to encourage this same principle in Manantali, by encouraging a rotation of maize with heavy fertilizer the first year, followed by peanuts the second year, and a cereal grain the third. This proved unsuccessful because the sales price of maize was generally too low to justify the cost of fertilizer.

Intercropping was also relatively low in most of the sites. There was virtually none on the irrigated rice perimeter, and it was also rare in Yanfolila and Manantali. In Tienfala, farmers often intercropped beans or roselle (*Hibiscus* spp.) with their sorghum, but rice, peanuts, and maize were grown in sole stands. Higher rates of intercropping were found at Finkolo, where 13 of 38 fields were intercropped, usually maize with millet, maximizing production on small fields. It was again at Dioïla where the highest rate was found; half of the 40 fields were intercropped, usually a mixture of millet or sorghum and beans. In general, women's fields were somewhat more likely to be intercropped than were collective fields.

In Yanfolila, it appears that Dogon migrants were changing intercropping practices in response to the different agricultural conditions there. In Dogon country, rates of intercropping were very high. S. Cohen (1981, 57) found only 14 percent of millet fields sole-cropped on the plateau, and even fewer (2.3 percent) on the plain. Yet in Yanfolila, 77 of 92 (84 percent) Dogon fields were sole-cropped, very similar to the indigenous sole-cropping rate of 90 percent in our sample. Little intercropping was also found in other studies there (I. Cissé, Coulibaly, and Sow 1989, 95).

Other practices to increase soil or water availability were very rare. A few Dioïla farmers reported making mounds for some crops, but virtually nothing else. Saul (1993) showed how wealthier Burkina farmers were able to lengthen use of parcels through a mix of techniques similar to those found in Dioïla. Other farmers relied mostly on fallowing and clearing new parcels to get more fertile land, despite government regulations to discourage clearing and the potential for deleterious environmental effects. The low use of soil conservation technologies underscored the importance of capital and associated access to state organizations for inputs to sustain soil fertility.

Patterns of access to equipment and inputs showed clearly that the government was able neither to control access completely nor simply to hand it over to the private sector. The existence of private market channels for equipment and animals meant that even when the government wanted to control access, it could not. Local production of both meant that artisanal markets remained active. In contrast, when structural-adjustment programs pressured the government to hand over input distribution to the private sector, it failed because production was concentrated outside the country and large-scale wholesalers preferred bulk sales to ODRs (Shea 1986).[5] Despite changing national and international policies, input access remained effective only through ODRs.

Production Strategies

We now turn to an evaluation of production strategies in light of the patterns of resource availability. As already noted, two different approaches toward agriculture could be distinguished. In most of the sites, migrants considered crop farming their most important activity, while in Finkolo and Tienfala, agriculture was usually meant to complement nonagricultural income. Among those for whom agriculture was a key activity, there were two further strategies. The first involved using crop farming to produce both the family's food and the cash needed to pay taxes and buy consumer goods, and it required farmers to produce a surplus commercialized either nationally or locally. The second strategy was to use agriculture to produce most or all of the family's food needs, but to use other activities, livestock or nonfarm, to generate cash. The choice to pursue agriculture or something else as primary activity was usually a conscious one, linked to the choice of migration site. In contrast, the ability to use farming to meet cash as well as subsistence needs was usually dictated by the particular configuration of opportunities in the zone. More farmers wanted to produce a commercializable surplus than could, since many met either ecological or economic constraints.

Production strategies began with a decision to grow certain crops. Ecological factors (level and distribution of rainfall, type of soils) obviously affected crop and variety choices. In addition, certain crops were "supported" by ODRs who offered input packages and technical recommendations particularly tailored to them. Some crops had well-developed large markets, while other had smaller niche markets. Land tenure conditions also affected some crop choices, especially that between annuals and perennials. Indigenous knowledge was also important; farmers knew the characteristics of some crops better than others. Family characteristics affected the size of the labor force and also reflected prior decisions about the division into collective and individual fields.

The information about crop choices came primarily from field census data, using the distribution of major crops. Since there was relatively little intercropping, this provided a reliable measure of major choices, even though fields were of widely different sizes. In all the OCP sites except Dioïla, this gave relatively complete information. In Tienfala, Finkolo, and Selingue, most fields were covered using the initial study design; in Yanfolila, the team changed the research strategy to include all fields. In Dioïla, however, the field questionnaire sampled only about one-quarter of fields, with a bias toward grain fields and away from cotton fields. However, the team also did a complete field census in 15 of the 30 sample households, which provided better information on field distribution, giving two figures for Dioïla. For the two cooperatives, we had only crop production information; we used this as an indicator of crop distribution. The trends shown were supported by ethnographic information.

*Growing Cereal Grains*

Food security gained through household production remained the most important part of agricultural production strategies. On average, all sample groups put more than half their censused fields into basic food grains: millet and sorghum, maize, and rice (table 8). Even at Dioïla, where farmers carried out highly commercialized cotton production, more than half of censused fields were in cereals. Since grain fields were often among the larger fields, these percentages likely reflect a larger field area in cereals as well. Farmers grew food in part to cope with unpredictability in the political-economic environment, which made marketing possibilities unsure. To cope with unpredictability in the physical environment, they usually grew several different varieties with differing capacities to withstand the usual environmental hazards.

**TABLE 8. Crop Distribution**

| Site | N | Sorghum Millet | Maize | Rice | Cotton | Peanuts | Other |
|------|---|------|------|------|--------|---------|-------|
| | | A. Based on total production of fields in kilograms | | | | | |
| CAMSEL | 41,000 | 0% | 20% | 80% | 0% | 0% | 0% |
| CAMUKO | 44,925 | 2% | 1% | 91% | 0% | 2% | 4% |
| | | B. Based on number of fields | | | | | |
| Selingue-migrant | 18 | 11% | 0% | 83% | 0% | 6% | 0% |
| Selingue-indigenous | 15 | 7% | 33% | 13% | 0% | 47% | 0% |
| Yanfolila-indigenous | 30 | 33% | 20% | 13% | 7% | 17% | 10% |
| Yanfolila-migrant | 92 | 35% | 13% | 22% | 5% | 13% | 12% |
| Finkolo | 34 | 9% | 62% | 0% | 0% | 12% | 18% |
| Tienfala | 17 | 35% | 12% | 41% | 0% | 12% | 0% |
| Dioïla-field sample | 40 | 80% | 0% | 0% | 3% | 18% | 0% |
| Dioïla-supplemental | 65 | 40% | 9% | 2% | 23% | 18% | 8% |
| Manantali | 61 | 28% | 13% | 11% | 0% | 28% | 20% |

*Source:* Manantali figures from seven households in Diarra et al. (1990).

The decision to emphasize a particular grain depended on the interaction of economic and environmental factors. Rice growing had the greatest constraints, both environmental and political-economic. All rice fields required some water control, if only the management of naturally occurring depressions. Since rice was the food grain of choice among urban, middle-class Malians, its cultivation and sale became highly politicized. Large-scale producers rarely grew only for home consumption, but also sold some, inexorably drawn into the politics of rice production and distribution. On the perimeters of Selingue, with full water control, the Dogon migrants had no choice but to grow rice; since they had few dryland fields, they could grow little else. The only other groups that grew much rice were the cooperatives, who were putting in pump-irrigation systems on their riverside fields. They chose to cultivate rice to meet their own food requirements and as an innovative way to earn cash. Those farmers growing rice under almost full water control were the only groups for whom their major food crop was also their major cash crop (cf. Little and Horowitz 1987). We would have liked more information on how the Dogon migrants to Selingue disposed of their produce, since they may have been under some pressure to sell rice rather than to keep it from home consumption. This could have come both from the OERHN management and their own realization that a single kilogram of rice could buy several of millet or sorghum. In 1987 average Third Region market prices of millet and sorghum were less than half that of rice, 36–38 FCFA/kg versus 83 FCFA/kg (PADEM 1988, 27). In contrast, the Soninke cooperatives had more freedom to dispose of their production as they saw fit, since they were on their own land and procured their inputs themselves.

The other groups that grew rice did so under artisanal conditions, partial water control on flooded rivers, stream banks or other depressions. This rice was generally considered to be a woman's crop, grown by women on individual fields, except among Dogon migrants to Yanfolila, for whom rice was a relatively new crop. Migrant men, not constrained by the same local traditions as their indigenous neighbors, had began to cultivate artisanal rice along the watercourses. Artisanal rice production in these zones was not supported by the ODRs, and growers retained the ability to dispose of their product as they chose. It appears that they often kept some for special occasions and sold part of it; rice rarely was an everyday food for rural Malians in the south.

Rather they turned to rainfed grains, maize, millet, and sorghum, for their basic foods. Since maize required better fertilization and more reliable water supplies, it was generally grown in areas adjacent to residences that received substantial amounts of household refuse and in better-watered areas. Fields were usually small, except in some particularly well-watered areas, for example, among the indigenous population of Selingue and the plantation workers of Finkolo. In other areas, maize was primarily used to tide the household over the hungry season, since it ripened well before either millet or sorghum. Millet and sorghum remained the grains of choice for dryland cultivation among most rural Malians. Farmers chose several varieties based on taste preference, predictions of insect or weed infestation, and estimates of future rainfall. In areas with many individual fields and/or well-established nongrain cash crops (indigenous Selingue inhabitants, Dioïla, Manantali), slightly more than half the fields had food grains as a primary crop. Where people concentrated more on grain production, either because they had no developed cash crop (Yanfolila), or because they had nonagricultural ways to earn money (Tienfala, Finkolo), two-thirds or more of their fields were in food grains.

In their choice of grains, farmers were first constrained by their desire to insulate themselves from the hazards of the political-economic context by producing their own food. They generally turned to grains that they knew well and fit the ecological constraints. However, not all farmers had sufficient land resources to follow this strategy. Most notably, the Selingue migrants were forced to rely wholly on irrigated cultivation of rice because they could get land only on the perimeter. Only among the cooperatives was innovation in grain production a positive choice.

*Grain Production*

Production levels can illuminate the adequacy of choices farmers made. This section assesses adequacy in several ways. First, households wanted to be able to meet needs for food. Second, farmers often evaluated their production levels in comparison to their neighbors. Third, variation within sites offered some insights about the varying effects of external constraints and the role of individual choice.

*Meeting Nutritional Requirements*
To evaluate levels of grain production, we first addressed the question of whether or not the household produced enough to feed itself. This is not an easy question because any choice of a subsistence figure has political implications. If the average nutritional requirement is about 2,100 (FAO 1986, 42) or 2,200 kcal/person/day (Hiebsch and O'Hair 1986, 180), and millet and sorghum provide approximately 330–340 kcal/100 g (Hiebsch and O'Hair 1986, 182), the yearly dietary requirement, calculated exclusively in grain, would be some 230–240 kg/person/year. Yet, grain provided only 65 to 90 percent of calories in most of Mali, and many have calculated minimum requirements to be significantly less. The Malian government and the WFP used 167 kg/capita for the 1987–88 crop year, while USAID adopted a higher figure of 188 kg/capita (Sundberg 1988, 4). Following USAID's example, we have used 190 kg/person/year as the food requirement for the average individual. To be sure, some household members needed less and others more. However, this figure can be used to compare the differential ability of the farmers at different sites to reach at least a minimum level of subsistence.

Farmers were asked three different times (in the household census, farm census, and field questionnaire) to estimate production. Figure 3 shows the highest estimates for each site and figure 4 the lowest. Usually the differences in the estimates were relatively small and/or easily explained. In Tienfala and Dioïla, the different estimates came from different samples. In Tienfala, the field questionnaire figures (which showed higher production levels) came from only two of the three sample villages, while household and farm censuses were done in all three. In Dioïla, the field questionnaire included only about one-quarter of the fields, while the other two addressed the production of the entire farm. The only time that widely varying figures came from the same sample was among the indigenous population of Yanfolila, the one group we considered to have given generally unreliable answers. Since many did not provide information on individual fields at this site, we believe that the esti-

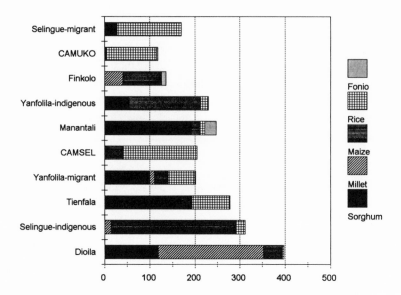

Fig. 3. Highest estimated 1988 production of grain in kg per person. (Note that the Tienfala sample has 5 households. Data for Manantali sample of 7 households, 194 persons, from Diarra et al. 1990.)

mates of around 200 kg/person/year were more reflective of production than lower ones.

Relatively small variations in the responses gave us confidence in these data rather than the reverse. Since they were obtained by recall, figures exactly the same across the three estimates would have been suspicious. Moreover, we think that some of these figures may be slightly underestimated. Many farmers did not weigh or even bag most of their crop. Since production was estimated from the average weight of a bag, estimated production may reflect only the bagged portion. Farmers also saw researchers as representatives of the government and therefore often underestimated production because of tax concerns. They believed that they were more likely to get government assistance for various projects if they could present themselves as poor rather than well-off. Nevertheless, we think these figures are reflective of gross food self-sufficiency levels and relative production among groups.

The samples fell into three categories in terms of meeting food needs. If the average production was less than 190 kg/person/year, the population was not on average self-sufficient. If production fell between approximately 190

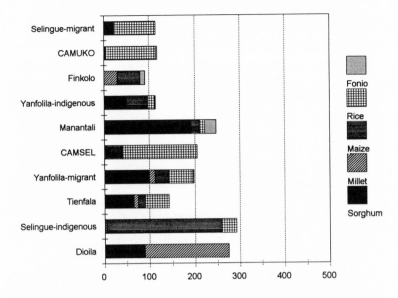

Fig. 4. Lowest estimated 1988 production of grain in kg per person. (Note that the Tienfala sample has 9 households. Data for Manantali sample of 7 households, 194 persons, from Diarra et al. 1990.)

kg/person and 250 kg/person, the zone was just at the level of self-sufficiency but produced little surplus. Households could not sustain themselves much more than one agricultural season and would likely have difficulty if agricultural conditions worsened the following year. If a zone produced more than 250 kg/person, they not only met subsistence requirements, but generated a surplus that could either be sold or stored against future bad years.

Only two groups were clearly producing beyond subsistence: the farmers of Dioïla (276–398 kg/person/year) and the indigenous population of Selingue (292–313 kg). In Dioïla, cotton and grains were planted in a mutually beneficial rotation, with continued emphasis on food crops. The indigenous inhabitants of Selingue would describe themselves as worse off than the inhabitants of Dioïla. They lacked a complementary crop to generate cash and had seen their land base decrease and come under greater population pressure; they hesitated to put land into fallow for fear of other claims on it. Moreover, the potential for soil degradation (lacking inputs and unable to fallow) raised the question of how long they could sustain production levels. The field census data from Tienfala also suggested that at least some farmers produced a significant surplus, although on average they did not since overall production ranged from 142 to 278 kg. Since the amounts of land available appeared to vary substantially from migrant to migrant, depending on the circumstances of migrant and lender, this greater variation was expected. None of these surplus grain producer groups sold grain as their major income-earning activity. Although their level of grain production was relatively high, they turned to other crops or activities to meet cash needs.

The following groups appeared to produce enough for subsistence, but not a significant surplus: the migrants of Yanfolila (197–202 kg/person/year), the Soninke cooperative at Selingue (205 kg), some of the relocatees of Manantali (247 kg), and the indigenous population of Yanfolila (114–230 kg). In the case of Yanfolila, many individual fields, which could increase overall production, were not included, so the 200 kg figure seems more accurate. In the other three groups, figures appear to reflect the actual situation. In Manantali, some people did quite well in the first few years after resettlement because the land on which they settled had not been cultivated for many years and had a significant reserve of natural fertility. Production levels in the initial years depended on whether the household had sufficient labor to clear the parcel quickly. Nevertheless, the long-term potential was questionable because the land base was restricted.[6] In contrast, the Yanfolila migrants and CAMSEL were both relatively well endowed with land, but as relatively recent migrants, were still adapting to the resource mixes at their sites. In both cases, they had the potential to improve production over the long term.

Although most of these groups were self-sufficient in food, they were not able to generate the cash they needed from agricultural production. In Yanfolila, both migrants and indigenous farmers were just beginning to take advantage of the CMDT's increased level of activity; in Manantali, ODIPAC's decline had begun negatively to affect farmer income. Yet these household farmers did not turn to food grains to meet cash needs. Only CAMSEL, which expected to sell its rice as well as use it for home consumption, found itself having to decide whether to sell or eat the food its members produced. Many of these farmers turned to nonagricultural activities to earn cash, but they often found production insufficient because they wanted to use agriculture to earn as well as to eat.

Finally, overall production was insufficient for most households among three groups: the Selingue migrants (114–170 kg/person/year), the Finkolo tea workers (91–136 kg), and the Soninke cooperative at Yanfolila (117 kg). The most problematic case was the Selingue migrants since they expected to make a living from agriculture but found it almost impossible to get sufficient land, either irrigated or rainfed. In fact, their situation was even worse since the figures show *gross* production before the in-kind payment in rice to the OERHN for inputs and services. In contrast, CAMUKO had sufficient land but suffered from inexperience. In light of a disastrous harvest in 1988, members began the 1989 agricultural season with more respect for local knowledge, that of both farmers and CMDT agents, and ready to learn from them despite initial beliefs in the superiority of their formal agricultural education. At Finkolo, people farmed mainly to complement their wages from the tea plantation and could buy additional food. The situation at Finkolo was acceptable, and the future could improve for the cooperative, yet at Selingue, the situation was not sustainable unless access to basic resources was improved, either through off-farm employment opportunities or by changes in access rules to irrigated land.

*Comparative Production*
Migrants judged production levels not only in absolute terms but also in comparison with their neighbors. Only in Dioïla was production high both absolutely and comparably. Here studies in neighboring areas also showed high levels of production. For example, estimated per capita annual grain production in two CMDT sites studied for a food security project was 285 kg in 1985–86, a season with relatively good rainfall (Dione 1987, v). Among farmers on the edge of the Sounsan classified forest, reported production was about 278 kg/person/year for the same agricultural season as our study, 1988-89 (Y. Cissé et al. 1989, 58). At the other sites, production of migrants was either below that of their better-established neighbors, or, perhaps more interesting, equivalent to that of their neighbors yet insufficient.

We expected that relatively new migrants, with fewer resources than the indigenous populations, would show lower production levels. This was indeed the most common situation. In Manantali, ODIPAC figures, not quite comparable to our own, but indicative, showed grain production levels of 84.2 and 54.4 kg/person/year in two subsectors composed primarily of resettled villages, but 177 kg/person/year in one composed primarily of hosts. The Finkolo tea workers were much less productive than neighboring full-time farmers, found in a 1978–79 study in Bambadougou, near Sikasso, to have production levels ranging from 291 kg/person/year among nonequipped farmers to 499 kg/person/year among the highly equipped (Whitney 1981, 165). In our own study, both the migrant sample and the cooperative at Selingue had much lower production than did their indigenous neighbors (fig. 3). In Yanfolila, the situation is more problematic because of the questionable accuracy of the indigenous responses. However, studies done for the Mali Sud III project suggested relatively high production levels among indigenous populations, although they did not give per capita production figures. For example, our indigenous Yanfolila households showed average production of 3,900 kg/year, based on the lowest per capita production figures to 7,900 kg/year, based on the highest. Yet their Yanfolila households with only a low level of equipment averaged 7,097 kg/year grain production. Well-equipped households throughout their study zone showed mean grain production of 10,082 kg/year (I. Cissé, Coulibaly, and Sow 1989, 178, 179).

Migrants were aware of the fact that their resources did not allow them to produce at levels comparable to their indigenous neighbors, although they had somewhat different perspectives at different sites. Manantali relocatees, who compared compromised production on new sites to good production on their old ones, were frustrated by the new conditions. In contrast, Dogon migrants to Yanfolila, who had come from the drought-plagued north, saw improvements in access to well-watered land and production levels, despite lower production than their neighbors.

The most instructive case was where some or all of our sample farmers were below self-sufficiency but so, it appears, were many indigenous farmers as well. Food security studies showed many farmers in the OHV zone to be far from self-sufficient. Only 30–32 percent claimed to produce at self-sufficiency levels (D'Agostino 1988, 68), and average production in the northern part of the OHV was estimated to cover only 70 percent of household needs (Dione 1987, 12). Tienfala was not far from these studies' northern site, Koulikoro; while our entire sample showed grain production levels around 140 to 170 kg/person/year, theirs found average production levels of 111 kg/person/year (Dione 1987, 13). Selingue, although not part of the OHV, was not far from their southern site, Ouellessebougou. There 1985 average production was about 125 kg/person/year, comparable to the figure for our migrants, and well below the production levels for the Selingue autochthones (Dione 1987, 11).

The question is how any of these farmers were able to sustain household welfare over the long term if they could not produce sufficient quantities of basic food grains. Other studies suggested that some farmers from the Ouellessebougou zone complemented grain farming with relatively large-scale vegetable cultivation because of their easy access to the Bamako market (SARSA/USAID 1994). They also sold livestock (Dione 1987, 38). In the north of the OHV as well, there were indications that cattle raising was used to supplement crop farming; the money from cattle sales could be used to buy food (Dione 1987, 39; SARSA/USAID 1994). These data make very clear the need to look beyond grain farming, or even crop farming in general, toward entire household production systems to understand the differences between migrant and indigenous households. The following chapter addresses the issue of whether migrants had access to resources needed for nonagricultural activities.

*Individual Variation*

Most studies of rural African farmers show striking differences in productivity among them, linked to a variety of national structural factors, including changing market structures, land concentration, and the privileged access of elites to nonagricultural wealth and knowledge of national land law (Reyna and Downs 1988). Some of these issues were important in Mali, but they often were most noticeable in contrasting our samples with other groups. For example, in Tienfala, civil servants and wealthy merchants were better able to get access to large farms, getting *concessions rurales* through networks with local administrators, while the households in our sample got small farms through existing village structures. Within the samples, productivity differences among households did not always link clearly with factors such as these. However, three instances were particularly instructive in elucidating other more individualized, local constraints on production: the Yanfolila migrants, the Dioïla farmers, and the tea plantation workers.

Yanfolila showed striking differences in production levels among migrants in the three different villages. In Yanfolila town, the mean grain production level was 92.1 kg/person/year and there were only two households that produced more than 190 kg/person/year. In the village of Wuru Wuru, mean production was 176.2 kg/person and yet again only two of the six migrant households produced more than 190 kg/person. In contrast, at Gwalafara, all the households but one produced more than 250 kg/person/year and mean production was 389 kg/person/year. The lower production in Yanfolila town in contrast to the villages appears to reflect a move toward a strategy that relied less on agriculture and more on multiple income sources, as in peri-urban areas such as Tienfala. It is not clear whether people chose to move to Yanfolila because they saw nonagricultural activities as a positive choice, or whether they were pushed there because indigenous villages were unable or unwilling to grant them sufficient lands. The difference was not only rural versus urban. The contrast in production levels in the two villages suggests that there were quite different resource mixes available at villages only a short distance from one another. In Wuru Wuru, people complained outright of the village's poverty, and many had moved elsewhere. In Gwalafara, in contrast, despite murmurings of "jealousy" on the part of autochthones toward migrant farmers, the most successful migrants there had already called upon relatives to join them (Dandenault 1987). The figures from the Tienfala zone, already noted above, suggest marked variation in the resources available from one village to another there as well. It may be difficult for new migrants reliably to assess the different resources available in adjacent villages, especially when they do not negotiate directly with village elders themselves, but rather pass through an administrative organization, as was the case in Yanfolila.

Dioïla too also showed different production patterns among villages. Most notable were relatively homogeneous production patterns within Miankabugu in contrast to more varied production levels in the other two villages. This village, which we will discuss again in chapter 7, appeared to have chosen to remain small, giving all inhabitants similar and significant access to resources. In the other two villages, the production differences between early and later migrants were marked. If the sample was divided into two halves, the early arrivals had larger families and higher production of both cotton and grain. Because the early arrivals had much larger households, their per capita grain production was slightly below that of the newcomers, but their cotton production was much higher. This suggested that later migrants found sufficient land to grow food grains, but not enough land or labor to produce large quantities of cotton. In contrast, early arrivals had been able to find good cotton land, while ensuring sufficient, if not always outstanding, grain production. As the rural population continues to grow, we expect that the difference between those who control access to large pieces of land and others looking for new lands will increase, although as long as land remains untitled, stratification will not occur simply or straightforwardly (Berry 1993; Saul 1988).

Finkolo showed marked variation among households rather than villages. Of the 30 households, 4 had no agricultural production while one produced between 9,000 and 14,000 kg, depending on the data set. The median household production was 200–225 kg/year, well below the mean of 656–983 kg/year in 1988, suggesting that means were raised by the presence of a few very large producers. Big producers were found in all three villages relatively evenly spread out; 2 of the 10 farmers in both Tominian and Camp I produced over 1,000 kg, as did 3 in Sokurani. High production was linked to labor availability, with big producers showing somewhat larger than average households, slightly over 10 in contrast to the Finkolo mean of 7.2. The biggest producer had a very large household, 24 people. Several of the larger producers were linked to early inhabitants. One at Tominian was brother of the hamlet chief, while one at Sokurani was one of the founders. The biggest producer, however, was not among the first inhabitants. In contrast, few came from among the more highly specialized workers; in fact the latter more commonly had no production, presumably because they earned more money. It appears that individualized connections helped farmers get agricultural resources.

Finally, production levels also varied over time. Factors like rainfall changed unpredictably from year to year. Some of the recent policy changes will probably lead to substantial changes in access to capital over the long term. Access to labor and knowledge also changed over time. Our data, concentrating on a single year, could not capture the effects of the changing production environment. This study needs to be complemented by others that look more directly at these issues.

*Complementary Crops and Crop Sales*

Although grain production provided an anchor for household stability, no farm household wanted an economic strategy based solely on grain. Some complementary (i.e., nongrain) crops were grown for consumption while others were grown for sale. Even though many households sold some grain, most farmers claimed to dislike the idea and felt uncomfortable with a strategy that relied on a single crop for both cash and consumption. Hence many were attracted to crops other than cereals as a way to earn cash. Because of this link between complementary crops and crop sales, we treat the two together in this section. However, the data about these crops and the incomes earned from them are not as complete as we would like. Malian farmers grew many complementary crops, sometimes on collective fields, but also divided over many individual fields. The sheer number and variety made it difficult to get a complete record and even more problematic to get accurate information about income earned. Table 8 shows where cotton and peanuts were most important.

The best information was about the cultivation of large-scale industrial crops, often cash crops supported by ODRs, cotton in some of the CMDT zones and peanuts at Manantali. Farmers, both household heads and those with individual fields, often cultivated these crops, using the ODR for access to inputs, credit, and aid with commercialization. At the time of the study, the CMDT was active in Dioïla and had begun to increase extension at Yanfolila. ODIPAC, formerly active at Manantali, had decreased its level of activity.

At Dioïla, where the CMDT had long been active, cotton production was high and remunerative. Cotton production averaged 1,933 kg/household in 1988 and 1,576 kg/household in 1987. Twenty-nine of the total sample of 30 farmers grew at least some cotton in 1988, although only 24 had grown it in 1987. Moreover, 88 percent of reported agricultural income came from cotton sales. Farmers in Dioïla reported earning a total of 6,533,605 FCFA (U.S.$19,799), or 217,787 (U.S.$660) per household from cotton alone. This was by far the highest average crop earnings reported.

However, production and income varied widely from one household to another. Household earnings from all agricultural sales (cotton plus other crops) varied from a low of 38,250 FCFA (U.S.$116) to a high of 1,530,900 FCFA (U.S.$4,639). The median was 167,080 FCFA (U.S.$506), below the mean of 246,797 FCFA (U.S.$748) suggesting the presence of some big producers. Three households of the 30 had sales superior to 500,000 FCFA (U.S.$1,515) while 12 households had sales less than 100,000 FCFA (U.S.$303). Income reflected production levels, which varied more in the villages of Fofoni Dogolen and Kolobugu than Miankabugu, the same pattern found in cereal production. In Fofoni, production varied from 160 kg/household to 4,800 kg, with a mean of 1,258 kg. In Kolobugu, it varied from 490 kg to 8,000 kg with a mean of 2,243 kg. At Miankabugu, mean production was highest, 2,713 kg/household, and varied relatively little. Except for one household that produced 6,500 kg, harvests ranged from 1,300 to 3,000 kg. Again, we were not able to uncover any obvious reasons for the differences among farmers, except longer settlement. Early migrants had been able to come at a particularly auspicious time and used their access to the CMDT at a period of growth to increase their resources. The highest observed production, 8,000 kg, was in the household of the man with the tractor, one of the first settlers.

The CMDT had only recently begun significant activity in Yanfolila, and there cotton activity was much more concentrated and production levels much lower. In 1988, five migrants and two autochthones grew cotton, while in 1987, only one migrant had grown it. Production levels were much lower than in Dioïla; Yanfolila cotton production in 1988 averaged 499 kg/household among the indigenous population and 373 kg/household for the migrants. Although cotton formed 86 percent of reported crop sales in Yanfolila, earnings were much lower than in Dioïla. Total income from reported crop sales was 401,500 FCFA (U.S.$1,217), or an average of 13,383 FCFA (U.S.$41) per household over the entire sample. In fact, these sales came from only four households, all migrants; three-quarters of the value noted was the sale of cotton from a single household. The CMDT hoped that through its extension services, both the number of farmers reached and the level of production would increase. This was a goal shared by a broad segment of the population who were aware of the Dioïla example. The success of the CMDT zone was also obvious to the Finkolo farmers, none of whom grew cotton. They were surrounded by cotton farmers doing well, but they were unable to participate because they were not full-time agriculturalists.

The other complementary crop with many growers was peanuts, which had earlier had high levels of ODR support at Manantali. Farmers in the zone continued to cultivate peanuts during and after the resettlement, although commercialization was transferred to private merchants, and credit for inputs became slowly more difficult and then impossible to obtain. As with cereals, there was some decrease in production during the resettlement, but Manantali farmers did not abandon peanut cultivation to devote themselves solely to food crops even in the first year of settlement. Since they received WFP food for two years, they did not have to rely totally on their own food production and were able to grow a separate crop for cash. Despite the demise of ODIPAC commercialization, farmers were at a loss to know what else they could sell on a significant scale, besides peanuts, with their significant domestic market. By 1989, private commercial peanut buyers regularly frequented the Manantali markets.

ODIPAC support for peanuts as a cash crop meant that many household heads grew them on collective fields to generate cash, as was the case for cotton in the CMDT, but peanut cultivation was much more widespread than cotton because it was a major cooking ingredient and had a very active domestic market. While cotton production was confined to only a few of the sample groups, all except CAMSEL had some peanut fields (table 8). The vast majority of these were women's individual fields, in which peanuts were the primary crop in an intercropped field of multiple sauce ingredients. In addition to using peanuts at home, women could sell them, either raw or processed into peanut butter and oil. Although a few people still grew cotton for home processing and sale in local markets, its place in local distribution networks was much smaller. We were not able to gather as much quantitative data as we would have liked on peanut sales, but it is clear that many farmers, particularly women, sold them.

Another set of crops that Malian farmers recognized as potential cash earners were fruits and vegetables, both of which faced production constraints. Vegetable gardens were grown in the cool dry season (December through February) to take advantage of cooler temperatures and to avoid competition for labor with grain. Yet they required somewhat more soil humidity than did many field crops. Farmers needed to have supplementary water sources, placing gardens next to rivers or streambeds if possible. Otherwise, they might dig wells within the enclosed gardens, or attach hoses to pumps attached to boreholes. Tobacco, as well as vegetables, could be grown in these gardens. Because of the constraints imposed by water access, gardens tended to be small but quite intensively cultivated. They tended to receive more inputs, including manure from animals and pesticides (SARSA/USAID 1994), because the amounts used were quite small.[7]

Those who wished to have orchards rather than vegetable gardens faced greater constraints. Fruit trees required not only relatively humid conditions but adequate soils and protection from animal depredations. It was difficult for many farmers to secure all these conditions except on very small parcels. While almost all farmers grew a few trees in their housing compounds, where they could be watched closely and watered regularly, only a small number had more. Farmers also needed secure tenure because trees occupied a single piece of land indefinitely. Many landowners did not permit migrants to grow trees, because it symbolized land ownership. Few migrants grew more than a few fruit trees in their compounds. Dioïla farmers claimed they had been settled long enough to grow trees, but in fact, very few did.

Farmers grew both fruits and vegetables for home consumption. Mangoes in particular were a welcome addition to the family diet, since most ripened at the beginning of the rainy season when there were not a lot of other things to eat. With their high sugar content they provided significant calories, as well as large amounts of vitamins A and C. Children who had access to either cultivated or wild fruit snacked on it regularly, a sure nutritional benefit. Women regularly grew vegetables in gardens to provide sauce ingredients for daily meals. Yet many farmers also wished to sell fruits and vegetables to supplement other cash sources.

Here they met marketing constraints. Farmers were often tempted to grow "European" vegetables (e.g., lettuce, carrots, green beans, cucumbers) because of their higher prices. However, markets were relatively limited. Outside of the few places where farmers were organized to grow them for export (none in our sample areas), they had to be close to large markets for the urban middle class, the most frequent domestic buyers. This most often required proximity to urban centers and reliable transport to get produce to market before it rotted. Some farmers tried to target civil servants in small towns, but this market could be quickly saturated if too many growers entered it. Thus, local vegetables (e.g., local eggplant, onions, okra, tomatoes), although receiving lower prices, were often more attractive because they had more active local markets. Farmers would eat them if they did not sell, and preservation techniques were widely known (e.g., drying onions and tomatoes). In more commercialized areas, there appears to have been some developing specialization in sauce ingredients.

In virtually all sites, interviews indicated that at least some farmers sold produce from gardens or fruit trees, but it only sometimes showed up in reported income data (table 9). For example, farmers at Yanfolila and Manantali sold some of these crops, but none was formally recorded in the study. Therefore, these sales figures are only indicative, and the quantity of sales was likely higher. However, they do reflect the processes discussed above. Notably, it was

**TABLE 9.    Garden Revenues**

| Site | Crops Grown | Total Earned in 1988 | Number of Households |
|------|-------------|----------------------|----------------------|
| Selingue-indigenous | onions, mangoes, oranges | 70,000 | 3 |
| Selingue-migrant | sweet potatoes, onions, hot peppers, potatoes, okra, squash | 72,000 | 5 |
| Dioïla | okra, tomatoes, tobacco, cowpeas, watermelon | 115,500 | 4 |
| Finkolo | onions, tomatoes | 86,400 | 3 |
| Tienfala | okra, tomatoes, green beans | 30,150 | 1 |

only among the indigenous group at Selingue that sales of tree crops (mangoes and oranges) were reported; despite the fact that Yanfolila was known for oranges, no one in the sample, either migrant or autochthone, reported selling them. One farmer in Tienfala, close to Bamako, sold a European vegetable (green beans) that could not tolerate long conservation, although migrants at Selingue, not that much farther from Bamako, also grew potatoes, which could support somewhat longer storage. Otherwise the crops sold were mostly widely used local annuals with good markets.

The Dioïla case, however, shows yet another process, that the growth of commercialization can lead to greater diversification in crop sales as well. Although only a minority (4/30) reported sales of garden crops, they provided a complement to cotton earning for a few households. Moreover, Dioïla households were also the biggest earners from grain sales, having reported total earnings of 721,355 FCFA (U.S.$2,186), mostly from millet and sorghum. Only in Yanfolila did other farmers report selling grains, but much less, 44,000 FCFA (U.S.$133) of sorghum sales and 12,500 FCFA (U.S.$38) of rice. The timing of these sales (many during the hungry season, and few directly after the harvest) suggests that farmers were selling surplus grain for extra cash (Dione 1987). Dioïla also had the most innovative seller, a farmer who began selling large quantities of watermelons.

Qualitative information about Malian farms suggests that studies have consistently underestimated the variety of crops and the number of farmers growing them. It appears that researchers simply got tired of keeping track of all the different crops and the variation from farmer to farmer. Our interviews uncovered many crops. Women sometimes cultivated okra, beans, or hibiscus[8] as secondary crops in peanut fields. In some areas (e.g., Finkolo and Manantali), fonio *(Digitaria exilis)* was also an important grain crop, accounting for all the "other" fields in Finkolo and most of them in Manantali. This grain, like maize, ripened early and assuaged people's hunger until millet and sorghum were mature. Other secondary crops included various members of the bean and pea families (including green beans, white beans, and Bambara groundnuts). Some Dioïla farmers began to cultivate beans systematically in order to renew soil fertility while simultaneously providing cattle feed. Especially appreciated was *niebe (Vigna unguiculata),* used for animal forage as well as an ingredient for the family meals. Root crops, especially yams and sweet potatoes, were grown where the rainfall was sufficient. Sesame and watermelons were also grown by a few farmers.

When a crop was not supported by an agricultural extension service, that is, when seeds, fertilizers and other inputs, marketing channels, and so on were not provided, farmers were much more dependent upon individualized supply and sales networks to get resources and markets for a crop. In all sites, there were marked differences among farmers; some grew many of these complementary crops, while others grew few. Some claimed to sell little or nothing, while others sold important quantities and earned relatively large incomes.

Overall, structural constraints led farmers to grow certain crops first. Habitual ways of eating affected the food they grew for subsistence; grains and common sauce ingredients were of primary priority. Market constraints affected secondary, commercialized crops. Large-scale sales of a single cash crop depended on the presence of an ODR that facilitated national and international sales, but where these existed, farmers would look first to that crop to earn money. In addition, they grew a wide array of crops for less highly organized, often much smaller and less predictable local markets. Then, farmer knowledge became a critical resource in deciding which crops had potential markets.

There was little correlation between who sold secondary crops and other characteristics of farm households. Among the indigenous population of Selingue, sellers of secondary crops were mostly successful grain farmers with animals. In Dioïla, however, three of four had below average cotton production, and at Finkolo they all had low grain production and no animals. Among the migrants to Selingue, there were a couple who had very good grain production and a few with next to nothing. To understand these processes better, we need more traditional ethnographic work to see how people got knowledge about new niche crops as well as access to the resources to grow them. Despite information from other areas that showed the importance of linkages to urban centers or elite networks (Saul 1988, 250; Goheen 1988), the only clear case of this in our sample were the Soninke cooperatives. In contrast, there was no evidence that successful family farmers came to settle with much more than average resources. In any case, decisions about secondary crops varied more widely than grain production ones, both from site to site and among farmers within a site.

We are forced to conclude that individual assessments of household and personal resources available were one factor encouraging people to try innovative farming activities. For example, since the households and individuals who decided to enter gardening did not clearly have access to either more land or labor than other households, this appears to have been an individual decision to do something different to earn money. Although the core of the farming enterprise did look quite similar among all farmers of one group in a single site, individual choice was often expressed in the decisions about secondary crops. Farmers could be especially innovative in choices about secondary crops, because failure would not compromise family livelihood. Some farmers searched for local niche markets, and if the environmental and labor conditions were appropriate, they began regularly to produce for them. No household pursued all possibilities. Each household had to evaluate the land, labor, and capital resources available to it to decide on strategies that would best meet cash and subsistence needs.

Successful complementary crops could substantially increase household or individual welfare. Nevertheless, it appears that certain activities remained successful only as long as few people undertook them. Overproduction could decrease prices for niche crops with relatively small local markets. We need much more information to understand how farmers determined where the niches were, and whether they had the resources to meet them. A more specific focus on local innovation would allow us to address these issues.

Conclusion

Rural Malians moved from one place to another in an effort to better their chances at pursuing successful economic strategies, but rural strategies almost always included agriculture. Structural constraints at a variety of levels affected resources available for agriculture. Local custom remained important in getting land and labor, although national laws affected land access. Access to inputs and other agricultural technology was affected by the world division of labor. Where technology was locally produced, distribution was also locally controlled, but in the case of high-technology imports, access remained through ODRs even when there was international pressure to change. Hence, international constraints were sometimes contradictory, as in input provision, where donor policy was not sufficient to counteract world economic structures. Nationally, the Malian government wanted to exert high control over local production, but was not able to realize the high degree of control it ascribed to itself in law, most probably because it lacked both the political and financial resources to do so.

Structural constraints sometimes led to unsustainable production systems, most notably among the migrants of Selingue who had to rely on small parcels from the irrigated perimeter. But in general, external constraints did not entirely determine farmer success. Migrants as well as indigenous groups attempted to use the possibilities presented to them in innovative ways to their benefit. While few hesitated to make use of the services offered by state institutions such as the ODRs, individuals also searched out specific niches and opportunities to complement them. For example, some autochthonous farmers joined the cooperative in Selingue, which clearly had privileged access to resources. Others began experimenting with garden crops or grew fruit trees. Some of the Dogon migrants to Selingue adjusted their family organization to get better access to irrigated land. Dogon migrants from the north to the south changed their crop mixes in light of the different ecological conditions. Dogon refugees used NGOs and local politicians to help them get land, as did the Soninke cooperatives, albeit it on a much larger scale. Despite people's skepticism of their government's intentions, they consistently used its programs and personnel to increase access to what they saw as benefits.

Although farmers claimed that local channels were traditional and stable, they were willing to try new things or to use innovative paths of access to improve resource access. Some of the innovations were relatively predictable in the sense that many farmers tried them in many places (e.g., vegetable farming). On the other hand, some were quite new. Some required considerable resources and risk; others took few resources and not much was lost if they failed. The large-scale cooperatives of returned guest workers were a rare and big experiment, but growing watermelons was a small one. Using a Land Rover to thresh grain was unique. Each individual had to look at the particular mix of human, financial, and natural resources available to him or her and make decisions about what might work best. While individuals were far from free to do whatever they wanted, they had much more space for action than is ascribed to them by theoretical approaches that look only at structural constraints or that conceive of agency primarily in terms of resistance.

Although farming formed a key part of rural production strategies, the diversity of farmer goals should serve to remind us that local economic security cannot be evaluated on the basis of agriculture alone. Farmers had different expectations of agriculture, depending on their complementary activities. The next chapter turns to these activities and their role in rural production strategies.

Chapter 6

# *Complementing Crop Production*

Virtually all rural Malians complemented crop production with other activities. Poorer farmers had no choice but to do so, since their survival often depended on earnings from complementary activities. More affluent farmers consciously searched for investments that would allow them to spread risk and increase income. Individuals and households created strategies that made use of resources they had, not only goods and labor, but also skills and knowledge. While there were systematic constraints on the possibilities for complementary activities, people also looked for individualized niches that offered less competition from others.

While most rural Malians took pride in farming well, those in our sample did not appear to attribute particular importance to farming as a "traditional" occupation. They were ready and willing to undertake other activities, judging them by a number of results-oriented criteria: size of potential return; long-term security of the return; ability to provide for their families. Many people would give up farming if they thought they could provide sufficiently for families in another way. Many independent artisans, entrepreneurs, and wage laborers continued to farm precisely because they could not earn sufficient incomes from nonagricultural work alone. The structure of the Malian economy meant that few individuals, either urban or rural, could survive economically on the basis of only one occupation.

This chapter looks at two major types of complementary activities: raising livestock and nonagricultural activities. To raise livestock, access to pasture and capital to buy animals were the most important constraints. In contrast, the constraints on nonagricultural activities were more variable. They depended on the structure of local markets, which varied significantly from zone to zone. Individual skills and knowledge also played a greater role, alongside the capacity for capital investment, which was important for some nonagricultural activities but not all.

Livestock

Only very poor Malian farmers had no animals. In fact, since animals were a major way in which farmers held wealth, livestock ownership was a direct measure of socioeconomic status. Farmers with varying amounts of money turned their cash into different species: goats or sheep if the amount was small; cattle if it was large. Livestock were easily turned back into cash if the need arose and were also used directly for payments such as bridewealth. Animals did not simply store wealth, however, but could help create new wealth. They performed needed farm work. Oxen were used to pull plows and donkeys pulled carts, and all animals provided manure. In larger herds, livestock reproduced themselves. Females provided milk, a welcome addition to the diet during the early rainy season, when the grain was not yet ripe. To be sure, keeping savings in the form of livestock was not risk-free, for they were subject to epidemics, wildlife attacks, and theft. But farmers still found them a better alternative than putting their money in the bank.

## Resources for Stock Raising in Southern Mali

Although capital was needed to buy animals, it did no good unless farmers were also able to get food, commonly in the form of pasture, and water for them. In our study areas, all relatively well watered, water was not problematic, but access to pasture was critical. Most stock raising in the sample areas was extensive, using little labor but much land. Relatively little feed was grown or bought, and livestock were fed on naturally occurring pasture, with the diets of small stock (goats, sheep, chickens) supplemented by the leftovers of family meals. In relatively well watered, densely settled areas, cattle were pastured primarily on areas considered marginal for agriculture. These included slopes and hills, areas too lateritic for cultivation, swamp areas, and those adjacent to swiftly flowing streams, the latter avoided by farmers because of the risk of onchocerciasis (TAMS 1983, D14). Pasture also included forests, and good soils in fallow or land uncultivated because sufficient fields existed elsewhere. The latter areas especially were pressured when farmers cleared new fields.

In the study areas, farmers perceived access to pasture as decreasing because of population growth and increased field clearing. Since successful agriculture usually implied the growth of herds as well as field areas, pasture problems were potentially most acute where agriculture was most productive. ODRs often included livestock initiatives in their portfolio of programs, and livestock agents from the Service d'Elevage, often veterinarians, were among the handful of government representatives in almost every rural area. Nevertheless, little attention was paid to pasture access for farmers. Most extension programs in well-watered areas accentuated crop cultivation.[1] Livestock programs often spent more effort on plow and draft animal projects, animal health and vaccination initiatives, or upgrading the central administration (Brett-Smith et al. 1987). Relatively little emphasis was given to the preservation of pasture for the growing herds of successful farmers, although foresters and ecologists did express concern about the potential degradation of forest and grassland by them (Warshall 1989).

Government actions also decreased available pasture. Village territories generally included pasture, but since these areas were usually not "improved," claims over them were generally not recognized by Malian law (GRM 1987). For example, in the Manantali resettlement project, the definition of the relocatee population as farmers meant that scant attention was given to the needs for pasture in the new sites, causing problems for both hosts and relocatees. In Selingue, the government encouraged the village of Selinkenyi to give a large piece of its pasture to the Soninke cooperative for their farm. In addition, onchocerciasis control could lead to increased agricultural use of river valleys and decreased pasture availability there.

Shrinking pasture led to increased competition between the herds of locals and those of transhumant pastoralists during certain periods of the year. Transhumant herders generally were based to the north of the study areas, but they moved cows, sheep, and goats further south during the dry season. In certain parts of Mali, transhumant herders and settled farmers created a symbiotic relationship where herders pastured their cattle on harvested fields, and farmers reaped the benefit of their manure the following season (Toulmin 1992). Elsewhere, however, herders moved in before crops were harvested, or remained there until the new fields were planted, potentially damaging crops. Their herds also competed with local herds for pasture in both forest and grassland, and with other forest users (e.g., those gathering fruits and medicine, hunters) for forest products.

In our study sites, relationships between farmers and transhumant pastoralists tended to be tense, especially in Manantali and Yanfolila. There, interviews suggested that the number of transhumant herders had increased substantially in recent years, as herders moved farther south in response to drought-related climate changes (Bassett 1993b; Brett-Smith et al. 1987). In Yanfolila, the closing of the northern Ivoirian border to Malian herders meant they stayed in southern Mali for a longer period. Even in other areas, however, there were problems. One of the Dioïla villages refused passage to transhumant herders, despite their desire for the benefits of manure. A second Dioïla village continued to let transhumants pass through but refused to let FulBe herders settle, even though their mother village had given its agreement.

There was also local competition over land use among settled herders, farmers with large herds, and those with few animals. One focus of this competition was debates over the use of classified forests, created mostly during the colonial period as reserves of untouched bush. Since then, farmers had cleared fields in them and sent animals to graze there. The Sounsan forest, near Dioïla, for example, was used by an estimated 60,000 livestock at one time or another in the rainy season; because the forest was surrounded by rivers, water was easily available and the risk of loss was low (Y. Cissé et al. 1989, 84). Donor funding to rehabilitate forests included experimental programs to integrate forest conservation with sustainable use by people and animals, yet many people wanted to cut forests down to create more farms (Y. Cissé et al. 1989). Although foresters joined herd owners on the other side of the debate, any program would have the effect of decreasing existing human and animal use of classified forests, thereby also decreasing the effective pasture available to herds.

There was also conflict over different forms of land use within and near villages, expressed mainly by continual complaints and intermittent conflict about animal depredations in fields and gardens. In the most extensive form of herding, herds were let roam during the dry season, but when the crops were in the field, boys took animals into the bush so that they would not destroy them. As herds got larger and pasture shrank or became more distant, families with large herds or the village collectivity would hire a professional herder to watch them during the cropping season. As these problems became even more acute, the professional herder was sometimes engaged for the entire year. A herd needed to be large and productive to justify the costs of hiring a herder, however, and even with reduced pasture, it was not always done. Roaming animals often entered fields, eating and destroying crops. Destruction of gardens appeared to be a greater problem than that of rainfed fields, because they were cultivated later in the annual cycle, when livestock were less closely guarded. People often built fences around their gardens, but determined animals sometimes got in anyway. Tensions among villagers over the potential and actual depredations of livestock and perceived pressure on pasture led the Yanfolila villages to require Dogon migrants to divest themselves of any stock before settling.

Villagers tried several methods to deal with increasing pressure on pasture. First, they became interested in programs that would demarcate village territories that included communally owned pasture and bush as well as cultivated farmland and fallow. They thought they could better control the alienation of land to those they chose and the use of their territory by transhumants and the livestock of adjoining villages. The programs would also inhibit the ability of government to dispose of their lands without their approval. At the time of the study, these programs were only in the experimental stage in Mali, although neighboring countries, for example, Burkina Faso, had more experience with them.

Secondly, there was a slow move toward more sedentarized livestock-feeding systems, under some pressure from government agencies. The government's interest was phrased in terms of concern about the environmental degradation of pastureland and expressed through projects such as those encouraging farmers to grow forage crops or create silage pits. There were also projects to develop commercial livestock feeds based on cotton and peanut residues. Farmers often hesitated to adopt these new strategies unless they had to because they increased the costs of livestock raising substantially. Only in Dioïla, where people had relatively large herds and good crop production did people buy much feed, mainly cotton by-products and seed during the dry season, and peanut and bean leaves. They also made systematic efforts to collect residues (e.g., millet bran and stalks, maize stalks, peanut leaves) from their own fields. Some also grew forage. The field census showed several cases of intercropped cowpeas where farmers noted that the crop was forage for the animals. In Selingue, a few immigrants bought animal feed, mostly during the dry season, and in Finkolo, farmers spent some on feed for cattle, but nothing for sheep or goats. Tienfala farmers spent almost no money, but did build silage pits. Otherwise, the sample groups relied primarily on natural pasture.

Although many were reluctant to purchase or grow food for their cattle, they were willing to invest in animal health. The Dioïla farmers and the indigenous population of Selingue spent the most of all the groups, mostly on salt, salt licks, and veterinary care, including vaccinations. A few among the indigenous population at Yanfolila also spent on these. The Yanfolila migrants spent little, mostly on veterinary care for a donkey owned by one individual. The livestock service also worked with CECI on health needs for the draft oxen placed with the migrant groups. Manantali residents also spent little on their animals. Generally, the amounts spent on livestock reflected the numbers of animals owned, except in Manantali, where people owned many animals but spent little on them.

Farmers were most likely to invest in care for animals that promised some return. They distinguished, for example, between draft oxen and other cattle. Since draft oxen in good health were key to agricultural returns, many farmers took great care of them, feeding them nutritional supplements, vaccinating them, and guarding them closely. As one agricultural agent remarked, "They treat their draft oxen like members of the family." They also took care of donkeys used to pull carts. They were much less likely to make significant investments in the health of other animals, for they did not believe that the potential return justified a significant investment.

At the time of the study, the sample farmers generally continued to see pasture access as a free good, even though ease of access had declined. The relatively low population densities in most of southern Mali coupled with the presence of uncultivable slope and lateritic areas meant that enough range remained to pasture at least some cattle, but not all who wished necessarily had easy access to the pasture. The decline in pasture led to an increasing role for capital in stock raising. Although farmers sometimes romanticized the old days where raising a herd was essentially cost-free, that was clearly no longer the case. Not only was money needed to buy animals, but more was necessary for herd survival. Farmers needed to pay for shepherds, vaccinations, and sometimes supplementary feed. Despite these expenses, virtually all farmers remained attracted to livestock raising as a place to invest their earnings. The ability of the farmers in the different sites to actualize this ideal varied with their economic resources and access to pasture. The following section looks at stock ownership in light of these constraints.

*Livestock Ownership*

Very generally, those with more wealth had more animals. The wealth came from access to capital to buy animals as well as stability of settlement, which led to greater rights over pasture and greater possibilities for natural herd increase. This meant that those with successful crop-farming enterprises, as well as indigenous populations, tended to have larger herds. The groups can be ranked roughly into four levels of animal ownership (table 10). Dioïla and Manantali both showed high rates of ownership; the indigenous inhabitants of Yanfolila and Selingue ranked second; next came the migrants to Tienfala and Finkolo; and at the bottom, with the least number of animals by far, were the Dogon migrants to Yanfolila and Selingue. We gathered no information about animals owned by the Soninke cooperatives.

*Dioïla and Manantali*

Dioïla showed the highest average per person animal ownership. The average household had the most of every kind of animal in the sample, with the exception of cattle, where it was second to Manantali (table 10). Successful crop cultivation gained cash that could be invested in livestock, and 87 percent of households had at least some animals, including draft oxen (table 11). Although

**TABLE 10.   Livestock Ownership**

| Site | Cattle | Draft Oxen | Sheep Goats | Donkeys | Total per Household | Total per Person |
|------|--------|------------|-------------|---------|---------------------|------------------|
| Dioïla | 5.63 | 1.83 | 7.17 | 0.27 | 14.90 | 1.52 |
| Manantali | 8.26 | 1.36 | 4.06 | — | 13.70 | 0.64 |
| Yanfolila-indigenous | 0.00 | 1.50 | 0.00 | 0.00 | 1.50 | 0.04 |
| Selingue-indigenous | 2.70 | 1.20 | 0.30 | 0.40 | 4.60 | 0.47 |
| Finkolo | 0.30 | 0.13 | 1.67 | 0.00 | 2.10 | 0.29 |
| Tienfala | 0.00 | 0.22 | 0.55 | 0.22 | 0.99 | 0.17 |
| Yanfolila-migrant | 0.00 | 0.31 | 0.00 | 0.04 | 0.35 | 0.04 |
| Selingue-migrant | 0.00 | 0.05 | 0.00 | 0.16 | 0.21 | 0.03 |

*Source:* For Manantali, the source is T. Diarra et al. (1990).

most livestock was reportedly owned by household heads as part of the household patrimony,[2] several women reported owning sheep, goats, and chickens, including one woman whose husband owned none.[3] In addition to using money earned from crop sales to buy animals, people also used earnings from trade or artisanal work when it was not needed for immediate family needs. That so many people at Dioïla were able to invest savings in animals is a reflection of the success of their agricultural strategies and the fact that few had to buy food.

Although animal ownership was widespread, sizes of herds did reflect different wealth levels. The largest cattle herd, owned by a FulBe in Kolobugu, had over 100 head when no other household had more than 21. Although he had high grain production, his cotton sales were below average; he apparently drew on his ethnic background and knowledge to specialize. In Miankabugu, levels of stockholding were less differentiated than in the other two Dioïla villages,

**TABLE 11.   Livestock Distribution**

| Site | Households in Site | Households with Animals | Proportion with Animals | Largest Herd | Smallest Herd |
|------|--------------------|-------------------------|-------------------------|--------------|---------------|
| Dioïla | 30 | 26 | 87% | 145 | 2 |
| Manantali | 50 | 45 | 90% | 77 | 2 |
| Yanfolila-indigenous | 4 | 3 | 75% | 2 | 2 |
| Selingue-indigenous | 10 | 4 | 40% | 21 | 2 |
| Finkolo | 30 | 5 | 17% | 30 | 1 |
| Tienfala | 9 | 2 | 22% | 8 | 1 |
| Yanfolila-migrant | 26 | 4 | 15% | 5 | 1 |
| Selingue-migrant | 19 | 3 | 16% | 2 | 1 |

*Source:* For Manantali, the source is 1985 preresettlement census.
*Note:* Smallest herd is for herd owners only.

reflecting the pattern already found in crop production. All households had some cattle and herd sizes ranged from 2 to 16; all households had either sheep or goats as well. Equipment was not an alternative investment even for the one farmer who had purchased the minitractor, whose purchase cost was equivalent to about 60–70 head. He had the second largest herd in his village.

Conservatively estimated, the total value of livestock owned by the Dioïla sample was approximately 6,447,500 FCFA (U.S.$19,538) or 214,917 FCFA/household (U.S.$651), a substantial sum and roughly equivalent to the average reported annual cotton earnings of U.S.$660. Slightly over three-quarters of this value was in cattle, the most valuable species. Development reports often accused farmers of using stock as nonproductive savings, but 68 percent of Dioïla owners sold some stock other than chickens. If those selling chickens were included, the proportion selling animals increased to 89 percent of owners. The value of reported animal sales was 1,244,100 FCFA (U.S.$3,770), an average of 40,803 FCFA/household (U.S.$124). Almost surely an underestimate, this formed a noteworthy addition to household income.

Manantali also showed quite large herd sizes, but unlike Dioïla, this appeared to be a temporary phenomenon linked to the resettlement. Residents had invested a substantial part of the cash compensation from the resettlement project in animals. According to the census done by the PRM prior to resettlement, the households in the ISH sample averaged 9.54 cattle and 6.64 sheep and goats in 1985. By 1986, the herds grew to an average 11.6 cattle and 25.46 sheep and goats, as households began to benefit from wage earning and project indemnities. By 1989, average household holdings decreased to 8.26 cattle and 4.06 sheep and goats, slightly lower than they had been before the resettlement, because there were more difficulties in finding food and water for the animals.[4]

The new villages had neither water troughs near their new wells nor cattle pens when animals arrived (T. Diarra et al. 1990). Neither people nor animals knew the bush around their new sites well, so that animals were more easily lost. They were attacked by wild animals who also had their migratory patterns and feeding areas disrupted by new settlements and changing river levels; others became stuck in the mud. They suffered from thirst and hunger, but farmers were unable to provide them with supplemental foods such as millet bran and peanut hay, since their own production was not yet established. Economic pressures also impacted herd size. Farmers who needed food often sold animals, both older animals and recent purchases, to buy it. Farmers complained about having to sell animals to buy food, because they were used to producing enough to eat, and stock sales did impact negatively on overall herd size. Nevertheless, because they had livestock to sell, they were better able to weather the food and cash crises that arose.

More recent studies at Manantali have shown that animal ownership declined even further after 1989 as pressure on pasture continued to mount (T. Diarra et al. 1995). The only kind of animal to show a significant increase was donkeys, whose numbers increased from none in 1985 to 118 in 1989, according to the Livestock Service. Improved roads built by the dam construction company and the resettlement project involved extensive clearing, which in turn decreased tsetse fly and trypanosomiasis infections. New roads also made donkey-driven carts more feasible.

Although Dioïla and Manantali showed very similar large herds in 1989, the two sites were at different points in accumulation processes. For Dioïla residents, animals were an integral part of an economic strategy whereby high earnings from cotton and grain sales could be saved and invested in animals, which in turn provided supplementary income. This strategy was so successful that as pasture came under pressure, residents could and did substitute capital for it. In contrast, our study found Manantali residents at a high point of stock ownership, when a temporary influx of capital from the resettlement allowed them to purchase livestock, but neither pasture nor ongoing earning possibilities could sustain those levels.

*The Indigenous Inhabitants of Selingue and Yanfolila*
The autochthonous population of Selingue also showed relatively high animal ownership, although lower than at the preceding two sites. It is likely that the autochthones of Yanfolila also generally had large herds, even though our sample reported only small ones, due either to an extremely skewed sample or to their consistent underreporting of economic resources.[5] Other sources suggested substantial livestock holdings for the indigenous Wassulunke. The 1986 administrative census showed animal ownership rates of 0.45 head per person, with cattle comprising 83 percent of animals (MATDB 1986, 224), while the Mali Sud III study found the average Wassulunke household to have a herd of 28.8 head, with cattle as the most important component (PIRT 1989, 2:13). These figures suggest even greater livestock ownership than at Dioïla, but to be conservative, we have grouped them with the indigenous people of Selingue.

These two groups had the privileged access to pasture that came from their position as indigenous inhabitants, even though neither site had a highly remunerative cash crop at the time of the study. Neither group invested much capital in its herds. However, pasture pressure was growing at Selingue. The creation of the reservoir and dam-related resettlement pushed villages closer together, affecting their ability to sustain their herds. As already noted, a large part of the existing pasture had been given to the CAMSEL cooperative. Notably, the administrative census showed lower per capita animal ownership,

0.20 head/person compared to 0.47/person in our sample (MATDB 1986, 229). This suggests that the pasture pressure had most affected immigrants, and ownership was becoming differentiated between indigenous locals and new settlers. Indigenous inhabitants at Yanfolila may also have perceived pasture pressure because of new settlers, but there remained significant areas of pasture, especially in comparison to Selingue.

Stock ownership was also relatively widespread in these two sites (table 11). A slightly lower proportion owned stock than at Dioïla and Manantali, but there were more owners than among the other groups. In Selingue at least, all four major animals groups (cattle, draft oxen, sheep and goats, and donkeys) were present, and some women reported owning cattle and sheep. Again, those with larger herds had a significant store of wealth. The Selingue resident with 20 cattle would have had savings of approximately 1 million FCFA (U.S.$3,030). Selingue residents also noted the value of herd reproduction, as many of their draft oxen were born into existing herds. However, no livestock sales were reported among these groups.

The experiences at these two sites underline the importance of being recognized landowners of the territory for access to pasture. However, the lack of sales, in contrast to Dioïla, suggests the importance of capital to sustain herd productivity and to use herds as an investment to produce more income.

*Finkolo and Tienfala*
Finkolo and Tienfala had stock ownership rates about half that of the high ownership sites, reflecting both a lack of access to resources and the fact that non-farm activities played an important role. Wage employment rather than stock raising was the main complement to crop farming among both these groups. Both sites were relatively near to urban centers, creating competition for grazing as well as farms. Nevertheless, both groups showed average animal ownership greater than among the full-time farmer migrants to Selingue and Yanfolila, suggesting that stock ownership remained desirable and feasible for at least some of them.

Small herd sizes reflected competing demands on pasture, capital, and people's time. In Finkolo, although the average per capita ownership was low among our samples, it was actually slightly higher than the reported figures for the arrondissement as a whole, 0.29 head/person vs. 0.21 (MATDB 1986, 170). In Finkolo, farmers said that getting access to pasture was less a problem than getting fields, yet the commitment of their time to wage labor meant that herds generally were small.[6] In Tienfala, in contrast, people noted competing demands on land for both pasture and agriculture. Tienfala had plenty of uncultivable land on its cliffs and slopes, but commercial herders dominated it. Tienfala was a pass-through zone for cattle moving from Banamba, north of Koulikoro, where many were raised for sale, to either Bamako or its neighbor, Kati, where they would be butchered and consumed. Small farmers were at a disadvantage in any competition with large-scale wealthy commercial herders. These peri-urban residents also had different investment choices. As noted earlier in chapter 4, their children showed higher rates of school attendance, and some of the Tienfala residents may have chosen to invest any surpluses in their businesses rather than animals.

The constraints and choices were reflected not only in herd size but also in the choice of animals. Cattle ownership was relatively low, and individuals showed a preference for small ruminants. Work animals (donkeys and draft oxen) were also valued, particularly in Tienfala (table 10). Animal ownership was much less widespread, less than a quarter of households owning them (table 11). A few nonheads did own however; for example, a dependent male at Tienfala had goats. For those who had animals, however, they could be a significant store of wealth. In Finkolo, a rough estimate of the total value of animals was 1 million FCFA (U.S.$3,030), or 200,000 FCFA (U.S.$606), on average, for each of the five owner households. Sales were less widespread with smaller herds; less than half of owners reported sales. One person in Tienfala and three in Finkolo reported sheep sales, which brought supplementary income.

Given the constraints on pasture, some of these migrants may have bought animals and sent them to home areas, a common strategy. Our study, focused on the resources used daily by the rural households, did not ask about cattle or other animals kept elsewhere. Because many Finkolo residents planned to retire in natal villages, they were the most likely to have had other animals. Nevertheless it is clear that most of the migrants to these to areas did not make stock-raising a major part of their production strategies because of the constraints on access to necessary resources. However, a few with access to pasture and capital were able to supplement savings and income streams with stock, especially small ruminants.

## The Migrants to Yanfolila and Selingue

The Dogon migrants to Yanfolila and Selingue had by far the lowest animal ownership rates. This reflected low resource ownership at their arrival as well as inability as yet to achieve sustained levels of surplus production. Should they do so, they would surely meet the problem of the superior access to pasture held by indigenous people. In Yanfolila, migrants started out worse off because of the requirement that they arrive without stock. Although some of the Dogon migrants to Yanfolila were dynamic crop farmers, they had not yet created successful production *systems* because they were not able to complement crops with stock. In Selingue, migrants could not buy livestock because they had neither capital nor pasture resources. The problems experienced by the migrants in crop production were both reflected in and exacerbated by their inability to have much stock. The lack of stock among both Selingue and Yanfolila migrants underlined their vulnerability, for they had limited options should crops fail.

In both areas, only a few owned animals, and they exhibited a clear preference for work animals, either draft oxen or donkeys (tables 10, 11). Donkeys became a good investment when ecological and infrastructure conditions permitted. Both Selingue and Yanfolila had been sufficiently cleared to decrease trypanosomiasis and had decent road networks for carts. Reported animal sales were also very rare. Only one Yanfolila migrant reported selling sheep. It appears that ownership by other than household heads was nonexistent.

Livestock remained an important part of the rural farm production strategy, yet it required a certain quantity of resources. In most zones, immigrant farmers had more difficulty in getting cash to buy animals as well as access to pasture since existing villages were more often hesitant to share pastureland than farmland. Thus, migrants had a more difficult time than did indigenous populations in putting together an agricultural strategy that included stock as a buffer against the contingencies of crop farming. This was reflected in herd mixes. Only those with high access to either range or capital had cattle, while those with low resources concentrated on work animals, complementing them with small ruminants when resources increased. Sites with high animal ownership showed many cattle, while those with low rates had mostly small ruminants and work animals.

High rates of animal ownership had significant spread effects. Once people had relatively large herds, the cost of gaining new animals decreased, since farmers could rely more on natural increase. Possibilities for sales also increased, and animals became an investment that brought monetary return as well as savings. They provided manure, making poorer farmers without animals more dependent on chemical fertilizers and the agricultural extension agencies that provided them. High levels of animal ownership in a zone did lead to greater differentiation in herd sizes among owners but also reflected more widespread ownership. Sites with low levels of animal ownership showed few people owning few animals.

Although generalized patterns of access to resources made for a low rate of livestock ownership among most recent migrants, there were at least a few individuals in all sites who were able to get and keep stock. These were usually among the wealthier farmers, but since animals were also viewed as an investment, they appear also to have been individuals who felt that this niche would bring them some return. The emphasis on work animals that could be rented to others as well as used to lessen one's own load and the trickle of sheep sales reflect this. Nevertheless because of the capital requirements to get stock, there were more constraints on using it as opposed to nonagricultural activities to complement to crop farming. Many of the latter required only a labor investment.

Nonagricultural Enterprises

The study sample also used nonagricultural activities to diversify risk and increase income. In two sites, Tienfala and Finkolo, nonagricultural activities were primary, and agriculture was a way to cope with the risks associated with wage earning. Among the other groups, mostly "full-time" farmers, nonfarm activities were an important supplement. Poor farmers who could not provide sufficiently from farming alone were forced to undertake nonagricultural activities to make ends meet. If these activities (e.g., agricultural labor for another) competed with the farmer's own agricultural priorities, his or her ability to farm successfully was even more compromised. In contrast, more affluent farmers, who earned sufficient income from farming to meet family needs, often tried to diversify their risks by spreading investments across agricultural and nonagricultural activities. They often searched explicitly for activities with high returns, often requiring significant capital investment.

Yet while the monetary resources available to invest in nonagricultural activities constrained their potential return, other resources were important as well, most notably skills for jobs in high demand. Local economic structure was also important, for it determined whether there was a market for goods and services produced locally. Where the number of consumers was growing, there were more opportunities for both specialized and unskilled labor. In contrast to livestock, nonagricultural options existed for those with any level of resources, but the returns depended on local market structure and the knowledge held by an individual as well as his or her ability to invest. We turn first to those who did not aim to meet most of their needs from full-time farming: the migrants to Finkolo and Tienfala. We then turn to the sites that accentuated farming. Because the study focus was on agriculture, much of the data on nonfarm activities was qualitative and came from informal interviews. The data illustrated major patterns, but detailed quantitative data on productivity or income were not available.

## Nonagricultural Activities as the Major Production Strategy

In both Finkolo and Tienfala, agriculture may have increased the probability of family survival, but it was rarely the major source of cash income. In Finkolo, salaried labor on the tea plantation was the key subsistence strategy, while in Tienfala, the strategy was more consciously one of the simultaneous exploitation of several economic niches, some agricultural and others not. The choice of a peri-urban settlement zone, as opposed to one either more urban or rural, was consciously done to facilitate this strategy.

There was not much point in migrating to Finkolo except for a job on the tea plantation. Skilled permanent jobs paid better than unskilled or temporary ones. Income from permanent positions was less seasonally variable and also appeared to be higher than for temporary help. Adult men were most likely to be permanent employees. Of the 15 household heads about whom we had information, 10 held permanent positions, 2 were temporary employees, and the status of the other 3 was unknown. Men occupied a variety of job categories. Although some were laborers, others were drivers, mechanics, carpenters, or well-diggers. Skilled workers, those who had gained specialized knowledge at some time in their past, could earn more than laborers. Unfortunately, we have no information on how individuals gained the skills that allowed them to get more remunerative positions.

Having the household head in a permanent, skilled position increased the attraction of remaining at Finkolo, but it did not assure household viability. To increase income, heads encouraged children and wives to work as temporary employees. In one case, up to 10 other family members also worked on the tea. Women harvested tea in the field and sorted it in the factory. Harvesting income was highly seasonal, and most women were temporary employees. Their revenues increased during the rainy season, when the harvest was greatest, and a woman could harvest 45 kg of green leaves per day. Paid at a rate of 25 FCFA/kg (U.S.$0.076), she could earn 1,125 FCFA/day (U.S.$3.41), which compared favorably to the daily rate for temporary help of 250 FCFA/day (U.S.$0.76). Many women encouraged their daughters to work on the plantation as well. This not only increased family revenue, but also helped the daughter to finance her trousseau and meet her own cash needs.

Workers were not content with their standard of living. Families only became better off when multiple family members became wage earners. For temporary workers, the dry season could be quite difficult. Women remarked that when the harvest became irregular, the money they earned was insufficient. Moreover, the demands of high-season wage work left people with little free time and made it difficult to pursue entrepreneurial activities. Few women, for example, were involved in trade, although one had begun to sell goods in her husband's small restaurant. Others cited both a lack of time (especially during the rainy season) and a lack of funds as constraints.

Nevertheless, many people stayed a relatively long time at Finkolo, although they rarely began to consider it home. They kept in close contact with home villages, and many did return home at retirement. They seem to have created adequate lives given the options in rural Mali. Individual monthly earnings at the height of the season were sometimes over 30,000 FCFA (U.S.$91), which compared favorably with the wages paid to many urban Malians. Although the daily rate of 250 FCFA for temporary help was quite low even by Malian standards, many of the tasks given for the "day" did not require a whole day's work. Once the task was completed, the worker was free to leave and could undertake other work on his/her own account. Many people sent money to families in their home areas, something they could not have done if their incomes were insufficient. As noted above, the rate of school attendance was among the highest of all the rural areas. It seems that at least some were able to put together acceptable economic strategies with the combination of wage work and some farm production.

In Tienfala, the Bamako market, with its many consumers, and many people looking for employment, influenced people's nonagricultural options. Tienfala was known since its initial settlement in the early twentieth century as a place for *débrouillardise,* or "making do," and migrants generally undertook entrepreneurial activities or opened small businesses rather than finding salaried jobs. Salaried employment was considered to be much less remunerative; the nearby commercial plantations for example paid wages so poor (12,500 FCFA/month—U.S.$38) that people preferred other activities.

The best returns came to those who had skills in demand; sometimes these skills had to be accompanied by significant investment to make them remunerative. Among the migrants were a blacksmith who marketed his products locally and a jeweler who sold his wares in Bamako. Migrants to Tienfala-gare and Tienfala-village were somewhat more likely to accentuate nonagricultural activities than were those who chose to settle in the more agricultural Fugadougou, yet even there one of the migrants was a housepainter who often worked in Tienfala-gare. All these men had skills in demand; jewelers and blacksmiths also had to maintain working capital. In general, older men tended to have more capital to invest than did women or younger men. Again, we have no information on how these men learned their crafts.

But even those with only everyday skills and little to invest could find work because the large Bamako market spilled over into its hinterland. Tienfala-gare had its own civil-servant and nonagricultural population that needed workers. Women were hired as domestic servants in some families and did women's domestic work (e.g., pounding grain, transporting water) for pay. Girls and young women often migrated to Bamako, where they found jobs as domestic servants. Because the zone was still rural, people also gathered natural resources, still mostly free goods, to sell. In addition to the migrants in the study, Bozo and Somono, ethnic fishing groups, settled in the zone. Women of many ethnic groups sold fish, buying it here and reselling it in Bamako. Local people also sold wood and processed it to make charcoal for sale.

For those who had few skills and little to invest, incomes were low. For example, young unmarried women working as domestic servants often found themselves working for minimal wages (i.e., 3,000–4,000 FCFA/month—U.S.$9–12). But again, as in Finkolo, households created acceptable economic strategies when multiple members had different activities. Activities often changed over time as families increased their local networks. As people become more settled, for example, women of migrant families worked less for other families and concentrated more on production on their own farms. Our sample, by including intact households, was biased toward those who were able to make this strategy work. Nonetheless, indicators such as the number of children in school, which showed the second highest rate among the samples, suggest that some people made it work sufficiently well that they stayed for a long time. Unfortunately, we were unable to gather data about the actual incomes earned by sample households.

The different patterns of nonfarm activities in Tienfala and Finkolo reflected primarily the larger economic context of the two zones. In Finkolo, the plantation dominated its local niche; there was no point in residing in the study villages unless at least some family members worked there. Yet it was the ability to enter agriculture and livestock raising alongside that allowed people to increase their standard of living. Earnings from one activity could be invested in another to make a reasonable subsistence strategy. In Tienfala, Bamako, with its large population and diverse market, dominated. While competition for certain types of employment was intense, there was also a great variety of opportunity and possibilities for quite specialized economic activities. But again, households looked to complement nonagricultural activities with agriculture and livestock.

## Nonfarm Activities as a Supplement to Agriculture

In the four other sites, nonagricultural activities were a complement to the main activity, agriculture, for most residents. Strategies for choosing activities varied with the success of agriculture and the particularities of the larger economic context. Our data suggest that sustained high agricultural production can stimulate nonagricultural activities, but boom phenomena do not lead to balanced growth.

### Farmers with Successful Cash Crops

There was only one group that earned much from cash crop production, the farmers of Dioïla. Here, high levels of crop production and livestock ownership were complemented by a rich mix of nonagricultural activities. More affluent farmers entered these activities to diversify income sources (and risk and dependency on the environment as well) and to improve living standards. Concurrently, successful farmers increased consumer spending, creating a market for people with rural consumer and farm-oriented specialty trades.

The high rate of equipment ownership meant that some men were able to rent out specialized agricultural equipment. The tractor owner for example, earned at least 126,500 FCFA (U.S.$383) from rentals to other sample households, only a portion of the village residents. Based on information by those who paid to rent equipment, men who owned trained draft oxen and plows could also earn money by renting to those who needed one or both. The high rate of equipment ownership also created opportunities for blacksmiths to make and repair it. The possibilities to benefit from these earning sources usually required capital to invest in the first place.

Although Dioïla farmers remained generalized producers who grew food as well as cotton, their high levels of production allowed them to specialize a bit and to buy more consumer goods, creating a local market. Men reported earnings from weaving and working as masons. There were also more opportunities in the zone for construction workers and mechanics as more residents built improved housing and bought mopeds and bicycles. Women also could benefit from these activities. One reported cotton spinning and a few others trade. Two, for example, made and sold small millet cakes for the market. Others reported gathering shea nuts and making oil and soap for sale. Some of these activities required some capital investment; many required specialized skills as well. Again, it would be useful to know how people learned these skills.

Finally, increased levels of economic activity also increased the opportunity to earn at least a little from activities that required neither specialized skills nor capital investment. In Kolobugu, for example, one man reported earnings from selling wood. Women's associations harvested and transported cotton and pounded shea nuts for pay. More recent migrants whose own farms were still small had increased opportunities for farm labor. Many of these possibilities had relatively low wages. But in some times and places, for example during the cocoa booms in Nigeria and Ghana, farmers working for others could earn sufficient income so that they could begin their own farms later (Berry 1993). Some women's groups in Kenya were able to turn earnings into significant investments (Moore 1988). Whether this might be possible in Dioïla was not clear and would require long-term study.

The amounts of earnings reported to us from any of these nonfarm activities were small, but Dioïla was remarkable for its range of them. It was also the only site where anyone reported earnings from processing agricultural products. As in the other sites, qualitative ethnographic data suggested that the importance of nonfarm income was more than the quantitative data indicated. Actual sums earned by some individuals may have been substantial.

Unlike Tienfala, where artisanal activities served urban markets outside the villages, in Dioïla, the major markets were rural. The kinds of nonagricultural activities found there stemmed directly from its agricultural success. As the availability of money in the zone increased, so too did the local standard of living and the level of commercialization. This created more opportunities to enter commercial activities for local markets, including food processing. Those who had knowledge or capital could find niches to complement agricultural earnings. In addition to the farmers in the sample, specialized migrants had also entered the Dioïla zone. For example, Bozo and Somono fished from camps near the sample villages and sold their produce there.

*Boom and Bust*
Bringing many short-term but highly remunerative jobs, dam construction at Manantali created a short-term boom, radically changing the economic framework and with it, the options for nonagricultural activities. Later, resettlement activities brought jobs and cash compensation, which could be used for investment. The zone's opening through construction and resettlement meant that greater commercial options remained even after those two activities had finished. Each of these changes offered specific options to the population.

Wage work for the dam construction company or its subcontractors, for the contractors engaged by the PRM to rebuild housing and village infrastructure, and for the PRM itself were all attractive to Bafing residents. Local residents were at a disadvantage in getting jobs on dam and housing construction since many of these jobs required specialized skills or previous building experience, relatively rare in this zone. However, many families, especially those with literate men with some urban work experience, did have one member or two who worked with one of these organizations over several years. Local residents also had an advantage in getting jobs to build and erect the thatched roofs for new housing, since urban subcontractors, who usually built flat tin roofs, lacked the specialized knowledge necessary. In contrast to other employers, the PRM gave priority to relocatees, especially for unskilled labor. For example, they hired villagers to clear the new village and field sites. Supervision was provided by a few of the better-educated young men (i.e., those who could read and write French), hired as foremen. Clearing work was very short-term, offering one season's work for most of those involved, but the benefits were quite broad-based, since most households had at least one young man to send. Only a few households with only small children and older members did not benefit.

Alongside wage-earning opportunities, the PRM provided cash payments to settlers in situations where lost resources could not be replaced. From its inception, the project planned to pay compensation for fruit trees and the few improved houses. Other compensation was added during the course of the project. As it became clear that there was neither the time nor the money for contractors to build granaries and kitchens, the PRM decided to indemnify relocatees directly. As of June 1988, 330,615,171 FCFA (U.S.$1,001,864) had been paid as compensation, according to official project figures. With roughly 10,000 people moving, this was about 33,062 FCFA (U.S.$100) per relocatee. Clearly, those who had more (more granaries, more trees) received more. Those who received large payments, mostly male heads of big households, had a substantial sum they could invest. Coupled with money earned from wages, possibilities for productive investments could have been significant.

However, much of this money disappeared as quickly as it came. Many Bafingois residents had not paid their taxes for several years and the *chef d'arrondissement* often arrived in villages soon after PRM compensation disbursements to collect them. Especially among smaller families, some money was used to buy food and meet other immediate needs, since agricultural production was disrupted for at least a year. Little money served to buy agricultural equipment, and the fruit tree compensation was rarely used to buy new fruit trees (T. Diarra et al. 1990, 80), although project funds supported a small nursery to supply trees at reasonable prices. People lacked knowledge about new venues in which to invest what was left and turned to old standbys. They invested in livestock, but epidemics and pasture pressure led to increased livestock deaths and investment losses, as we discussed earlier in this chapter. They also "invested" in people, as many used compensation to pay bridewealth. Young men married and their families began to grow. Our 1993–94 return to Manantali found a mini–population boom following all these marriages (T. Diarra et al. 1995).[7]

The nonagricultural option with the most long-term potential revolved around the commercial expansion of the zone. This started during the days of dam construction when opportunities for small entrepreneurial activities abounded for those who could provide necessary goods and services to the wage earners. One host village, for example, entered vegetable cultivation on a large scale, selling lettuce and other green vegetables to expatriate and African workers. Women also sold charcoal and sauce ingredients, and some began small restaurants. Those locals downstream from the dam who did not have to resettle had more access to these activities than did relocatees preoccupied by the move, and they provided an example for the entire population.

The consumer market declined substantially after the dam was built and only a small core of salaried employees remained at the dam site. Unlike Selingue, only two hours from Bamako on a paved road, Manantali remained relatively isolated and did not attract many migrants. However, from the perspective of the locals, who had lived in the old Bafing, the zone had experienced a commercial opening. Prospects for future employment (when the turbines would be up and running) kept a few outsiders in Manantali town, and young local men who might have otherwise left on wage labor migration remained in the Bafing. By 1989, Manantali inhabitants were making use of new opportunities linked to the greater commercialization. Several village markets in or near the Bafing had opened or increased in size, reflecting the greater ease with which merchants could come from nearby towns. Professional traders bought farm products and sold industrial goods while local artisans hawked their wares. Many local women also sold produce and processed foods to either other locals or traders. Since cash crop production stagnated after the resettlement, Manantali residents had to rely on these newly created opportunities to earn money. Their long-term potential was not yet evident in 1989.

The Manantali experience, although relatively rare, is instructive on several counts. It shows once again that the most revolutionary changes were brought about by more powerful actors who could change the entire economic context. It shows also the relative ineffectiveness of a short boom, as opposed to more balanced long-term growth in catalyzing economic change. But the Manantali experience illustrates as well the ability of people to adapt creatively to a series of very rapid changes, mixing options in different ways as new opportunities arose. Constraints of traditional culture did not keep people from trying new activities; they showed instead great willingness to try new things. Success at new activities depended on a complex interaction of the larger economic contexts with individualized resources and dynamism.

*Complementing Subsistence with Nonagricultural Work*
Yanfolila and Selingue showed a similar pattern to Manantali in the sense that there was no cash crop to provide basic income. They too relied on nonagricultural activities. Their experiences show the difference it made to be an indigenous inhabitant versus a migrant, but this had different results given the different local economies in the two zones.

In Yanfolila, the *cercle* town provided a small center with some consumers and active markets. In 1989, the town, having just received an improved road and scheduled to be electrified, was slowly growing. Agricultural services were improving as the CMDT began to expand. But the town was still small, population density remained low, and access to bush areas relatively easy. Despite its growing urban center, Yanfolila remained the most rural of the study zones. This mix of resources affected the nonagricultural opportunities.

The indigenous Yanfolila population had privileged access to the extensive bush resources, and they used them as their entry into the growing commercial opportunities. For example, people who fished and hunted could sell fish and game. Cutting wood for sale was an important source of income for men in the dry season and for women throughout the year. Men and women also looked for shea nuts in the forest, so women could make oil. As landowners, the indigenous population was more likely to have fruit orchards, and in Yanfolila town and Wuru Wuru, indigenous women sold the fruits from their husbands' gardens. Placer mining was also practiced, although none of the sample reported income from it during the study. People's established social networks also generated collective activity. Indigenous women created agricultural work groups in Yanfolila town and Gwalafara. We did not get any estimates of the amounts received from these activities, but it is likely that people could get a small steady income from them.

Migrants had different possibilities. Lacking access to bush resources, they looked particularly for the opportunities afforded by the growth of Yanfolila town: trade, artisanal work, and services. Four men reported making bricks; a mechanic worked primarily on mopeds; and there was an active blacksmith in the sample. There were also jobs for unskilled workers; nine men reported working as laborers; two carried out unspecified artisanal activities; and three men sold wood. Most men worked primarily during the dry season, except for the smith, who worked all year. Migrant women in Yanfolila town washed clothes, pounded grain for pay, and sold wood. One woman reported earnings from shea butter sales and a second from laundry. Dogon girls often entered domestic service to earn money to aid their families, something rare among the indigenous Wassulunke girls. They were continuing a tradition begun in their home region, where they had often gone to Mopti as servants. Women in particular maintained that their incomes were insufficient to meet their multiple needs. Dogon women undertook diverse activities but still failed to earn enough. They were looking for new activities that would be both more remunerative and less consuming of time and labor. They wanted to learn how to make soap or baskets, or to dye cloth, which they believed had better returns. Although people needed nonagricultural work to make ends meet, it is likely that those who had skills and capital had more remunerative possibilities.

The involvement of migrant households in nonfarm activities was high. In Yanfolila town and Gwalafara, 8 of the 10 migrant households in each sample had some nonfarm income, while in Wuru Wuru, 4 of the 6 did. Even where agriculture was successful, in Gwalafara, men entered nonfarm activities since they still saw the possibilities for self-sufficiency in agriculture alone as rather precarious. In contrast, women in the villages saw agriculture as the best way to earn money. However, migrant women accentuated their own fields and did not participate in indigenous women's work groups. Earnings among migrants were highest in Yanfolila town, where rough estimations suggest that six of nine activities earned 25,000 FCFA (U.S.$76) or more annually. In the villages, no activities earned more than 15,000 FCFA (U.S.$45), and even that was rare. The ability to get work in Yanfolila town induced some migrants to settle there rather than the villages, even though it was somewhat more difficult to get land and hence agricultural production was lower.

Although these were only rough estimates, the reported earnings of immigrant households from nonfarm income were on average twice as large as those of indigenous households, 21,040 FCFA/household (U.S.$64) versus 10,063 FCFA/household (U.S.$30). Again, this reflected the hesitation on the part of the indigenous sample to reply openly, but it also reflected greater reliance on commercial activities among the migrants. Neither group could use surplus crops to generate additional investments or income. As the autochthonous owners of the land and long-term residents, the Wassulunke had greater rights over, and knowledge of, bush resources. They turned to these to generate goods and incomes. In contrast, migrants tried to meet the demand for artisanal goods and commercial services in the zone. Resources for both indigenous and migrant groups were in relatively good supply in relation to demand. The indigenous population had much bush available. There were not a lot of jobs in Yanfolila town because it was small, but there were also a relatively small number of people competing for them. Because of its relatively balanced growth, migrants to Yanfolila could find work *and* land and thus create acceptable production strategies.

This was in contrast to the Selingue population, which had to cope with less balanced growth. It appeared to many, including the migrants who went there, that Selingue, with its dam and rapid population growth, should generate opportunities for nonagricultural employment. Kangare, the arrondissement and dam headquarters, had indeed grown into a small commercial town. However, appearances were deceptive since the number of people looking for employment outstripped the work available. In this, it contrasted with other sites. The Selingue market, for example, could not begin to compete with the size and diversity of the Bamako market. While the Bamako market did indeed have many more looking for work, it also had more niches to exploit. The Selingue market was also much narrower and smaller than Dioïla, which although it had limited opportunities at any one place, was spread over a large zone of successful farmers. While one of the facets of Mali's underdevelopment was that there were often more people looking for work than remunerative work available, the situation was worse in Selingue. Moreover, the many poor people that went to Selingue looking for work created very little consumer demand, especially for specialty goods.

Both farmers and potential farmers competed for land and a small range of nonagricultural employment opportunities. More settled residents appear to have had privileged access to the possibilities that did exist. Former dam construction workers had developed social networks that allowed them to create remunerative economic strategies, and they appear to have been able to benefit from nonagricultural niches, although we did not study them directly. The indigenous residents of Selinkenyi also were able to gain some access to the small market for specialized skills. Two men, for example, reported that they were tailors in addition to farming. Others took advantage of the active markets to sell; one woman reported earnings from sales of shea butter.

More importantly, Selinkenyi residents took advantage of benefits they gained from their position as the indigenous inhabitants of the zone. For example, the men who left their own farms to relatives and joined the CAMSEL cooperative as a means to diversify earning had that possibility because their village hosted these migrants. Others took advantage of their knowledge of the bush and its related resources. Selinkenyi women could sell shea because they could gather it; indigenous women were more knowledgeable about where trees grew and had greater rights to them. Indigenous women also did placer mining for gold during the dry season. Only one woman reported earning any money, and the sum was relatively small. However, women hoped for the big strike that would liberate them from the daily grind. This activity had become common for local women, who knew the local sources. None of these activities appear to have earned substantial sums for the indigenous residents, but they did allow them to earn some cash to complement their crop farming.

This was in contrast to the Dogon migrants. For them the need to earn cash income was among the greatest of all the samples since it was virtually impossible to produce enough to support a family on the produce of irrigated land alone, all that most of them had. Theoretically, the situation for finding non-agricultural employment was similar to that among the indigenous population of Selingue. Yet, these people joined the many without significant long-term networks chasing relatively small opportunities for employment. Unlike the autochthones, they had little direct access to bush resources (except for fuelwood) to earn income. In our sample, no migrant reported any nonfarm income at all. Unlike the other sites, where ethnographic information suggested that the quantitative information was an underestimate, this source added little here. Although some probably did earn something, the possibilities appeared to be fewer than at the other sites. How the migrants made ends meet over the short term was not clear. Nor was it clear what they could do over the long term.

The experiences of the migrants to Selingue show that it was indeed possible that all the pieces of an economic strategy could be compromised simultaneously. While the economic strategies of the other groups had at least one piece that provided relative security, there was none for them. Should we return in the late 1990s, we would expect that they would be the group most likely to have moved back home or on to another new site.

Their experiences also illustrate the importance of balanced growth. Successful farming complemented by a balance of other investments and opportunities could create rural employment for full-time and part-time laborers, artisans, and merchants. Unbalanced growth, in contrast, created both economic and environmental stresses. While individuals could creatively follow new opportunities, they could not create conditions of balanced economic growth. That depended instead on the creation of a facilitative framework by central and local government policies.

*The Soninke Cooperatives*

Neither of these cooperatives had yet reached a stage where they were producing sufficient crops to sell as well as to assure their subsistence. CAMUKO, the Yanfolila cooperative, was not even producing that much. However, these groups had different possibilities for nonagricultural activities. First, they had accumulated savings and benefits from their participation in programs for returning French immigrants. Second, many were literate, and both groups had members trained in accounting and mechanics, which offered them possibilities for earning income. Finally, they had learned new skills and new technologies in France. We got no information from CAMSEL, and only hints from CAMUKO, but it appears that these groups intended to build on these resources.

The Soninke women of CAMUKO had the most explicit plans for nonfarm income earning. They had brought a variety of electrical appliances from France, including sewing machines, food processors, and irons, that they wanted to use to generate income as well as for their own family needs. In 1989, they were anxiously awaiting the electrification of Yanfolila to begin small businesses. Whether they were able to do so was not clear, since their husbands were encouraging them to move to the village of Wuru Wuru, where there was neither electricity nor a market. Despite the problematic future of this particular activity, it was clear that Soninke migrants were taking steps to improve returns from both farming and nonfarm activities, and that they had some of the resources necessary to do so. These activities built both on specialized knowledge and capital resources that allowed a potentially greater return.

Nonagricultural activities were essential to increase income and spread risk. Possibilities for these activities increased in zones with balanced economic growth but were less where growth was either unbalanced or nonexistent. In the rural areas, expanding agriculture or stable rural employment could provide the motor for growth. Yet people needed resources to invest to get the most out of nonagricultural activities. Although capital was the most obvious one, people also invested in specialized knowledge, the access to bush resources that came from being an autochthone, and social networks.

Conclusion

For Malians, rural and semiurban production strategies virtually always included a variety of pursuits, usually combining agriculture, livestock, and nonfarm activities. The ability to enter these activities depended on access to resources, including knowledge, capital, and natural resources, such as pastureland or bush.

In turn, access to resources depended on the larger economic and ecological context. Economically dynamic zones offered more opportunities for commercial and artisanal activities, yet the growing populations associated with them also meant that land-based resources such as pasture and bush could decline. Access to national infrastructure such as roads, transport, rural-development operations, and markets also constrained some possibilities and enlarged others. The balanced development of a number of sectors at one time appeared to lead to multiplier effects, while booms only in one sector could lead to unbalanced growth. In that case, parts of the population usually found making a living extremely precarious.

Balanced economic growth appeared simultaneously to lead to greater potential for all economic sectors: farming, stockraising, and nonagricultural activities. Capital could substitute for natural resources in stockraising, and growing consumer affluence provided income possibilities for those making needed consumer goods and providing important rural services. Data from Dioïla show a sample with growing economic differentiation, but also with broad-based access to resources. Although the difference between top and bottom may have been greater there, more people had wealth: incomes, livestock, and equipment.

In all sites, distinctions between indigenous populations and migrants affected access to resources. New migrants usually had less access to the natural resources of the zone than did the indigenous population, which had prior recognized claims. While long-term residents were more likely to turn to exploitation of bush resources and livestock, new migrants were more likely to make use of commercial and wage options generated by small urban centers to meet cash needs. Long-term residents were also more able to use social networks to create collective income-generating activities than were new migrants.

To be sure, our samples, with their focus on intact households, were biased toward people who had been able to create somewhat sustainable economic strategies. Individual migrants who had not been able to maintain at least minimal subsistence would likely have moved on. In this sense, our sample shows optimal potential rather than failed possibilities.

Yet within the constraints posed, many individuals responded creatively to opportunities. People showed little evidence of being "bound by tradition" as they responded to opportunities and began new activities. In Manantali, those who did not resettle began to grow vegetables and other foods for the workers; relocatees worked for the PRM and its contractors to clear land and build roofs. Everyone who could tried to find a job with a construction enterprise. In Dioïla, people began to rent out agricultural equipment, and in Yanfolila, women used agricultural work groups to generate income. As the Malian urban middle class grew, more rural girls began to enter domestic service.

Alongside the changes open to relatively large groups, individuals looked for particular niches to exploit, based on specialized knowledge and talents. The Soninke women had their electric sewing machines and food processors. The tractor owner rented it out. A few in Finkolo began to raise sheep. And in each site, there were a few tailors, a few masons, a few blacksmiths, each responding to specific needs and opportunities. We need more information about how people discover these niches and learn the skills to exploit them. The balanced growth of a variety of nonagricultural occupations appeared to be more sustainable than the large-scale entry of many people into a single occupation and should be a long-term goal of development initiatives.

In the concluding chapter, we will look directly at the interaction of the various components of the rural household economy and the ways in which human agency interacted with structural constraints. Before doing so, we turn in the next chapter to negotiation, a process used to lessen the effects of structural constraints and increase the scope for individual choice.

## Chapter 7

# *Negotiating New Relationships*

People approached problems with their cultural frameworks as a rough guide for action, and within a context of political and economic inequality. Yet neither context was determinative. As new neighbors dealt with one another and interacted with government representatives, individuals and groups endeavored to create representations of rules and events that favored their future action. In the two previous chapters, we looked at the interplay of larger constraints and individual initiative in the choices that people made in regard to economic strategies. Here we turn to the negotiated interactions among the different parties. While Malians of all regions and classes renegotiated social relationships, this process appeared to be more consciously pursued in situations like those of our study where people had self-consciously to forge relationships with new neighbors.

Social and cultural negotiations occurred at many levels, within households and outside of them, between more or less equal partners, and between those of unequal power. The results were constrained by larger contexts and structures but also depended to a significant degree upon the resources and knowledge available to those involved. Resolutions of similar problems in similar ways sometimes led to social or cultural changes, since many Malians were presented with comparable economic constraints and opportunities. Although most claimed to value their traditions, Malians also recognized the substantial changes that their society had undergone in recent years and pressed for new ones.

In the field, we saw negotiations in full swing, yet because the data were gathered over a short period, we were rarely able to follow the entire process. In some cases, we never learned how ongoing negotiation was resolved. The Manantali case becomes particularly important because the series of field visits allowed us to see both negotiation and results. Because we saw so much negotiation in process at the different sites, however, some of the social patterns we found, especially those counter to cultural ideals, seem best interpreted as the outcome of prior negotiation. This chapter focuses on three arenas of negotiation: within the household; between neighbors, both between new settlers and old residents, and among new settlers; and among locals, government agencies, and local elites.

## Domestic Negotiations

The literature on Africa is full of discussions about the relationships of different household members, particularly those between male household heads and women, and between household heads and dependent men. A significant part of the literature on household heads and dependent men has focused on the ways that this relationship has been renegotiated over the years as young men began to earn their own incomes (Meillassoux 1981; chap. 2 here). These negotiations have often led to changing power relationships, family structures, and cultural ideals. The literature on the relationships between men and women has been in stark contrast. Little attention has been given to the negotiating process, and it has more commonly been argued that women lost resources and power as a result of changing economic contexts and negotiations with the men in their lives (Moore 1988). Instead of a seeing range of diverse effects, many have argued that the effects of economic change have been almost universally bad for women (Gladwin 1991a; B. Rogers 1980). Although the patriarchy of both African and European colonial societies led to greater opportunities for subordinate men than women, there has almost surely been more negotiation between men and women than has been recognized in the literature. Moreover, the social consequences of economic change have not been universally to women's detriment. In light of this history, and because we have more data on the relationship between men and women anyway, our discussion highlights that relationship.

### Negotiations between Husbands and Wives

Mariam Traoré, the wife of deposed president Moussa Traoré, used a rural idiom to justify her large commercial farms and extensive business holdings. She claimed to be like any wife with fields and businesses to support her children. Her family depended on her contribution since her husband had other, more public, needs to serve. Although many realized that this statement was a political ploy, the theme nevertheless resonated with Malians, men and women, rural and urban, most of whom believed that both men and women had a duty to contribute to their children and the upkeep of their households. In farm households, this was commonly expressed through an ideal cultural division of labor. Household heads were to use the produce of the collective fields to provide household grain and cash necessities. Women, in turn, had individual fields to provide family sauce ingredients and other necessities for themselves and their children. Adults kept separate budgets, which they used to meet these responsibilities.

However, as people moved to the cities, this ideal came under pressure. Men were more likely to find formal-sector or commercialized informal-sector jobs, and many women grew economically dependent on their husbands. Although many urban women earned some income, they often did not earn enough to meet their responsibilities.[1] So husbands began to give their wives "sauce money" (*prix de condiments* in French, *nasongo* in Bambara). As in many parts of Africa (Moore 1988, 56), this was envisioned as an economic transaction between men and women, as each continued to keep an individual budget and meet gender-linked responsibilities to family upkeep. Both rural and urban Malians recognized these two alternatives as two ideal ways to meet family responsibilities, a difference between rural and city dwellers that came about because of the different constellations of economic resources offered by cities and villages. People did not evaluate either the urban or rural option as morally superior and rarely did they attribute the choice of one to differences in education, social class, Westernization, or modernization. In fact, people expected that men and women might well change the specific ways in which they made their familial contributions when the configuration of economic opportunities changed. The cultural value with moral force was that each adult make some contribution.

As economic circumstances changed, the resulting male-female division of labor could entail a degradation of women's status: less autonomy, less income, and more work. Yet more common were contradictory effects. Women might trade off some autonomy to work less when male production systems became more remunerative. Moreover, women could move out of agriculture into artisanal or entrepreneurial activities if these were more remunerative and if the men's agricultural activities produced sufficient food for the family. Although women were responsible for providing sauce ingredients, they could gather, cultivate, and/or purchase them, depending on what made most economic sense. Although many Malian households used wild foods (Warshall 1989), rural women were often quite content to cultivate or purchase a more restricted, yet still adequate, range of sauce ingredients because it usually entailed less work.

As the larger economic context changed, couples appeared to enter into negotiations about the distribution of work, income, and budgetary responsibilities. These were rarely formalized but were expressed in a variety of culturally accepted statements and behaviors. Choices about remunerative work, and hence relationships between men and women, evolved somewhat differently in each of the sites because of the different economic contexts. But even within sites, men and women came with varying cultural ideals and resources, creating variation among households. On the whole, our data allowed us to see general trends at each site better than variation within sites.

In Dioïla, the general agricultural success affected the division of labor between men and women. Women contributed a substantial amount of work to collective fields and were not as likely to have their own fields as in some other sites. However, they had less need to farm grains on individual fields to meet the deficit of collective grain production, since the collective fields produced enough. If they had fields, they could emphasize sauce ingredients and cash crop production. The data suggest moreover that farming sauce ingredients became a choice; while women still needed to provide these, they had the option of growing them or entering another income-earning activity and buying them. Some Dioïla women appear to have followed each option. Some continued to have fields, but women also showed more income from food processing than at other sites. Increased household resources bought by the head for collective fields were used by women to lessen workloads as well. Some used carts bought by their husbands to transport wood, and virtually all who had fields used their household's agricultural equipment on them. Although, as others have noted (McMillan 1986), women did appear to lose some independence by working more on husband's fields, greater household resources also appear to have decreased their workloads while the increased regional resources opened new income-earning options. How women chose and families encouraged certain among the different options was not clear, but this likely depended upon their personal knowledge and skills and family constraints.[2]

In the other sites, economic growth was not sufficient to increase the range of options for a broad base of women. In two, Manantali and Tienfala, women worked hard to preserve their "traditional" role in agriculture as the best way to meet their family responsibilities and appear to have been supported by other household members. Involuntary resettlement often has had a negative impact on women's access to remunerative resources (Koenig 1995; B. Rogers 1980), and indeed at Manantali, women lost bush areas for gathering when they moved. However, they did receive farmland and tried to use agriculture to compensate for this loss. Since land was allotted to mostly male household heads who were in turn responsible for dividing it among all household members, women's farmland clearly was a priority for all, not just the women themselves. Information from the 1993–94 study made it clear that household heads realized that they were incapable of directly supplying all the household's needs and felt they had no choice but to make sure that women had access to fields. In turn, women were rarely expected to work on collective fields.

A few households tried different strategies. One well-off household head, a rather authoritarian man, decreed that there would be no individual fields for the first several years after resettlement, and all, men and women, would work on the collective fields. The household prospered and was able to put aside significant grain stocks. In fact, however, women did continue to have vegetable gardens and rice fields and worked less on the collective fields than did men. In return for their work on collective fields, the head provided peanuts and other sauce ingredients to each cook, reducing the quantity women needed to provide themselves. Yet once production was established, the head began to decentralize production, allowing both women and men to have individual fields.

In Tienfala, while some women did nonagricultural work for pay when recently settled, women in the households of established settlers were more likely to work in agriculture. Migrant women also joined collective agricultural work groups to earn cash; they were not excluded from these as in Yanfolila. They continued their "traditional" way of meeting family responsibilities, while men were more likely to pursue cash-earning or artisanal activities that depended on the Bamako market. We do not have any data on how the division of labor may have affected internal family dynamics.

In both these sites, the decision of women in migrant households to meet their family obligations through the "traditional" means of cultivating individual fields appears not to have been simply a resumption of they way things were done before migration, but a conscious choice. In Manantali, in fact, women perceived a change from a mix of gathering and farming toward more farming, an improvement in their minds since they found gathering dirty and hard work. In Tienfala, agriculture appeared to be a valued choice that not all women could achieve. Lacking sufficient data about internal family dynamics and a rigorous study of comparative returns from different jobs, we nevertheless think it likely that in these sites, women's decisions to meet their responsibilities through agriculture were the result of negotiations about the best ways multiple family members could meet economic responsibilities and fulfill social obligations.

Finkolo saw the greatest reallocation of family responsibilities. When many family members worked on the tea plantation, both wives and sons gave their earnings to the head. Heads in turn gave back to their wives money to buy food, clothes, and other household needs, as well as to complement the money a girl earned for her trousseau. This was the closest that households in any site came to a pooled budget, yet men and women each kept control of a certain part of the income and were responsible for meeting certain needs. Finkolo also had the most centralized agriculture, with only collective fields. Since fields and the time devoted to farming were small, both men and women found the idea of individual fields ridiculous.

This division of labor likely did give women less autonomy than when they had exclusive control of the money they earned. However, their complaints were not about how husbands used money, but about the difficulties of the household in getting access to more resources, both natural and national. Women especially wanted more access to national resources, such as schools, to improve the lives of their children. Some also wanted independence from the demands of wage work, for which they would need more land, rather than from the demands of their husbands. They blamed the land shortage on the external situation, not on the allocation of fields within their own families.

In these groups, women retained some ability to make independent household contributions, hence some autonomy over household expenditures. The results suggest that choices about which activities men and women ought to undertake were not guided only by cultural ideals and intrahousehold negotiation but also by the larger regional configuration of economic opportunity and constraint. Both sexes were willing and able to enter new activities when they had the potential to improve the lives of household members. The ability of certain members to benefit from new possibilities could lead to changes in the internal division of labor, and as long as the family was being supported to their satisfaction, women appeared to accept, and even to welcome, these changes. In most cases, women judged alternatives by whether changes sustained or improved family living conditions.

This becomes clearer when we look at the migrant households of Yanfolila and Selingue, where women generally believed that they had few options and were frustrated by their own inability to generate income. This was especially problematic when other household members were not able to earn adequately either. Some migrant women turned to extremely low investment, low return activities such as cutting wood for sale. The Dogon women of both Selingue and Yanfolila expressed some of the strongest desires for income-generating projects, so that they could better meet their household responsibilities.

Frustration and potential conflict between the sexes was particularly strong among the Soninke at Yanfolila. Women could not farm, since the migrants were living in Yanfolila town until houses were built. The men commuted each day to their fields, working on house construction when farmwork was done. Some women wanted to move out to the village since they would then be able to cultivate their own fields. Others, however, were very skeptical about the move. The years they had spent in France had led them to consider new possibilities, that is, the motorized machines that they planned to use to generate income once Yanfolila was electrified. In the village, there would be neither power source nor clientele. They also had higher expectations for their children than many village women. They wanted them to attend school and also wanted good access to health centers, more difficult in the village than in town. Virtually all the men claimed that when the group was ready to move to the village, the women had no choice but to follow their husbands, but women were less sure. The problem had not been resolved when we left the field, but it was clear that negotiations were taking place. Whether the women used their resistance to get better conditions in the village, or whether a few of them remained in Yanfolila we do not know, but these would be among the more likely resolutions. Clearly, the tension was exacerbated by the failure of many of the economic activities. CAMUKO's agricultural production was very low, while Yanfolila was not yet electrified and women's machines just sat there without earning money.

The only group of women totally dependent on their husbands were the Wahabiyya Dogon, and we were not able to interview them directly about their concerns. While in Saudi Arabia, some had joined this sect, which secluded their women. Their husbands were required to support them and their families completely, an ideal not shared by most urban or rural Malian women.[3] Women did not work on the fields, and their husbands collected wood for them, although women did gather some wild foods. They did not appear to have begun household-based income-earning activities, as have secluded women in Nigeria (A. Cohen 1969, 64–66). Given the difficulties faced by their men in rice production, it is hardly likely that women faced economic constraints serenely, but we were unable to gather information about allocation of familial responsibilities in these households.

This study was not designed to track intrafamily negotiation of roles and responsibilities in light of larger economic changes, yet the data suggest that this occurred. While men and women did have some divergent interests, they also lived together and, in so doing, had overlapping interests as well. In light of new options and pressure on old ones, people innovated socially as well as economically, as they worked to find ways that could satisfy individual needs for autonomy and social status as well as shared needs to create sustainable household earning strategies.

In general, more options were open to men than to women. Agriculture remained one of the prime activities for rural Malian women, in large part because it gave them better returns than many other options (Luery 1989). Yet women were not tied to it. They were willing and able to enter other income-earning activities when men were able to provide enough food and when more remunerative options were available. They felt most limited when they had access to neither "traditional" resources nor new ones, and when the men in their lives were not able to earn enough.

*Elders and Juniors*

The relationship between household heads and dependent men was less important in our samples because most households did not contain adult men other than the household head. In fact, a certain percentage of migrant households were likely created by dependent men who had decided, with their families or alone, that they preferred forming an independent economic unit rather than remaining in the household of their own family head. Where there were elders and juniors, however, they continued to negotiate.

Manantali showed the greatest number of dependent men living with senior household heads. There, negotiations between elders and juniors were catalyzed by the fact that most of the new resources generated during the resettlement came from the activities of young men. They cleared the new field and village sites, had the few dam construction jobs held by locals, and served on the liaison committees established by the PRM. These five-man committees, charged with project-village communication, demanded extensive travel between new and old sites, so younger, stronger men were generally chosen by the elders. Although they were not empowered to make decisions, they gained a power base through their access to information and their privileged status as interlocutors with the PRM.

To keep control, household heads demanded that young men turn over earnings to them. Bridewealth payments increased throughout the period as a way for elders to control funds, a common phenomenon in African resettlement projects (Scudder, personal communication). Young men contested this control, and some families split, dividing the PRM land allocation, the WFP food allotment, or both. Near the end of the project, the youth organized through the political party to bring about a decrease in the size of bridewealth payments. Nevertheless, much power remained in the hands of heads. After all, young men who might have migrated elsewhere before the dam construction were living at home and earning in Manantali, where elders had a better idea how much they earned and how they might spend it. Elders were willing to use much of the compensation money they received to pay bridewealth for their sons, which influenced many of the latter to remain in the extended household. Certain PRM activities also increased the power of the heads. Between the first and second seasons, the PRM changed from an hourly to a task rate for land clearing accompanied by a change in payment modality. Instead of the PRM paying individuals directly by the project, village chiefs were given funds to pay those who worked, reinforcing the power of the elders.[4] So while some households experimented with new opportunities that emerged after the dam construction, they mostly did so in the form of the large extended family, where the household head retained a significant degree of power (T. Diarra et al. 1995).

In general, people appear to have approached social organization, including all sorts of social relationships, as a resource to be used to profit from existing situations (cf. Moore 1988, 124). Although the indigenous Tienfala residents usually disliked working on large plantations because of their low wages, some youth did so expressly to learn arboriculture. Once they learned about new varieties, techniques such as propagation by cuttings or grafting, and new technology such as motorized pumps, they returned home to start their own tree farms, even creating a cooperative of tree and vegetable gardeners at Tienfala-gare. At Selingue, migrant families split expressly to qualify for multiple parcels of land on the irrigated perimeter. The most self-conscious innovation was the creation of the two Soninke cooperatives, where each member had an equal share of the produce and a voice in major decisions. The membership held formal meetings on a regular basis where they discussed and decided on major issues. This was done in the hope that they could improve production in a way that they could not on individual family farms.

Except in the case of radical innovations like the Soninke cooperative or the adoption of Wahabiyya Islam, Malian villagers did tend to talk about household structures as if they were relatively homogeneous and unchanging. This did not mean, however, that the degree of behavioral diversity was low. Our data clearly indicated that intrahousehold structures were not as homogeneous as the household ideology would indicate. The diversity seems most readily understood as a function of negotiation and choice among household members. The next step is to design studies around the hypothesis of intrahousehold negotiation. These should lead us to a more sophisticated understanding of how the relationships between elders and juniors and between men and women have changed, as well as generating better ideas about how to raise the standard of living for all household members.

Negotiating with Neighbors

When migrants came into a new area, they had to create relationships with the people already living there. Cultural traditions provided guidelines about how to go about this, but these generally maintained a hierarchy where the earliest

residents were considered privileged compared to later ones, with the latter de-
pendents of the former (Kopytoff 1987). Many migrants appeared unwilling to
accept this valuation and the subsequent constraints on their actions uncritically, leading to much negotiation. In general, migrants negotiated to increase
their autonomy, but varying conditions led to diverse alliances and coalitions.

*Negotiating with Hosts*

Where resources were perceived as relatively abundant, and where hosts felt in
control of the settlement process, there was relatively little conflict between
hosts and settlers. Only in Dioïla did hosts perceive both conditions. Government and national elites had least involvement in the settlement process, and
migrants and indigenous residents appeared to respect "traditional norms" of
firstcomerness and latecomerness with one another. Yet settlers, with their own
hamlets, had considerable autonomy in the way they led their daily lives, and
the first migrants and their families gained the power that came from being first
in the hamlets. Not much obvious negotiation occurred since both economic resources and social roles were adequately allocated by existing norms.

In the other sites, there was perceptible competition over resources between hosts and migrants, a necessary although not sufficient condition for conflict. Hosts and migrants showed various patterns of conflict and cooperation.
The most important factor appeared to be the degree of control that hosts felt
they could exert over guests. This was affected as well by preexisting social and
cultural linkages, and the extent to which alliances between host and guests
might permit access to new resources unavailable to hosts otherwise.

In Manantali, a situation of involuntary resettlement, hosts had perhaps the
least control. Even though the PRM made an effort to gain hosts' cooperation,
the mere existence of a government agency took ultimate control away. Moreover, the relocatees were not willing to grant hosts privileged status in this situation, and the PRM helped engineer ceremonies that gave relocatee villages
equal status to hosts. Hence hosts were faced with a loss of control over their
land, over new settlers, and increased competition over resources as villages
moved closer to one another. Conflicts increased, and village-level dispute-set-
tlement procedures were often inadequate to solve problems. Villagers on both
sides called upon government agents to intervene, as we will discuss in the following section.

Nevertheless, close cultural and social linkages between hosts and settlers mitigated conflict. They had had previous relationships with one another
through marriage, and some of the relocatees had previously cultivated seasonal

hamlets in the resettlement areas. Hosts had formally accepted relocation based upon these linkages. Some aspects of the relationships between hosts and relocatees remained amicable. The inhabitants of one relocated village helped its host neighbor by lending it grain after the latter's fields were flooded in very heavy rains right after the resettlement. Individuals from host and resettlement villages continued to intermarry regularly.

In contrast, at Yanfolila, hosts felt little control, and there were important cultural differences between northern Dogon migrants and cosmopolitan Soninke on the one hand and the southern Wassulunke on the other. This site had the most overt conflict between settlers and migrants, even though natural resources were abundant. The large numbers of migrants who arrived at one time probably did affect localized access to resources, but the most important issue appeared to be control. Because of government and political-party involvement, the villages appeared to believe they could not refuse to help drought victims.

Once the Dogon arrived, village chiefs were anxious to assert their authority over them, as well as toward the government and NGO representatives. Some of them considered the donkeys and carts brought by the CECI project to be their own property (Dandenault 1987, 13), and, as noted in chapter 5, the draft oxen and plows in Gwalafara were confiscated by the chief. Host villagers wanted access to all aspects of the project, even if they did not use them. For example, in one village, the Dogon alone cleared a collective garden area, but then indigenous villagers took half of it and planted only a third of their half (Dandenault 1987, 7, 9).

One way Dogon and Wassulunke expressed their conflict was by invidious comparisons between their own use of the environment and that of the other group. The Dogon, who had migrated from some of the most densely populated zones of Mali, relied heavily on intensive agriculture and gardening. They had changed some of their agricultural practices (e.g., tools, the number of weedings of a single parcel) in light of new environmental conditions, but they still worked very hard and put most of their effort in agriculture. They complained about the "laziness" of the locals (Dandenault 1987, 8), who made more extensive use of their environment, because of their privileged access to pasture and bush resources. In turn, locals complained to the Forestry Service that the Dogon exploited forest resources unsustainably, although the local forestry representative claimed to see no difference in activities of locals and migrants. Successful migrants claimed that the indigenous population was "jealous" of them because they worked harder and produced more.

The competition erupted in conflict, the most spectacular case being the eviction of one of the most dynamic Dogon farmers from his rice field in Gwala-fara just prior to the study team's arrival. The situation here was among the most conflictual because of the village's long-term grievances against the Selingue dam and its flooding. It had viewed accepting migrants as a chance to get additional resources through the NGO programs, but the Dogon agricultural success only showed a kind of superiority and exacerbated problems with their hosts (Dandenault 1987). Moreover, the Dogon turned away from the village to solve those problems. To fight the eviction, they called upon the local Dogon association based in Yanfolila town to help them. Its members included literate retired civil servants with sufficient knowledge of the law to help them bring a favorable interpretation of Malian land law (GRM 1987) to the local authorities. Because the administration was involved, this case will be discussed in the next section. However, this strategy was a clear indication to the Gwalafara indigenous leadership that the migrants lacked respect for them.

Relationships between hosts and migrants were hindered rather than helped by the involvement of local government and NGOs, who simply ignored the political dimensions of settlement. Local elites believed that the policy of settling Dogon within existing villages would hasten assimilation. Yet this strategy only made more visible the differences between hosts and migrants, as each group had daily contact with the other. Moreover, the NGO planned a number of activities (gardening and cart, donkey, and draft oxen ownership) as community-wide collective interventions, involving both hosts and migrants. None of these worked because each group was jealous of the other's control and access to new resources. For example, even though the Wassulunke had alternatives to gardening, they did not want to let the Dogon monopolize the benefits of the new resources brought by them.

The future resolution of the conflicts between hosts and migrants at Yanfolila was far from clear in 1989, but clearly it had been a mistake for outsiders to force the two groups to work together, giving each little autonomy. Local norms would suggest that a large group of settlers be given their own hamlet, on village lands to be sure, but at some distance from the core settlement. Even though migrants would have to recognize the privileged position of the mother village, they could develop their own practices as they saw fit, as had the residents of the Dioïla hamlets. The CECI evaluation noted that many of their development efforts would have worked better with a more homogeneous population (Hazel and Dandenault 1989). Since conflict does appear to decrease when hosts as well as new settlers benefit from development projects (Scudder 1991), a better strategy might have been to start parallel initiatives among Wassulunke and Dogon.

There were also problems between the village of Wuru Wuru and the CAMUKO cooperative, again because the land transfer was outside of the mother village's control. However, there was less overt conflict, as CAMUKO had its own parcel at some distance from the mother village; its members also planned to live there. Potential for future conflict came from different perceptions held by villagers and cooperative members of cooperative land rights. Villagers maintained that the cooperative had only been given use rights like those given to any other outside group, while CAMUKO claimed that they had permanent ownership rights. Conflict remained potential, perhaps because the indigenous villagers did not at that time need the land on which the cooperative had settled. Nonetheless, many locals claimed that future conflict was likely. Since CAMUKO's attempts to involve villagers in its activities had been fruitless, no ongoing mutually beneficial relationships had yet been established between the two that could serve to mitigate potential conflict.

The importance of local control in amicable relations between hosts and migrants is underlined by the experiences at Selingue and Finkolo, where there was greater resource pressure, but less overt conflict. In Finkolo, locals perceived land to be in short supply but controlled migrant access. When they lent land to plantation workers, they impressed upon them the extreme tenuousness of their tenure. Most workers accepted this constraint, since they did not plan to remain in Finkolo over the long term but instead planned to return to the area from which they had emigrated at their retirement. Should they wish to remain at Finkolo, the difficulties in getting sufficient land for a large farm surely would have made this problematic. Presumably, they would have been accorded land only if they clearly recognized local dominance.

In Selingue, the land situation had become so problematic that locals became reluctant to cede land to migrants. Unlike Yanfolila, national authorities did not aid individual migrants to get rainfed fields, since they envisioned them primarily as farmers on the irrigated perimeter. Whether this was a conscious strategy to encourage more effort on rice cultivation, an attempt to dampen conflict between the indigenous population and migrants, or done for other reasons, we do not know. Nevertheless, this hands-off policy meant that the autochthonous population retained more control over the use by migrants of indigenous resources. Since they saw little benefit to collaborating with the Dogon migrants, they mostly refused to lend them land. Conflict over rainfed fields did not develop because migrants had almost none.

In contrast, the authorities did intervene by "encouraging" the village of Selinkenyi to let CAMSEL create a large farm on a part of its pasture. This process did not augur well for the relationship between the two, but their experience shows how locals tried to turn a situation disadvantageous on its face to their benefit. Given that no ODR worked with rainfed agriculture in the zone, village farmers had minimal access to new agricultural technologies and inputs. CAMSEL, in contrast, brought those with them. When CAMSEL opened its membership to locals in 1988, several Selinkenyi residents decided to participate. Among our sample, autochthones who joined CAMSEL in 1988 had had lower production on their own fields in 1987 than those who did not, 153 kg/ person of grain in contrast to 239 kg/person among nonparticipants. Yet in 1988, CAMSEL participants increased their production 34 percent, to 205 kg/ person/year. By increasing production possibilities in a resource-stressed environment, CAMSEL membership offered a beneficial alternative to some indigenous villagers and helped mitigate potential conflict between the two groups.

The ability of locals to use migrants as a resource to achieve one of their goals was even more vividly illustrated at Tienfala, where the continued loan of land to immigrants under more or less "traditional" procedures was a strategy to keep land control in local hands, resisting permanent alienation to urban and commercial elites. Since many Tienfala residents themselves were emigrating, their lands risked falling vacant, vulnerable to being taken out of their control, unless they were used by someone. So locals lent them to other relatively poor, uneducated migrants like themselves, who would accept the hierarchical relationship and ultimate control of land by local landowners. At some point, pressure from the growing Bamako population for both housing and farms was likely to lead to permanent alienation, a process that has occurred again and again in Bamako's peripheral suburbs (Konate 1994), but collaboration between hosts and migrants delayed it. Migrants got land they needed while locals continued to enjoy ownership rights.

These experiences show that relationships between hosts and migrants were affected not only by short-term competition over land resources, but also by long-term competition for political control. Local landowners were willing to lend land even when resources were tight when they were fairly sure that they retained ultimate control but hesitated to grant even minimal amounts when it meant ceding control. When land transactions remained between migrant and host, control mostly did remain in local hands, but when national elites or state organizations became involved, locals could quickly lose. They mostly had no choice but to lend or cede land to migrants. In this situation, land conflicts multiplied unless locals could get some pragmatic benefits from their lost land. The latter case was rare, however, found only in the case of the CAMSEL cooperative. Although the actions of central authorities seemed to favor migrants more than hosts, either could turn to them to help resolve conflicts, a process to which we will return in the final section of the chapter.

*Relationships among Migrants*

New migrants were neighbors to one another as well. They decided who would be accepted in their new communities and under what rules. Although people worked with similar cultural frameworks, community structures could not usually be created according to a single cultural ideal. Even where they might have been, individuals could take advantage of new conditions to renegotiate relationships and create communities more to their liking. Our data showed cases where some people had consciously done this.

In Manantali, the explicit policy of the PRM was to move villages as units, and to duplicate existing village maps in the new sites with a few "improvements,"[5] preserving existing political relationships. Most villages, which did see themselves as communities, moved as units, but others took advantage of the move to create new configurations. Most common was to split, often after years of intravillage conflict over access to resources and power. One of the largest and most politically prominent villages split into three, along lines that Fortes (1953) could have predicted, first between two sets of cousins (the sons of two brothers), and then again, between two of the brothers (Grimm 1991). This was nevertheless expressed in claims about the place of the village in the contemporary world and fought out in both "traditional" and "modern" arenas, including Malian courts. Other villages split into an official village downstream from the dam and an unofficial upstream fraction. Two villages, which had been neighbors in the old site and had peacefully shared a large low-lying area of mango trees, took advantage of the resettlement to move, acrimoniously and loudly, far away from one another. There were also a number of individual families that simply picked up and moved to other villages where they felt more welcome.

In contrast to the splits, one resettlement village, Diokely, was a conglomeration of hamlets that decided to create a new village together. Diokely became one of the most dynamic of the resettlement villages, expressed by its establishment of a new market, which, by 1994, was the most active in the zone. This decision and its successful results appeared to upset some of the hamlets' mother villages, who were losing some of their political prominence to it.

Dioïla, where residents created new villages from scratch, with people from many different areas, had the possibility of consciously creating desired communities. The three villages looked very different. Kolobugu's compounds stretched out in a long line with fields surrounding the settlement area in a single oval crown. Fofoni Dogolen had a dispersed settlement pattern where houses, each surrounded by its own fields, were separated by up to 200 meters. Miankabugu was a nucleated village, with all compounds grouped around a central public plaza, with fields around the village. The residential focus around a central plaza in Miankabugu reflected a choice to become a community rather than a congeries of individuals as in the other two villages.

Kolobugu and Fofoni continued to grow over the years, and, with time, the differences between firstcomers and latecomers grew. The half who had been settled longer had larger families (11 persons vs. 5.2 for new arrivals), higher cotton production, and greater ability to generate cash. The tractor was purchased by the original settler of one of the two halves of Kolobugu, who also owned much other equipment, a large herd, and the only modern house. There appears to have been little sense of common identity and interest among the inhabitants of these two villages.

This was in contrast to Miankabugu, which chose to create something like a "traditional Mianka village," despite the fact that only a few village residents were ethnic Mianka. To avoid the need to clear new fields outside the crown of original fields, Miankabugu decided to keep itself small, allowing only eight households to settle. New settlement stopped only 10 years after the first settler arrived. This led to much less differentiation between early and later settlers, and a greater sense of egalitarianism within the community. Not a single Miankabugu resident lacked equipment, although three in Fofoni and two in Kolobugu had none. The relative size of herds and production levels was also more equitable. Yet average wealth was higher in Miankabugu than in the other villages. Excluding one Kolobugu herd with over 100 head, the value of household animal holdings averaged 148,544 FCFA (U.S.$450) in Miankabugu but only 44,964 FCFA (U.S.$136) in Fofoni and 95,467 FCFA (U.S.$289) in Kolobugu. Not including the tractor, the value of equipment per household varied from an average 114,425 FCFA (U.S.$347) in Miankabugu to 55,710 FCFA (U.S.$169) in Kolobugu and to 44,000 FCFA (U.S.$133) in Fofoni.

Other sites also showed that people had made choices about new village structures. When the two new Finkolo villages were created, people made religious affiliation an important criterion for settlement. The two Soninke cooperatives were notable for attempting an innovative form of production organization. These distinctive arrangements illustrated that people made diverse decisions about social arrangements as well as production. Unlike some production choices, which depended on individual or household decisions, village configurations needed the agreement of a substantial proportion of individuals and households. Hence we would argue that inhabitants made relatively conscious choices about the kinds of living arrangements they wanted and negotiated with one another to bring them about. People did not talk spontaneously about this process of community-level negotiation, except for the Soninke who saw themselves as self-conscious innovators, educated cosmopolitan people bringing new ideas to ordinary farmers. Nevertheless, it appeared that people did enter community-level negotiations relatively consciously. Since the creation of new village units was relatively rare, people need to be more conscious of the choices they made, even when they used existing models of cultural practice.

Coping with Outside Organizations

Individuals made choices in a context where the actions of government organizations and elites favored some choices over others. Yet the often conflicting interests of donors, national government, and other elites meant that locals had a space to exploit their own interests. Locals used that space to ignore directives from above, as well as to pursue negotiations among themselves, local elites, and government representatives. There were at least three distinct interaction strategies between national organizations and local populations. When locals found the options offered by outside organizations to their benefit, they simply followed government policies, more or less along suggested lines. Second, local individuals and organizations tried to involve regional or national groups or resources in their conflicts with others, as a way to increase their leverage. Third, locals attempted to turn the activities of large-scale organizations to their own ends, either by negotiating with or resisting these entities. In all cases, the results could turn out in a variety of ways. Locals believed themselves successful often enough that they continued a wide range of strategies.

*Collaboration with National Policies*

People usually approached national initiatives with skepticism, anticipating that the agencies' own interests would be primary. However, they did not automatically resist national initiatives, since they also had enough experience with them to know that local and national interests overlapped often enough that they could get some local benefit. While they rarely took the words of elites at face value, they were nonetheless ready to make use of national or regional institutions that they thought responded to their needs. The major rural institutions that people thought brought some benefits were the ODRs, and they participated often in their programs.

The activities of the CMDT and the possibilities for cotton cultivation and sales drew migrants to Dioïla. Most migrants made substantial use of CMDT programs, facilitated by the presence of an agent in Kolobugu. In Manantali, farmers used ODIPAC for credit and to facilitate peanut sales when they could; many formed AVs when ODIPAC began that activity. Even in sites where ODRs were less active, people made use of them. In Yanfolila, Dogon migrants were beginning to participate in CMDT initiatives, and the Soninke cooperative, realizing that it had much to learn about farming under local conditions, lent a part of its land to the CMDT for an experimental field. The ODRs were such a valued part of the local scene that farmers who had no access felt they were cut off from prized governmental services. Farmers in Selingue, lacking a rainfed extension service, had written to both the CMDT (to their south) and the OHV (to the north) to ask that they be integrated. The part-time farmers of Finkolo felt that they were discriminated against because the CMDT concentrated its activities with full-time agriculturalists. Most farmers complained bitterly when structural-adjustment policies caused ODRs to cut back on their activities. Although some farmers were better served than others, most rural people preferred some ODR programs to none at all.

People perceived other national initiatives to be in their interest and participated in them as well. The AVs in Fugadougou and other Tienfala villages were part of a program started by the Centre d'Action Cooperative to strengthen local cooperative structures. Tienfala also had entered a sister relationship (*jumelage*) with a French NGO, as had a group of Manantali villages with a French town. These relationships provided funding to small village projects; for example, residents of one Manantali village had built a maize mill and bought several sets of agricultural equipment. In Yanfolila, some enterprising Dogon took advantage of a program offered by the Forestry Service to build improved beehives. Other immigrants moved to town because they could get legal house plots there. People saw the possibilities of having a deed, even if only to a house plot, as a real advantage.

People had few hesitations about their involvement in what they perceived as beneficial aspects of national programs. To ensure continued access to these benefits, they developed personal as well as professional relationships with field representatives. Educated migrants, like the Soninke and some of the Dogon, were able to talk to local representatives as equals, surely providing them greater access. Others simply bribed them. In Dioïla, some people regularly gave gifts, usually in kind, to the local extension agent, often reporting this quite straightforwardly in the price that they paid for their inputs. But access was not limited to local elites, and the benefits of many programs were relatively widespread. Since many government representatives lived in villages, in conditions much like those of villagers, continual give-and-take occurred. Agents did not simply bring state programs and ideas to rural areas but were influenced by rural residents in turn. Nonetheless, while people expected that some national activities would be in their interest, they never expected that they would be exclusively so. So, local people also attempted to benefit by turning programs toward their own ends.

*Local Co-optation of National Programs*

People realized that national elites and institutions could be used not only for their stated purposes but also to pursue other ends. They could sign on for programs and then use what they got from them for their own goals, rather than official uses. They could sometimes use entire institutions to pursue new locally defined ends. One group of locals could use national programs and resources in their dispute with another group.

Using pieces of programs for their own purposes rather than stated ones was very common. One example, found all over Africa, was taking credit from an organization for a specific purpose and then using it for something else. An analogous example was found at Manantali, in regard to the WFP food allotments. While most people ate the food right after the resettlement, many had established their own fields by the end of the two-year distribution period and were successfully growing preferred foods. Against WFP regulations, much of the food found its way into local markets, providing extra income to the sellers. Since the food distribution was soon to terminate, officials simply turned a blind eye to it and considered market sales an indicator that people had indeed been able to reestablish their agricultural-production systems.

Using the resources brought by national organizations for local ends was found in other sites as well. The indigenous population of Gwalafara, for example, believed they had a right to co-opt the benefits of Dogon settlement, in light of their earlier poor treatment by the Selingue resettlement. From the chief's point of view, his confiscation of the plow and draft animals was appropriate and successful, an example of local expropriation of outside resources. In the same vein was the tendency of Dogon migrants to Selingue to split their households to get more land on the perimeter.

Locals even adapted "successful" programs to their own constraints and needs. For example, internal CMDT documents suggested that the strategy of putting two to three times the field area in grains as in cotton was an old pre-extension strategy. Nonetheless, about half of Dioïla farmers retained more fields in food grains than in cotton, despite high input use and cotton production. Even though the CMDT recognized that farmers used manure from cattle on their crops, their recommendations concentrated on imported fertilizers and domestic rock phosphates to renew soils. Farmers, however, integrated manure systematically into their fields. Farmers did not passively accept ODR rules and regulations but attempted to adapt them to their own needs.

Attempts to co-opt resources to other ends did not always work. In Manantali, for example, the PRM ran a program in pump repair to develop local capacity to fix new project pumps and boreholes. Many young men signed up for the program in the hope that they could use this skill to find employment outside the zone, defeating the aims of the PRM to increase ability to solve a local need. When the young men wanted tangible evidence of their new skills, specifically, certificates attesting to their successful completion of the course, the PRM refused, wanting to discourage emigration. In a sense, both sides failed. The young men did not get their certificates, but some left anyway, necessitating a second training session.

Sometimes, locals used institutions in a conscious way to pursue collective ends that they could not have otherwise done. At Manantali, the PRM had initially planned to allocate total field areas to villages, leaving village authorities to distribute them to households according to "existing" criteria. From the villagers' point of view, they had no existing criteria for distributing all the land within a village at once, even though they had processes for allocating new plots of land to single immigrant households. They were concerned that well-placed villagers would take advantage of local-level distribution processes to benefit themselves. Therefore, they proposed that the PRM distribute household parcels by lot. Although there was friction between relocatees and the PRM, locals also saw the PRM as a disinterested party as far as their internal quarrels were concerned. In light of the request, the PRM set up a commission of local administrators, PRM representatives, and villagers to oversee the process, which worked quite well.

Attempts to get institutions to change activities in favor of local concerns were not universally effective. The Finkolo workers, for example, were consistently unable to get the plantation to provide certain services. The plantation was willing to provide or facilitate some services that increased the ability of individuals, particularly women, to work, for example, grinding mills, a maternity hospital, and day care. In contrast, where services did not appear to have a direct positive impact on workers, for example, a school on the plantation or better access to agricultural extension for their private fields, the plantation did nothing to help workers. Moreover, the plantation did not provide sufficient potable water for those living outside the official workers' camps, even though this would have improved worker health and capacity to work. Because the plantation did provide so many services, local administration geared its limited services toward other areas. This meant that when the plantation did not provide services, workers had few alternative sources.

Even more common than using national institutions to pursue collective ends, one group might use these as a resource in their conflict with another local group. For example, the youth of the Bafing used the Union National des Jeunes du Mali (UNJM), the youth wing of what was in 1989 the single political party, to decrease bridewealth. As in many other African resettlement projects, effective bridewealth payments increased as elders attempted to maintain control over juniors. Bafing youth put up with this when they had significant earnings during the construction boom, but after resettlement they saw their earning potential decrease significantly and used the UNJM forum to hold a Bafing-wide meeting to discuss the bridewealth problem. In this way, they were able to convince elders to come to a regional agreement on lower bridewealth payments.

In Yanfolila, national governmental structures were used to pursue land conflicts between migrants and indigenous inhabitants, through arguments about the interpretation of Malian land law (GRM 1987). Dogon claimed that the fact that the state owned all land meant that, even as migrants, they had rights over uncultivated land in the surrounding villages. In contrast, Gwala-fara villagers argued that the recognition of customary rights in this same law meant they could control who cultivated their village territories. This dispute brought out the important role of knowledge as a resource. The Dogon relied on their organization in Yanfolila, particularly the two retired civil servants in it, to help them conduct local negotiations and handle disputes. At the time of the study, this discussion was still under way, but it was clear that the ambiguities and vagueness in the land law were there to be exploited by those who knew it. Literate people not only had an advantage here, but could also more easily convince local civil servants that they were valid interlocutors. The important role of education and literacy was also instrumental in giving privileged access to local elites by the Soninke cooperatives in Yanfolila and Selingue. Their cosmopolitan experiences and the fact that they could deal with administrators in French rather than the local language helped convince administrators of their superior status. However, even where no group had privileged access, locals often involved government organizations in their dispute resolution processes, especially when local efforts alone had been unsuccessful. In

Manantali, villages went to the local administrator in the arrondissement to help solve farmland conflicts and to the Forestry Service representative in conflicts over pasture.

There were, however, cases when groups were unwilling or unable to use government regulations to pursue what appeared to be local interests. For example, few hamlets became villages, even though government regulations said that any agglomeration of 100 or more inhabitants could petition the administration for recognition and receive it. Hamlets hesitated to alienate their mother villages, which would have seen this as a repudiation of their authority. In some cases, the mother village might even have attempted to take back the land that they had allocated to hamlet residents. There may have been certain advantages to remaining a hamlet, especially concerning tax collection (as we address later in this chapter). Yet refusal to become a village had some negative repercussions on hamlet residents since both NGOs and local administration tended to work first in recognized villages. Although the Dioïla study hamlets had access to CMDT services, they had bad roads and no schools, health clinics, wells, or NGO projects. Markets were also rare. Given the agricultural dynamism of these villages, this was rather surprising. Clearly, they were unwilling to enter into overt conflict with mother villages, who valued their greater ability to attract resources and services.

Locals were not always successful in using national institutions, in whole or even in part, for their own ends. Yet it happened often enough that locals often chose this strategy. The local presence of national representatives who virtually always spoke local languages as well as French made people feel that these institutions were potentially part of their own cultural repertoire. As the Manantali residents said, people in the more isolated villages would have run from national government representatives before the resettlement and would have lied if forced to talk to them. But the intensive interaction they had during the resettlement years gave them a new understanding of national organizations and taught them that elites were not really very threatening. They ended the resettlement years with a readiness to use those institutions and services that they could. The relative ease of dealing with national institutions perceived by many rural Malians also made them ready to confront these organizations more directly when their attempts at co-optation had failed.

*Confronting National Organizations*

Sometimes local goals and interests were clearly opposed to national ones. Then, locals often entered into explicit negotiations or direct confrontations with national representatives. They also resisted what they saw as unreasonable demands in more subtle ways (cf. Scott 1985). The latter tended to be somewhat more successful, because rural inhabitants were less powerful than national institutions. Yet direct confrontation was by no means always unsuccessful. This section looks at successful and unsuccessful examples of resistance and confrontation.

One arena where locals and national agencies had divergent interests was rural tax collection. Rural people evaded taxes because they did not perceive any benefits from them, in contrast to ODR activities. In the late 1980s, the Malian government was beginning to give local communities more control over a portion of taxes collected. But as of 1990, this strategy still had not given people much say over expenditures because decisions remained monopolized by local bureaucrats (Hall et al. 1991). Moreover, the purposes to which local taxes were put tended to serve the administration more than locals. In the 1980s, over half of the funds collected for local uses were directed by presidential request to specific ends (Hall et al. 1991, 7).

Much resistance was expressed through manipulation of the household members listed on the *carnet de famille,* a registry held by the household head, used to determine the appropriate taxes. All household members were to be listed, although not all were *imposable,* that is, subject to the head tax.[6] Only people within certain age groups had to pay, and women with more than a certain number of young children were exempt. However, rarely did the *carnet* correctly represent the number of persons who actually lived in a household. There were almost always some members living elsewhere, and households who were economically and residentially separate often remained on a single card. People often delayed reporting births, to decrease family size, even though infants were not immediately *imposable.*[7]

In their efforts to collect taxes and to make local appropriations reflect effective population, local administrators generally tried to get households in their jurisdictions to hold independent *carnets,* as well as to get hamlets declared villages. Both these processes facilitated tax collection since taxes were collected from recognized village chiefs. Hamlets paid taxes through their mother villages, not their own hamlet head. Local administrations also collected taxes for each *imposable* individual on the *carnet* of the household heads inscribed in their jurisdiction, hence their desire to get migrants to establish their own *carnets* rather than remaining on one in their region of origin.

Where local authorities played a role in settlement, they could arrange for settlers to transfer their *carnets* as well, as they did for the Dogon who moved to Yanfolila. In Dioïla, where authorities had no means to pressure residents, they tried to convince them that hamlets would only get services when their residents were censused (and hence given *carnets*) in Dioïla, but the residents got local *carnets* only very slowly. At the period of the study most residents did have them, but many simultaneously held others in their home villages. Only in Finkolo was the issue of *carnets* not important, since plantation laborers, as wage earners, paid income taxes on their pay rather than the head tax.

Despite these efforts to get rural residents counted, rural inhabitants generally resented paying taxes and undertook a number of strategies to avoid doing so. Among these were making themselves difficult to count, by such strategies as remaining on the *carnet* of the home village and retaining the status of hamlet. The latter worked simply by adding more layers and distance between the local *chef d'arrondissement* and themselves, making hamlet residents, for example, somewhat more difficult to count accurately. Although pressure from mother villages to keep their predominant status was probably the most important factor in retaining hamlet status, it also facilitated tax evasion. Another strategy was to keep a *carnet* in the area (home vs. migration zone) that had the lower tax rate, since rates were not uniform across jurisdictions. In particular, tax rates in poorer areas were usually a little lower than in more affluent ones. Since many migrants moved from poorer to wealthier areas, they could expect tax rates to increase if they established a new *carnet,* so they often tried to avoid doing so.

Resistance to paying taxes could be more direct. Certain villages pleaded poverty and simply refused to pay, as in Manantali prior to resettlement, when villages were relatively isolated and had restricted opportunities to earn cash. Here, the *chef d'arrondissement* profited from the resettlement to collect taxes, as already noted. He was able to collect some arrears as well as what was owed during that period. By 1994, however, despite growing commercial activity, people had again begun to plead poverty, and Manantali had the lowest tax collection rate of the entire *cercle.*

Not only tax collection but other interventions as well evoked direct resistance. We discussed in chapter 5 the situation in Tienfala when the *chef d'arrondissement* wanted to exercise his power to allot house sites to new inhabitants. Although he had implemented a domanial commission to grant these sites, the local chiefs of Tienfala-gare, Tienfala-village, and their mother village Djinkoni all ignored him and continued to attribute land within their areas of control. It was a race between the two levels of authority, and the *chef d'arrondissement* was not able simply to use his superior position to win.

Tienfala residents also protested against new forms of onchocerciasis control introduced in 1989. The Niger River, on which Tienfala lay, had been treated with insecticides for some time, and Tienfala residents thought that the resultant decrease in black fly had lowered disease rates. In the late 1980s, the drug ivermectin was recognized as an easy and inexpensive way to treat individuals with onchocerciasis, and perhaps keep down new infection rates by interrupting the vector cycle. The OCP hoped that ivermectin programs could replace their expensive spraying and manual river treatment programs, and began experimental programs to test this hypothesis. Among the sites chosen was Tienfala, which had relatively high infection rates and was close to Bamako and OCP scientists. As a part of the experiment, the OCP ceased treating fly-breeding sites in the Niger River. But the population protested the suspension of river treatment, complaining that they would be more vulnerable to the disease. Some refused even to become part of the experimental treatment program. These protests convinced the OCP to resume river treatment at least temporarily while simultaneously continuing and expanding the ivermectin treatment program.

Because of the power differences, local populations often lost confrontations, as shown by a host of examples from Manantali, where people tried to change village sites, wage rates, compensation rates, census counts, and a whole variety of policies. Only rarely (most notably in the village site changes) were they successful. The most dramatic confrontation occurred when one of the villages, which the PRM thought recalcitrant about clearing their lands, did not receive land-clearing pay when other villages did. They decided to take hostage the first PRM employee who passed by. When this man, a topographer, left his car to talk to the villagers, the latter, armed mainly with axes and machetes, surrounded him. His driver managed to leave with the car, returning several hours later with the head of the PRM's Social Section, the *chef d'arrondissement,* and several policemen. After extended discussion, the villagers released the topographer, and five people were arrested. The controversy had deeper roots than land-clearing pay. The new village wanted to force a hamlet from another village, on the edge of their new territory, to move. They had not, in fact, cleared much land because they were preoccupied with negotiations over the hamlet. The PRM was unable to resolve the issue and the *commandant de cercle* decided that the hamlet would stay and the village would have to accept its site.

Villagers also protested plans for structure compensation rates. Initially, the project had intended that all structures would be rebuilt by contractors, but the time frame made that impossible. Moreover, a change in contracting mechanisms between the first and second year of resettlement made housing more expensive than originally planned, increasing budget pressures. The PRM decided that granaries and kitchens could be rebuilt by villagers themselves, a procedure agreed to by the population. The problem was the pricing. Contractors had been scheduled to receive 80,950 FCFA (U.S.$245) for each granary and 99,000 FCFA (U.S.$300) for each kitchen, but local people were to get only 30,000 FCFA (U.S.$91) and 20,000 FCFA (U.S.$61) respectively. The population protested what they saw as discriminatory pricing, but the PRM, under pressure from donors and their Malian superiors to keep to the project budget, had no choice but to remain firm.

These two controversies made an important issue clear to the Bafingois, even though they "lost" each of the battles. The PRM itself was relatively powerless in comparison to its own superiors. Donor and ministry representatives, as well as the *commandant de cercle,* came often on supervisory missions to Manantali to make sure that their directives were followed. The *commandant de cercle* was the closest (only 90 km away) and came most often. He made great efforts to keep the PRM in line with his plans, threatening to call out the army if they could not keep the population and the project "under control." The locals had learned that PRM staff were accessible and ready to listen to them, but they only later learned that the PRM was itself constrained by higher-level organizations. These organizations sometimes overturned PRM decisions, although at other times their involvement allowed the PRM to resolve intractable problems.

Villagers tried to capitalize on the situation in two ways. First, they realized that they could openly manipulate many of the PRM rules. For example, to get kitchen and granary payments, they hastily put up shoddy structures. The payments, originally seen as cash for structures built, came to be seen (by virtually everyone involved) as compensation for lost structures. This led some villagers to demand recounts, claiming that granaries had been left out of the initial census. In one village, for example, a man went to the PRM saying that he had ten granaries instead of the six listed on the census and deserved more compensation. He complained so much that he provoked a recount, which actually reduced the total number of village granaries from 100 to 60. His covillagers got so mad at the results that they made the man go live on the fringes of the village.

Second, villagers decided that they too could involve higher levels of authority on their side. Since the PRM was already allied with the bureaucracy, they turned to the party apparatus. Specifically, they tried to involve the political party, the UDPM, by influencing the most highly placed local, General Filifing Sissoko, a former member of the party's executive committee, who came from a neighboring area. The UDPM national representatives were persuaded to call several local meetings to deal with resettlement problems. However, the main interest of higher party members remained their own fights in the nation's capital, and they attempted to use the local issues to advance their own agendas there. The priorities of the local population were never primary, and although many of the population's complaints led to changes in PRM policy (through pressures brought by the party on the PRM's superiors), these were rarely the changes originally envisaged by the population when they made the complaints. For example, complaints about poor house construction in the first project year influenced the change in contracting mechanisms that in turn made the people build their own granaries and kitchens. People had simply wanted houses built faster and better. In later years, people had begun to question whether this means of dealing with local problems had not been counterproductive.[8]

The continuous attempts made by the Bafingois to make the resettlement project more directly meet their needs were often unsuccessful in the sense that they did not lead to the changes they had originally envisaged. Nevertheless, from an anthropological point of view, the fact that the population continued to try to negotiate better outcomes, even when they lost many of their confrontations, suggested that they continued to believe that they could actively affect their future (Horowitz et al. 1993). They were not rendered passive by the power differences between themselves and administration. In part, this was because there were few negative sanctions against losing, besides the mere fact of not getting what they wanted. The army was not called out, despite the threats of the *commandant de cercle,* and even the five who were arrested in the kidnapping incident did not remain in jail long. It was always worth trying to negotiate with a government that was either unwilling or unable to use the full degree of control that it claimed to have.

This high degree of confrontation was rarely observed in the other sites. In part, this was because the extended fieldwork in Manantali provided data not available elsewhere. But it also was due to the more traumatic nature of involuntary resettlement where confrontations and lack of confidence between populations and resettlement agencies are the norm. These confrontations illustrated the limits as well as the strengths of local and government power in the Malian context.

Conclusion

Neither the existence of local cultural norms for action nor power differentials prevented local people from negotiating with each other and with local representatives of national agencies in order to pursue their own interests. Local people proved to be savvy negotiators who got what they wanted often enough that they continued to negotiate. Our data suggest that we should assume neither homogeneity nor opposition of interests among household members, classes, or other social groups. As individuals and groups came to reasoned goals, interests sometimes overlapped and sometimes diverged. When interests overlapped, coalitions, sometimes quite unexpected ones, could form, and when interests diverged people took a variety of actions. They sometimes ignored the divergence and simply found niches where it made little difference. They could manipulate the system. The relatively powerless could resist, passively, subtly or more confrontationally. Or the two parties could negotiate. Neither the strategy chosen to deal with divergent interests nor the outcomes were predictable simply on the basis of structural factors or the distribution of power.

The process of dealing with divergent interests underlined the importance of knowledge as a resource. Manantali relocatees were pushed to negotiate construction payments because they knew that contractors were supposed to get a higher price. Yanfolila Dogon knew aspects of Malian land law and used it in their negotiations with both autochthones and administrators. In contrast, Manantali relocatees knew less about national agendas and so were unprepared for what happened when they called upon national figures to help them negotiate with the PRM.

As divergent interests were resolved, or new coalitions created, norms sometimes changed. No matter what their original strategy was, the CMDT began to serve hamlets as well as established villages and recognized that farmers would use manure to complement the use of chemical fertilizers. Their recommendations began to take these patterns into account. Or, as in the case of Tienfala land disputes, so many different parties negotiated in so many different ways with inconclusive results that the situation appeared to be without any overriding norms. We need to develop theories and models that recognize this range of possibilities, and that go beyond a focus on resistance as the defining relationship between rural residents and the state. In the following chapter, we turn to the theoretical and practical implications of using a perspective on rural activity that includes innovation, individuality, and negotiability as an integral part of human action.

Chapter 8

# *Toward an Improved Anthropology of Development*

This research began with the expectation that general models of ecological and political-economic constraints would provide sufficient understanding of farm patterns in the six zones under study. Nevertheless, our data presented so much variation and diversity that when we attempted to use these models, we were confronted by many exceptions. We were forced to look for other concepts that could help us understand the patterns, or more importantly, the lack thereof, in local production activities. We found this in the role of human agency, as expressed in active negotiation, individual choice, and innovation. These concepts need to complement those that look at structural constraints on access to resources.

Individual choice cannot, however, simply replace an understanding of larger structures. The physical environment as well as the national and international political context did limit people's choices. Nevertheless, they cannot account for the variation and diversity in behavior. Moreover, focusing on structural factors has had the unintended effect of exoticizing rural people by treating them as undifferentiated groups (the poor, women, working classes, etc.) rather than as active, reflective individuals who did not always act in ways that could be predicted by group membership.

Incorporating human agency into models can pinpoint refinements of development theory. It also suggests changing strategies of development practice. This chapter looks at each of these in turn, after a summary of our findings.

## Structure and Agency in Malian Agriculture

In their attempts to create successful production strategies, rural Malians were constrained by larger structures, but the effects varied widely from place to place and among the different components of the rural household enterprise. This section looks first at the constraints and then turns to their economic impacts.

The central government of Mali and its local representatives wanted to exert a high level of control over rural areas to galvanize rural development. They created policies that attempted to conserve environmental resources, sustain production, and encourage growth. These policies were primarily implemented through the ODRs, which concentrated on agriculture, had some impact on livestock, but mostly ignored nonagricultural activities. ODRs were most important in structuring access to certain essential resources for farming, notably credit, inputs, and markets, but had relatively little effect on the resources needed for stockraising and almost none on those for nonagricultural activities.

The government attempted to control rural production in other ways as well, but those policies sometimes led to unanticipated or secondary consequences, not in line with stated goals. Examples included poles of development created by infrastructure such as the Selingue dam or cotton gins, or rural production enterprises such as industrial gold mines or the tea plantation. Rarely if ever were these planned as sites for diverse rural growth. Rather, once infrastructure was built, people migrated, drawn by what they saw as economic opportunities. This led some rural poles of development to boom-and-bust cycles.

Other attempts to control rural production were simply ineffective. This was particularly notable in many early governmental attempts to transform existing labor practices and to control market prices but also was reflected in the minimal attempts to control land access. The government lacked either the will or the capability to enforce its policies systematically. Nevertheless, because these policies existed, the government could and did call upon them in specific circumstances. Depending on an analyst's point of view, this led either to flexibility or arbitrariness. In this study, this pattern was especially notable in the government's varying willingness to participate formally or informally in land procurement discussions.

The government's unwillingness to implement fully all policies was due primarily to its poverty. It had neither the human nor financial resources to see that its policies were effectively carried out. Many rural areas had government personnel without transportation or sufficient operating funds. Hence the government was dependent on international donors to fund activities and the willingness of local people voluntarily to comply.

Donor pressure to carry out some policies and ignore others affected Malian agriculture. Donors also worked at cross-purposes, since different donors, as well as various programs of a single donor, might stress different objectives. Structural-adjustment programs privatized credit and input access and discontinued fertilizer subsidies, yet stressed environmental sustainability. Programs for environmental sustainability cost money to implement; national governments needed greater funding for them at exactly the time they were told to improve their economies through greater cost effectiveness and spending less. At the local level, many farmers who had grown accustomed to production organized through ODRs met severe problems of input access. Farmers were told to sustain and increase soil fertility at the same time as fertilizer subsidies were cut.

Even before structural adjustment, the systematic ways in which donors ignored certain parts of the production system meant a dearth of access to external resources in those areas. Since the role of livestock and nonfarm activities in so-called agricultural zones was usually ignored, individuals who undertook them were rarely able to benefit from organized training programs, credit access, or marketing information. Their own local networks and knowledge thus became essential. This pattern may change as recent efforts by donors to encourage rural entrepreneurship have led to the development of loan programs for small- and medium-scale nonfarm activities, but the long-term effects of these have yet to be determined.

Because of the varying targets of donors and the inability of the Malian government to pursue all its goals simultaneously, access to many resources remained in local hands. Local custom remained important in land and labor access. Local marketing channels with considerable time depth were important for agricultural equipment and animals, and for marketing crops and goods in local and regional markets. People learned how to raise crops and livestock, as well as many craft activities through locally controlled family, kin, and neighborhood apprentice systems, and through their own individualized experiences on wage-labor migration. While local custom did provide culturally defined models for many activities, it also led to distinctive individual experiences as people created individualized social networks and acquired new knowledge from a variety of persons and places.

The resulting system allowed for a significant degree of individual agency in putting together a household production system. Two particular circumstances in Mali may have led to somewhat greater-than-average scope for individual initiative. Since Mali was among the poorest countries in the world, its government was less able than most to use coercion to meet its goals. Second, a recent census of African countries showed Mali to have the largest number of net emigrants (Russell, Jacobsen, and Stanley 1990, 2:123), meaning that Malians had above-average opportunities to gain knowledge of alternative technologies and social arrangements. Nevertheless, we do not believe that the degree of choice open to Malians was unusually high.

Human agency always plays a role because of the nature of the structures that constrain human action. External structures that constrain local action rarely if ever operate seamlessly. In part, the different structures do not have identical interests. At the international level, the operations of the world economy do not work to favor consistently the actions of even the most developed countries, as shown here, for example, in the way that cotton prices reflected arguments among the three major producers. Even among Western donors, policies toward a single country were not identical; France as former colonial power, other Western European countries, and the United States all had different priorities for Mali. Moreover, each structure was itself made up of individuals who had private agendas, sometimes their own career advancement, sometimes priorities at variance with national policy. These individual agendas affected the way that policy statements were transformed into action. The most obvious example here was the way that French colonial policy was differentially implemented as army and civilian administrators fought for control of the colonial enterprise.

The end result was a degree of local space that people at the bottom could use for their own pursuits. While people were also constrained by their own cultural traditions, these, like external constraints, contained their own inconsistencies. In addition, rural Malians did not expect that everyone would follow cultural norms. The interactions between inconsistent goals and individual agendas at different levels of constraining structures led to varying importance of structure and agency in the diverse components of the rural farm enterprise.

Of all the components, structural constraints were most important in economic choices within agriculture, and within agriculture, among the major crops of the farm enterprise. The least evidence of innovation and individual choice was in the decision to grow food grains. Risk from both the economic and physical environment remained high, and people used cereal-grain production for food security and protection from risk. Structural constraints were also key in the large-scale production of export cash crops such as peanuts, cotton, or vegetables, which was most effective when inputs, agricultural extension, and marketing channels were provided by regional structures. Farmers mostly followed local custom in patterns of food grain production and the advice of ODRs in cash crop production; individualized choices were relatively unimportant.

At the other extreme were the production of secondary crops and the choice of nonfarm activities. Although these choices were clearly constrained by outside factors, most notably markets, the market constraints were quite fragmented and acted in different ways in different places. Producing for or finding jobs in local markets required an appreciation for quite localized characteristics, and there was scope for farmers to produce an array of secondary crops and to enter a variety of nonfarm activities. Households dissatisfied with existing structural constraints could and did move elsewhere to find a different set. Successful rural households were those able to analyze the particular characteristics of the local economy and deploy their specific configuration of local resources to meet them.

Opportunities in livestock raising showed yet another configuration of constraints. Two were especially important. First was the level of the household's economic resources, which depended upon its success in the other activities. Second, the difference between new settlers and older inhabitants had a great impact on pasture access. This difference had an impact as well on access to other bush resources, since indigenous populations were more likely to know and claim them than were migrants. Indigenous people were more likely than migrants to enter livestock and nonfarm activities using uncultivated bush.

People innovated not only in economic arenas but also in social ones. With the rare exception of the Soninke cooperatives, social innovation usually began by tinkering with existing social forms to increase resource access incrementally rather than as a conscious decision to try a new social organization. Households negotiated over the division of labor and the distribution of fields among household heads, women, and other men. Villages negotiated over internal organization and jurisdiction. Locals manipulated, resisted, confronted, and negotiated with government programs. This led to significant variation in household, farm, and village structure as well as in the nature of relationships between villagers and outside organizations. Although small-scale incremental change could lead to large-scale social changes, new customary practices were difficult to pinpoint because people's choices were so varied.

Toward Improved Development Theory

Our data led us to look for development theory that integrated local variation and individual choice with larger structural constraints. This section is a step toward that theory, identifying some of the elements that need to be included. More needs to be done before they can be integrated into a single model so we include some suggestions for future research.

A new theory needs to move away from an emphasis on Western domination as the single defining experience of developing countries. This emphasis both overestimates the level of control that developed states have had and underestimates the level of control within developing countries. A more locally centered view would continue to recognize Western colonialism and subsequent Western political and commercial domination, but only as several of a number of factors affecting the development potential of a particular country.

It would focus not only on the ways in which wealthier states have dominated poorer ones but also on negotiations between states, which sometimes have given poorer countries considerable leverage.

An analogous process has also occurred within countries, between national elites (state representatives and capitalist bourgeoisie) and local groups. Since government initiatives were rarely either totally compatible with or opposite to local interests, local people had a number of responses to them. At times, national and local interests overlapped, for example, when cotton cultivation improved farmer incomes as well as national foreign exchange. Other national initiatives were formulated in the interests of local people, as in some aspects of the ODR activities such as functional literacy programs. While national governments no doubt dominated local people, they were unwilling or unable to use their power continuously. Local people expected that government interests would never be identical to their own yet simultaneously believed that many state initiatives would include activities that met local goals and interests. This led to significant interchanges and negotiation between locals and national elites.

Anthropological accounts sometimes give the impression that no project ever worked, at least until the development anthropologist came to the rescue to set everything right. This perspective blatantly underestimates the capacity of local people to deal constructively with their own problems. In his review of World Bank evaluations, Kottak (1991, 435, 437), for example, noted that even though the average rate of economic return was higher on projects with good sociocultural compatibility, the single project with the highest rate of return was one ranking low on this variable. "People put themselves first, even though planners had not" (441).

A new theoretical framework needs to account simultaneously for two social facts: the general tendency as well as substantial diversity. The variation in any sample is often so great that to look only at the central tendency and not the exceptions is to oversimplify analysis so much that we end up with neither adequate models nor practice. We need to follow the counsel of Bernard (1994, 361) to "try to fit extreme cases" into theories.

There are at least two ways to do go about doing so. One is to widen the search for independent variables within and outside the political and physical environment that affect the path of rural development, looking for multiple factors that condition people's responses, or at least, complicate the interactions among them. The second is to accept more explicitly the role of human agency and hence a level of unpredictability in the outcomes of any development activity.

Although the former is a valuable effort, we think that it is time to emphasize the latter. To paraphrase Marx, human beings make their own history but not under conditions of their own making. Much recent effort, even among non-Marxists, has concentrated on understanding the conditions. We now need to increase our understanding of the ways in which human beings make their own history. The processes we have discussed here, negotiation, innovation, and individual choice, are among them.

The negotiability of human relationships has been one focus of anthropology for a long time, but few in the field of development studies have used it as a central concept. Berry (1993) made one attempt to reintroduce this notion, in her analysis of negotiations over land and labor in four African countries. She hypothesized that negotiation is universal human behavior, but that the levels and kinds of negotiability of social roles are variable and determined by historical events. She suggested that recent levels of negotiability in Africa have been so high as to be almost pathological, making life relatively chaotic. The Malian data documenting negotiability since the eighteenth century do not support her hypothesis (of increased recent negotiation), but it is reasonable to expect that even if negotiation is a normal tool, levels would vary with a number of factors. Certainly Berry offers a testable hypothesis. However, it cannot yet be tested, since so few researchers have looked at negotiation in detail. We need more studies that use this concept as a central focus to understand how levels, kinds, and results of negotiation vary from one situation to another.

While negotiation is an important concept, individual choice and innovation need to complement it. Although some negotiation takes place through formal or informal groups,[1] much also depends on individuals trying to make the best of the possibilities before them. Innovation, the process of putting together ideas or resources in new ways to meet individual or group needs, is an important aspect of coping mechanisms. This is an experimental process that sometimes works and sometimes does not because all innovation is subject to unanticipated consequences. Innovation usually does not occur in dramatic new choices, but in smaller incremental changes. Sometimes individual changes lead to innovation at the societal level, hence social change, but other choices may simply remain individual, leading to heterogeneity in individual behavior.

Statements claiming that rural people are not interested in "learning a better way" (Kottak 1991, 438) are oversimplified, since we were surrounded by individuals who were trying new things to try to improve their lives. Most people did not care much about the source of the ideas for their innovations: if they were from the "West" or from "tradition," from a government representative or from a neighbor, on the radio or through an old proverb. Rather, they judged them on their results. Nevertheless, they did appear to want to keep the process under their control, that it be as predictable as possible. Although they were not resistant to change, they often wanted, as Kottak (1991) has also noted, to innovate to safeguard what was best about their existing life. Hence, they often clothed their pursuit of change within the garb of tradition.

Changing to a perspective that emphasizes human agency, as well as the unpredictability of such processes as negotiation, innovation, and individual choice, led us to reconsider some basic anthropological theory. These included the relationship of peasants and the state, the role of knowledge as a key resource, and patterns of rural stratification.

*Peasants and the State*

Anthropologists have often focused on the antagonism between peasants and the state, seeing resistance as the most salient of peasant reactions to state penetration. Indeed, peasants *have* resisted state activity, but there have been other responses as well. Malian farmers, peasants who produced for themselves as well as the state and the market, embraced what they saw as the beneficial aspects of both institutions.

Particularly through the ODRs, the state became a standard institution of Malian rural life. Although they fled the tax collector, Malian farmers flocked to the ODRs and their services and felt that access to them was their right. They used markets throughout precolonial and colonial periods to the present, and when local markets were depressed, they went elsewhere looking for better ones. In contrast to some analysts who conceptualized state and market as oppositional institutions (e.g., Hyden 1983), farmers saw them as complementary, each offering distinct opportunities and constraints. They resisted those aspects they saw as constraints, but they collaborated with the state and the market in those aspects they perceived as opportunities, and played off one entity against another as it suited their needs.

Theory that concentrates on the oppositional relationship between peasant and the state suggests that a practical strategy of state withdrawal from economic activity makes sense. Yet, many analysts have described disasters resulting from the radical state withdrawal accompanying structural adjustment (Gladwin 1991a). Our approach, which recognizes state and peasant collaboration and overlapping interests as well as opposition, appears to account better for empirical results.

*The Importance of Knowledge*

We need also to incorporate explicitly the role of knowledge as a resource. Innovation demands that people have the capability of learning about different alternatives. The tradition of migratory wage labor has been studied primarily for its economic consequences, earning funds that can pay for various family needs. But migrants also learned about different ways of life.

Since the colonial period, Africans who went to Dakar or Paris or served in the French army gained knowledge and experience, as well as tangible returns. Almost every Malian village had at least a few people who had lived in other countries, and almost every Malian seemed to have a relative who had lived elsewhere. Even though many migrants lived in ethnic enclaves, they learned new things.

Villagers knew how to make use of the knowledge of their more cosmopolitan members. Until recently, many village chiefs were military veterans, who had learned much in their tours abroad and in their dealings with military bureaucracies. Since large-scale involvement of Africans in the French military ended by the early 1960s (after the wars in Indochina and Algeria), most veterans have died in recent years. A new strategy appeared to be evolving, as villagers began to call on retired civil servants to serve as chiefs. Again, these men were often conversant with the government bureaucracy and could use their knowledge to the benefit of the village.

Not every individual or group was as self-conscious about their innovative approach as were the Soninke former factory workers in our sample, but many people used their knowledge to improve their coping ability. Poor people may have had fewer options because they often had less knowledge about national issues and trends than did elites. But elites too had imperfect knowledge, often remaining ignorant of local issues. The outcome of negotiations remained unpredictable because all involved parties lacked optimal knowledge.

*Rural Wealth and Stratification*

We also need to refine our perspectives on rural stratification systems. There were power and wealth differences in rural Mali, but they were not always due to class differentiation, that is, structured differences of access to basic resources of land, labor, or capital (Hill 1986). Although people had different quantities of resources, the structure of access among our local groups remained quite similar. No one had deeds to land, for example; almost everyone relied mostly on their own household's labor. Possibilities for social mobility were open to many, and some migrants used them to became quite affluent.

Many studies stratify rural Malian farmers into wealth groups (e.g., Koenig 1986), yet these are not necessarily class strata. Neither are these differences simply a product of the developmental cycle or the fact that the lands of large farmers are redistributed through inheritance, as Hill (1986) has suggested. Indeed, certain characteristics did make a difference: in this study, time of settlement, extent to which land was already settled beforehand, and so on. We need a more subtle understanding of how economic stratification and social differentiation are intertwined in a context where all may be of one "class," but where there are clear wealth differences. We need, for example, to look in greater detail at what role negotiation and individual choice make in the identification of relevant social characteristics such as ethnicity or indigenousness, which in turn affect access to resources and social mobility.

*Methodological Implications*

Improvements in theory demand improved research techniques. People did indeed talk as if there was a single "traditional way," and as if villages were homogeneous entities with single sets of interests. Only by studying very concrete and specific reports of behavior did the patterns of wide variation became clear. For example, only when people were asked to give cropping histories of specific fields did the extent to which they ignored ideal rotations became evident. Studies that want to discover variation and diversity, individuality and innovation, must concentrate on specific behavior as well as cultural knowledge.

In fact, the wide range of diversity found was likely an underestimate. Even when reporting their own behavior, people tend to regularize it (Bernard 1994). By observing actual behavior rather than relying on reported behavior, we would expect to find even more variation. Future studies need to rely on observation to a greater degree.

As suggested in the introduction, our relatively deep knowledge of the field allowed us to look more systematically at diversity. Inexperienced fieldworkers spend a lot of time identifying the patterns in what seems like chaotic behavior. Experienced fieldworkers understand the major patterns already and can spend more time looking at variation. More longitudinal studies and greater indepth knowledge should lead to better theory.

Future research should look explicitly at the interconnections of ideology and behavior. Potential research problems include transactions between individuals, state agencies, and national elites; the role of knowledge in people's decision making; how people get their knowledge and the uses to which it is put. We need to look at the ways in which goals and empirical consequences diverge and whether this is common or uncommon. We need to look at the behavioral impacts of wealth differences and their connections to individual social networks. While keeping in mind the uneven playing field on which many rural poor live their lives, we need to use analytical perspectives that appreciate the unanticipated effects of political economic and environmental constraints, and the ways that these create spaces for individual choice.

Toward New Development Practice

For those of us concerned about development practice, the sufficiency of a new theory or approach has to be evaluated, at least in part, by its ability to generate strategies that can lead to improved lives for rural people. We end this chapter with some of the implications of our approach for rural-development programs. Some of these have already been suggested by others for other reasons, in which case, we simply add one more rationale for trying them.

In Mali, cotton was the success story of focused support on a single cash crop for international markets. Significant investments were made in cotton research and extension; large harvests were grown by many farmers who substantially increased their standard of living. Cotton sales on international markets brought increased foreign exchange to the Malian government as well as cash incomes for small farmers. Nevertheless, there was concern about the long-term effects of cotton cultivation on the environment, and the international cotton market remained susceptible to the conflictual relationships among the largest national producers. Not only did cotton as a crop need to be complemented by others at the family level, so too did the national cotton strategy.

If small farmers can benefit from increased income from large-scale cash crops, the next step is for local industry and markets to develop to meet their growing consumer demand. As other studies have suggested as well (Scudder 1991), farmers with growing incomes often wanted to improve their housing and get new and better consumer products; they invested in their children's education. Here, they also invested significant amounts in improving agricultural equipment. In contemporary Mali, these needs could be met by local artisans, who made bricks and built housing, furniture, and agricultural equipment. Local people were teachers as well. While a certain amount of increased consumer income went toward purchasing imported goods (most notably bicycles and radios), much was spent on goods and services produced with local materials and fabricated by local artisans or industries.

The successful specialization of some farmers encouraged both women and men to leave farming and to turn to artisanal or entrepreneurial activities. This increased possibilities for specialization in commerce and production (cf. Guyer 1991). Local enterprises that serve local consumer demand need to be encouraged and supported on a number of levels, including credit programs and training opportunities as well as market expansion initiatives.

Greater production and consumer demand stimulate development of local, national, and regional markets. Regional international markets, for example, other West African markets, are also important for development. Anecdotal evidence after the 1994 devaluation of the CFA franc suggested that Mali was able to benefit from the competitive advantage of its savanna location in much the same way that it had done in precolonial and colonial days. Livestock (for meat), oil (from cotton and peanuts), and rice were all moving toward the coast. One of the most graphic examples was reflected in the complaints of Bamako consumers unable to find cooking oil in the summer of 1994. The manager of the oil factory admitted that it had sent most of its production to neighboring countries because of higher prices there. This short-term problem suggested a long-term opportunity for both Malian producers and local processing industries.

In the introduction, we pointed to self-sufficiency, diversification, and intensification as three of the most important issues confronting African agriculture. The above processes have implications for the way that we look at these different issues, as well as at the relationship of the state to farmers and the gender division of labor.

## Economy: Self-Sufficiency, Diversification, and Intensification

Many countries, including Mali, have valued food self-sufficiency as a national goal, and we see no need to question this. Yet to translate the national goal into one of self-sufficiency at the household or village level is problematic. Farmers in this study did not necessarily value food self-sufficiency, although they definitely were concerned about food security. Although even employees and artisans often continued to grow food, this was a response to volatility in food prices and markets, as well as stagnating wages. They did not grow food simply because of attachment to the land or a "traditional" way of life.

To be sure, few farmers would have considered becoming commercial farmers who sold all that they grew and bought all that they ate. However, many farmers were interested in specializing in a few crops in which they had a competitive advantage because of ecological conditions, ODR support, market niches, or their own knowledge of that crop. They were more than willing to sell those crops and buy other foods that they wanted to eat but were unable or unwilling to grow. The development goal should not be large numbers of farmers growing large amounts of the same crop. Rather, projects should encourage the development of diverse crops to serve local and regional markets as well as to earn foreign exchange through international sale. The long-term goal might be a regional strategy with a mix of major crops, and more diversity in a region's crops than in any single farmer's or even household's crops.

Most farmers in our sample followed subsistence strategies that included diverse crops and activities, either as a necessity for survival or as a conscious way to manage the risks of environmental and political unpredictability. We would guess that most households did not see this as a positive choice, since to specialize in one or two crops would have been too risky to contemplate seriously.

But is this diversification? If diversification is seen not just as a choice to grow different crops, but as a conscious strategy to invest in a number of different venues as a way to increase income, then only among a few of the wealthier farmers was true diversification found. Among both middle-income and poorer farmers, following a diverse set of activities was primarily a survival strategy to cope with a hazardous environment. We cannot expect that this strategy will change soon because Mali's general poverty means that it is subject to greater environmental and political riskiness than other places with greater resources.

Nevertheless, development can and should build on the existing diversity in farmer strategies. The first step is to recognize explicitly the diversity present in farmer strategies, which existed at several levels: among the crops grown by a single farmer; among the specialties of the different farmers within a single household; and the combination of crop farming, other agricultural, and nonagricultural activities in the same household. At present, development programs need to pay particular attention to the mix of agricultural and nonagricultural activities. Development programs in Mali have tended to categorize people by their most important subsistence strategy; they were farmers *or* herders *or* wage earners. Once they had categorized clients in this way, programs paid significantly less attention to secondary activities. Wage earners did not get ODR services and were seen as only part-time farmers. The animals owned by farmers were mainly seen as the target of animal traction programs, and farmers' herds were more or less ignored, except when they caused environmental problems.

Once the diversity in income strategies is recognized, development programs can focus on improving farmer allocation of resources among the different options. They might provide small-business training for people considered farmers, as well as agricultural services for people considered artisans. Improved animal husbandry options need to be available to everyone. Programs need to recognize the particular constraints on resource availability that exist precisely because people undertake a mix of economic activities.

Moreover, more effort needs to be spent on the development of special niches alongside the major concentrated efforts of many agricultural agencies. Although many people benefited from agricultural research and extension work on major cash and grain crops, no household lived by these crops alone. Some of the most innovative production and cash-earning opportunities were found among secondary crops and entrepreneurial activities for local or regional domestic markets.

This suggests a quite different format for rural extension programs. The range of activities ought to be expanded, even as many agencies are cutting back in light of structural-adjustment initiatives. But they need to expand in a new way, not re-create what existed in the past. Then ODRs focused on one or a few crops and offered vertically integrated services, from credit through commercialization. Now that credit and commercialization have gone, leaner and meaner organizations are supposed to focus on agricultural extension and improvement of farming techniques, with little way to recover the costs of doing so. Instead of returning to vertical integration, ODRs need to expand horizontally by increasing the range of extension and technical improvement options to a number of crops. It would also be valuable to expand nonagricultural initiatives, including small-business and livestock components, through either the ODRs or livestock agencies.

This approach has implications for the training of extension agents, which has often been quite poor, too poor to offer farmers quality information on a range of topics. ODRs need to offer training to upgrade agents' capabilities, improve their technical knowledge, and inculcate different attitudes toward farmers. Agents should learn to respect the specific local knowledge that farmers have of their own land and crops. They should be encouraged to see themselves as technical consultants and joint problem solvers with farmers. If agents have better education and a new set of expected behaviors for career advancement, they can be more confident of their own knowledge and become more comfortable discussing problems with farmers as colleagues.

Even with a greater level of education, it would be unreasonable to expect agents to have a comparable level of competence in an entire range of crops and activities. There needs to be a reconceptualization of them as nodes in a network that will enable farmers to get more specialized information from other sources. They need to be trained in conceptual activities as well as content. For example, rather than telling a farmer whether a market exists for a certain crop, they should be able to work with a farmer to evaluate whether or not there are market opportunities for that crop. If someone wants to begin a small business, in addition to figuring out the market issues, they should be able to let rural residents know where they could find further training. Agents need libraries where farmers can get more information.

All this might sound rather idealistic, except that a number of the pieces already exist in rural Mali. Since economic liberalization, private schools and individuals have begun to offer training programs on new topics like community development alongside old standards such as truck driving. Individuals with the means to do so are willing to pay privately to gain skills that will put them in a better position in the changing economy.

Second, many rural inhabitants are potentially in a position to benefit from written material in local languages. In the process of creating AVs, villages held literacy classes and produced literate individuals. People often let literacy lapse afterward, because there was not that much of interest to read. Mali, nevertheless, has organizations to produce local-language literature, if there are incentives. If there were more pamphlets about different crops, livestock issues, and rural enterprises, people would read them. In addition, most villages have some young people literate in French because opportunities for urban and international migration have decreased.

Essentially, development needs extension services that serve farmers rather than directing them, that see them as customers or clients rather than as the next link down in an authoritarian chain. Agents should have some technical information on major crops for the zone but could also serve as information links enabling farmers to get greater oral or written information, as well as appropriate training in a diverse array of activities. Some extension agencies are trying some of these activities already in an ad hoc way, but they need to do it more systematically.

## Society: The State and the Gender Division of Labor

We also need to reconsider the appropriate role of the state. The trends toward political and economic liberalization in recent years have meant state retrenchment. Our results verified the value of certain aspects of this movement but questioned the appropriateness of others. There were activities in which the state retained a competitive advantage over the private sector, as well as a role for the leaner state to play in rural areas.

Since the Malian state was never able to play the role that it envisaged in commercialization, all that it had previously achieved was to disrupt private-sector commercial activities already in full swing. Its exit from commercialization was useful. The movement away from credit provision is too strong to counteract now as well. Problems appeared in other areas when the state removed itself, however. The most notable was in Selingue, where the farmers without dryland extension services felt themselves cut off from the services of the ODRs. The role of the ODRs in input distribution was particularly important. For whatever reasons, private distribution networks had not developed by 1989. And later data (SARSA/USAID 1994; Bingen, Simpson, and Berthé 1993; our own 1993–94 study in Manantali) suggest that private input distribution networks have not appeared in the interim, except in very restricted places (e.g., Bamako) and for a restricted number of inputs (mostly pesticides).

The state needs to retain a role in encouraging the development of private distribution networks (e.g., providing infrastructure, facilitating loan access) or through the continued direct provision of inputs. By this, we mean sales, and not credit, for we recognize that the state is no longer able to provide the latter. But many of the farmers we talked to were willing to purchase at least some inputs for cash. The problem has been and remains availability, especially in areas where private vendors do not think they can earn enough.

The state must also continue to support ODRs, especially if they are going to function primarily as information diffusion centers. When the ODRs performed credit and commercialization functions, they could at least theoretically use these for partial cost recovery and as a self-funding mechanism. Although it was questionable policy to finance themselves in this way, it was at least a practical possibility, especially for organizations like the CMDT (SATEC 1984–85). But if ODRs no longer provide credit or commercialize crops, the question of how they are to recover costs is inevitable. Given the highly speculative nature of some of the information they would provide under our scenario, it is doubtful that farmers would be willing to pay much for it, if at all. There needs to be a recognition that certain services such as agricultural extension and infrastructure development ought to be provided by the state and financed from the central treasury.

Among the services that governments should support are those deemed essential for the national welfare, but where farmers do not yet see practical benefits. This brings us back to the issue of intensification, promoted by the Malian government to decrease land clearing and minimize ecological degradation. However, intensification can only be successful when farmers find ways to build up soils so continued cropping of the same land does not lead to decreased soil fertility. Farmers were willing to try various means to increase soil fertility, but chemical fertilizers will remain a component in most of these strategies. Farmers needed a way to pay for these. They preferred credit, and those who were relatively poor had no other choice. The need for credit or subsidies also was important with suggested new alternative techniques that were still experimental and risky.

Many farmers saw uncultivated lands around them, and lacking funds to intensify the parcels they presently occupied, would clear new fields rather than continue to cultivate what they presently had, even if they had to pay a fine. If the government wants to preserve uncultivated areas, they must return to credit or subsidies for selected inputs or procedures in critical areas, and donors must be willing to support them in this. These programs could theoretically be done in conjunction with private-sector partners, and governments can be creative in the means they use. They should not, however, simply pull out and leave national priorities to the private sector.

The state also needs to take a role in regional planning, something that cannot be done sufficiently by the market. Scudder (1991) has noted the importance of small-town development in planned resettlement projects. It was equally important in areas of spontaneous migration and resettlement. Market and artisanal centers offered migrants income-earning possibilities in independent and wage employment. Having access to these jobs could make a difference to family survival, especially in the first several years after migration. Transport and roads linking villages and centers were important. Most buses, trucks, and other transport were and should remain in the private sector, although governments can encourage the development of new routes through various incentives. In contrast, road planning and transport infrastructure remain a state responsibility.

The other place where government needs to strengthen its role is in licensing and oversight issues. For example, the growth of private schools and training centers did indeed offer people more possibilities for learning new jobs, but there was little way for prospective students to judge the quality of training. This was especially problematic for specialized adult training where the proof of success was the ability to find remunerative employment afterward as opposed to passing a national exam. Licensing was also an issue in private agricultural input sales, since many had potentially deleterious effects on the environment or on the individual user. In those products, especially pesticides, where input distribution was privatized since 1989, many sellers did not know what they were selling. Yet many buyers, with little knowledge as well, depended on the vendors to give them appropriate information (SARSA/USAID 1994).

The final question raised in the introduction had to do with how best to improve women's access to development opportunities. There are a variety of entry points because women, like men, were involved in diverse occupations. Some wanted to improve agriculture, while others were looking for nonfarm alternatives. Yet even when women were included as potential program clients, they were rarely offered as many options as men. While OHV agents worked with women, there were less than a dozen in contrast to the 80 for men (Bingen, Simpson, and Berthé 1993, 21). In a project in Guinea to improve small-business efforts, women were generally offered fewer and less remunerative possibilities while men had greater choice and more remunerative options (Koenig 1993). Clearly women need access to the entire range of programs offered: agriculture, livestock, small-business development, literacy.

On the other hand, conditions were not quite as dire as much of the women-in-development literature has suggested. Women, like men, were active negotiators who made choices and tried new things. The division of labor between men and women was not rigid, nor did it change only to women's detriment. Many village technological changes such as wells or grain mills benefited women. Women also had access to plows even when they did not own or drive them. They may have lost some autonomy, but they often welcomed it because they were able to work less time or increase their family's standard of living.

Women's programs still need to pay attention to their particular needs. Malian society remains highly sex segregated, and women field agents increase women's access to programs. But women as well as men can benefit from an approach that offers them numerous possibilities from which they can choose those that seem most appropriate. Programs should look for ways to increase the range of choices open to women, since one problem has been that markets for certain of their "traditional" products become quickly saturated.

An approach to rural extension that concentrates more on individual choices also implies that there needs to be greater focus on the individual, and correspondingly less on collective forms of local action. To be sure collective action does offer greater bargaining power to poor rural groups (Cernea 1991), and in Mali, the ability to combine in groups has assured credit to villages since privatization. But not all improvements need to go through groups, particularly through groups as large as the AV or *ton villageois*. This stifles individual innovation and creativity and ignores the development of market niches that have room for only a few people. We need to develop approaches to development that foster individual initiative alongside collective responsibility.

*Intervention Points*

One of the questions of development practice concerns the level on which practitioners ought to work. Theories concentrating on structural constraints imply that development practice ought to concentrate on changing those structures. However, a theory looking simultaneously at structural constraints and individual agency suggests that practitioners ought to work at both levels. Different kinds of practitioners are better placed to work at certain levels than others.

It is of course incumbent on analysts to continue to point out the structural constraints that impede positive social change. Social scientists from donor countries are particularly well placed to have an impact on the policies carried out by their own countries (Ferguson 1990), while developing-country social scientists often can have an impact on their own national policies. Some external constraints cannot be changed; Mali will always have to deal with a hazardous physical environment.

On the other hand, social scientists working in the field and at the project level have a privileged position to look for those niches that allow individuals to make the most of their opportunities. Until now, working with individuals has mostly translated into training programs and educational initiatives, many of which have worked under the assumption that people need to learn about new things to overcome the constraints imposed by local traditions and culture. Our approach, it should be clear, suggests a somewhat different approach, one that builds on patterns of individual choice and innovation already present in rural areas.

Conclusion

Mali remains poor, in part due to its historical place on the periphery of the modern world system, in part due to its hazardous and difficult physical environment. But Malians are active persons manipulating and changing their environment through the choices that they make. They are not any less reflective than Westerners about the possibilities that they face, nor do they more blindly follow cultural traditions. Development theory and practice both need to take into greater account the role of individual choice in farmer behavior, as well as in its effects on social change.

Nevertheless, any development model focusing on individual choice as the key to understanding behavior, without reference to social context, is equally deficient. This has not been a serious problem in development anthropology, where even those theorists who have stressed individual decisions have typically done so within a larger political or environmental context. It may, however, be an underlying assumption in other development disciplines. An emphasis on individual choice should not lead us to ignore the national development actions that need to be taken by a centralized authority.

We have made an argument for theory and practice that take into account the active interplay among international concerns, national state activities, local culture, and individual choice. Anthropological theories that have stressed the conflicting interests of the state and individuals ignore the beneficial aspects of this interplay and have inadvertently emphasized the exoticism of rural inhabitants in developing countries. In contrast, theories accentuating the primary role of individual choice have ignored the necessary role of the state in social change. What we have proposed here is an initial attempt at improving theory and practice by bringing these threads together. We hope that others will join us in moving these ideas forward.

# *Notes*

## Chapter 1

1. Marx's work has inspired at least four different approaches to development. They are (1) modes-of-production analysis, which looks at the internal working and intersection of different modes; (2) structural-dependency theory inspired by Andre Gunder Frank; (3) world-systems theory inspired by Wallerstein; and (4) classic Marxist evolutionary theory, which suggests that the underdeveloped world should pass through a stage of capitalist development before turning to socialism. We cannot do justice to these differences here; see Long (1977) or Harrison (1988) for further discussion.

2. In 1993, Koenig received a grant from the National Science Foundation to do further collaborative research with ISH on the consequences of resettlement at Manantali, but this book did not benefit from any systematic analysis of those new data.

3. For one view of the *ton,* see Lewis (1979). The kinds of labor done, the frequency with which the group is hired, the forms of payment, and the effective membership all vary widely from village to village. See chapter 3.

4. Even today, many Malian farmers speak disparagingly of their experiences with socialism, which to them means primarily this experiment with collectivization.

5. This was true even for the American among us, who does not have sufficient local language skills to carry on a lengthy conversation. Nevertheless, she has sufficient cultural knowledge to enter the discourse framework with an interpreter.

6. We use the words *indigenous* and *autochthonous* interchangeably, simply to mean the people living in an area and claiming ownership of it when study migrants arrived. Whether they themselves had been migrants much earlier was not a research question.

## Chapter 2

1. Europeans entering Africa wrote African names and words using a variety of orthographic conventions. Today the scholarly trend is toward using an international alphabet that avoids the idiosyncracies of particular European languages. Nevertheless these spellings may not correspond to those used now within the country. Mali, for example, continues to use French conventions to write family names and place-names. Many historical places still exist, and most family names are still in common use. So that the nonspecialist reader can more easily match historical to contemporary place or word, we have usually chosen to use spellings found in Mali today.

2. Contemporary Malians commonly refer to their leaders by their individual names, rather than by their clan names, now used as surnames. Because many people

share the same clan, they do not distinguish among people easily. Hence we will refer to leaders by their first names after the initial reference, a practice common to historians as well.

3. Those who want further information on these states can turn to Africanist historians. For Segou, see especially Willis (1985), Abitbol (1992), and Izard and Ki-Zerbo (1992). For the Toucouleur, see especially D. Robinson (1985), Ly-Tall (1989), Kanya-Forstner (1971), and Oloruntimehin (1972). Person (1968–75) has written the authoritative work on Samory; English renditions of specific issues are found in Person (1971, 1985, 1989). For an anthropological perspective on state formation during this era, see Meillassoux (1991).

4. The process of negotiation did not end there, however. Slave masters were also known to deny the paternity of some of these children, presumably to avoid freeing them (Klein 1983).

5. Although women were subject to more constraints than men, they too were sometimes able to use institutions of slavery to meet their own goals. Oromo women of the Horn arranged to be taken to the coast, where they could find husbands in Arabia, and Voltaic women went south to the lagoon area of Côte d'Ivoire as slaves so they could marry (Manning 1990, 90).

6. Before 1922, the colony was called Upper-Senegal-Niger (Haut-Sénégal-Niger), after its two main rivers. The upper Senegal River formed the Western boundary, and the Niger ran through its center. It included parts of today's Burkina Faso and Mauritania, removed when it became the Soudan, sometimes referred to in English as Western Sudan.

7. It took war in two former colonies, Vietnam and Algeria, to convince the French of the inevitable end of colonialism.

8. Private land tenure existed in other areas in Mali not a part of our study, e.g., in the Niger flood plains of Massina. For further information, see R. Roberts (1987).

9. The following argument and data are from R. Roberts (1987).

10. Some people do retain memories of the background of enslavement. However, outsiders often remain ignorant where precolonial status plays virtually no role in contemporary economic opportunity, as in our study sites. The situation is different in areas where slavery was renegotiated to a sharecropping system.

Chapter 3

1. For a discussion of the complex impacts of the suspension of rail traffic and the growth of Bamako-Abidjan road traffic, see Jones (1976, 93–96).

2. Throughout the twentieth century, sub-Saharan Africa accounted for only a small part of world cotton production (Porter 1995).

3. The largest producers throughout the 1980s were India and China, but they did not export much since they were also major consumers (Commodity Research Bureau 1990, 176). By the early 1990s, both had become major exporters.

4. For the United States, these included a desire to gain influence in French-dominated areas and to provide work for development personnel hired during the Vietnam War (Somerville 1986).

5. Most former French colonies in Africa share a single currency, the CFA franc. It was tied to the French franc at a rate of 50 FCFA to 1 FF in 1949, where it remained until it was devalued to 100 FCFA to 1 FF in January 1994. There were multiple reasons for the devaluation, but among the most important were European Community requirements on France and continuing IMF pressures.

6. For further information on the development and failure of the Senegal-Mali federation, see Jones (1976).

7. Changing relationships between Mali and France were reflected in currency choice. In June 1962, Mali withdrew from the African Financial Community and created its own currency, the Malian franc. The Malian franc was retied to the French franc in March 1968, and Mali readopted the CFA franc in June 1984.

8. Figures for 1962 and 1967–68 are from Jones (1976, 360) and were calculated using the single exchange rate of 249 FM = U.S.$1.00. In subsequent years, as Mali moved through various currencies, U.S. dollar equivalents were calculated using appropriate exchange rates. Expenditure figures are from Encyclopedia Britannica *Book of the Year* 1981, 525; 1987, 699; 1990, 667, as are exchange rates for 1980 and 1986. In 1989, the exchange rate used was U.S.$1.00 = 330 FCFA, the average exchange rate during the study period and the rate at which all study data were converted.

9. Malian *bogolanfini* or mud cloth, of hand spun and hand woven cotton, has become one of the two best-known African textiles in the United States. Its designs have inspired machine-printed copies as well (P. Rogers 1993).

10. In recognition of this problem, Mali has more recently been moving toward a system of village-level management of bushlands.

11. In Bambara, the world *ton* simply means group and can refer to groupings for different purposes. More accurately, the collective farm labor group is a *demisenw ton,* or young people's group, and should not be confused with the *ton villageois,* the legal cooperative structure formalizing the Association Villageoise, where mostly household heads are members.

12. This ODR was abolished in early 1996, and the CMDT was moving into the areas where it had formerly worked.

13. It is not clear why donors so favored irrigation, yet postdrought foreign assistance commitments to it (U.S.$24.58 per capita) were the highest of any aid sector, in contrast to commitments of only U.S.$9.39 per capita for rainfed agriculture (Somerville 1986, 186).

Chapter 4

1. There was little migration southward from the northwestern part of Mali near the Mauritanian border, an area equally affected by the drought. Evidently, remittances from overseas migrants, mostly Soninke, were sufficient to buy food (DNAS 1985, 4).

2. Assuring wage earners of farmland should not be an excuse to pay low wages, but evidence from around the world suggests that rural proletariat in developing countries expect to be able to grow food to complement wages. See Koenig (1977) on Cameroon and K. Robinson (1986) on Indonesia.

3. The center was also usually the site of an arrondissement, the smallest unit of

local administration. A number of arrondissements made up a *cercle,* while several *cercles* were found in each region, the largest unit of territorial administration.

4. In those rare cases where an individual did move, it was always a man and never a woman.

5. The Tuareg rebellion in the north in the 1990s began in the context of regional poverty but turned to an idiom of ethnic conflict. This turn of events led many Malians to question their confidence in peaceful ethnic coexistence.

6. This pattern was found in other centers of voluntary migration as well. For Tanzania, see Arens (1987).

7. A comparison of adjacent IGN maps (Dioïla 1961 and Bamako-Est 1985) shows much higher village density on the 1985 map.

8. This is a standard story about the founding of many villages. Since many men do hunt and travel widely to do so, it also is a plausible account.

9. It is generally believed that the 1987 census undercounted the population, and that the country as a whole grew more than 1.7 percent per year between 1976 and 1987. Nevertheless the census figures can be used to compare growth rates in different areas.

10. The 1985 exchange rate of U.S.$1.00 = 402 FCFA was taken from Encyclopaedia Britannica *Book of the Year* 1986, 731.

11. Perhaps the Selingue dam was named after this village, while deforming its name. The change facilitated distinguishing between the dam and the indigenous village.

12. Malian law accorded the status of town only to agglomerations of at least 5,000 inhabitants.

13. Construction on the perimeter had still not begun in 1994.

14. Most of the ISH information comes from published reports, since the raw data were destroyed in rioting just before the 1991 coup d'état.

Chapter 5

1. In one Burkina Faso study, big farmers could sustain shorter fallows because more intensive techniques preserved soil quality (Saul 1993, 93, 94).

2. The ability to define land as occupied or vacant is one reflection of political power (Shipton and Goheen 1992).

3. Evidence from Bamako and elsewhere suggests that when the city boundaries move even closer, local community control becomes untenable (Konate 1994; Dickerman 1988), but this situation had not yet occurred at Tienfala.

4. There is no labor information available for Manantali, although patterns of labor allocation were similar.

5. Mali did mine and sell local rock phosphates to complement imported fertilizers. However, production was concentrated in one nonagricultural zone in the north (Tilemsi), and distribution followed lines similar to those for imports.

6. In fact, preliminary results from our 1994 study of Manantali relocatees suggest that restricted land area has led to insufficient fallowing, thereby decreasing soil fertility, leading to lower yields, and causing other production problems.

7. Pesticides were one of the few imported inputs widely sold in local markets, perhaps because they were sold in small quantities. Many buyers relied on vendors for in-

formation about use, but vendors usually knew little about correct use rates or potential environmental or health hazards (SARSA/USAID 1994).

8. Hibiscus seeds were used in sauces and to prepare a condiment called *datou.*

## Chapter 6

1. Some OHV and CMDT documents recognized that farmers kept livestock but hardly integrated this into planning (Bingen, Simpson, and Berthé 1993; internal World Bank documents on the CMDT); others, e.g., an ODIPAC planning document, barely recognized the role of livestock (FAO/World Bank 1986).

2. Cattle ownership patterns in rural Mali are very complex, with different people having varying rights over individual animals. Moreover, animals may be left in the care of others for a variety of reasons. Our study did not begin to penetrate these complexities, but only gave an indication of general ownership levels.

3. Because women were somewhat hesitant to report livestock ownership, and because the head sometimes reported all the household's stock as his own, the rate of stock ownership among women may be higher.

4. The disproportionate vulnerability of small livestock to relocation was also noted by Scudder at Kariba (personal communication).

5. Village chiefs in two of the Yanfolila study villages said that epidemics in early 1989 had devastated their herds. This may have affected figures as well.

6. The importance of cattle to farming was underlined by the fact that the tea plantation itself kept a herd of cattle to provide manure and had shepherds on its payroll.

7. Even highly paid dam workers appear to have been unable to invest their incomes productively. It seems that most families in southwestern Mali had members who went to Manantali during its active years to "search for their fortune," but few succeeded.

## Chapter 7

1. In Ghana, changing terms of trade for the specific items that each partner was to provide meant that women's responsibilities slowly grew (Clark 1994). We do not have comparable data for Mali.

2. Since Dioïla and Tienfala had no female team members, we had less data on women there.

3. Even our team's female researcher at Selingue was surprised at this choice, despite the fact that she claimed that other rural women's responsibilities were too demanding.

4. The PRM sociologist was aware of this consequence but saw it as secondary to the main reason, which was to simplify pay procedures.

5. These mostly consisted of enlarging spaces between compounds and in courtyards that had grown substantially in recent years.

6. By 1994, the rural head tax had been suppressed, although taxes on goods—e.g., livestock and firearms—remained.

7. There were local concerns as well involved in establishing *carnets.* Establishing a new *carnet* meant explicit recognition of household segmentation, which, although a normal part of the developmental cycle, was often perceived negatively by the existing

household head. Having formally to recognize the independence of his younger brother or son meant that he had lost authority. Households often put off establishing separate *carnets* until it was obvious that segmentation had occurred.

8. Further information about the complex political coalitions engendered by the Manantali Resettlement Project are discussed in Koenig (1988).

Chapter 8

1. The work of contemporary political science on associational life and the growth of civil society builds on the idea of group negotiation (Hyden and Bratton 1992).

# Bibliography

Abitbol, M. 1992. The end of the Songhay empire. In *Africa from the sixteenth to the eighteenth century,* ed. B. A. Ogot, 300–326. UNESCO general history of Africa, vol 5. Berkeley and Los Angeles: University of California Press.

AFRAM (Association pour la Formation et la Réinsertion des Africains Migrants). 1988. *Avant-projet de développement integré de la coopérative de Ourou-Ourou à Yanfolila (Mali).* Paris: AFRAM.

Arens, W. 1987. Mto wa mbu: A rural polyethnic community in Tanzania. In *The African frontier: The reproduction of traditional African societies,* ed. I. Kopytoff, 241–54. Bloomington: Indiana University Press.

Bassett, Thomas. 1993a. Introduction: The land question and agricultural transformation in sub-Saharan Africa. In *Land in African agrarian systems,* ed. T. Bassett and D. Crummey, 3–31. Madison: University of Wisconsin Press.

———. 1993b. Land use conflicts in pastoral development in northern Côte d'Ivoire. In *Land in African agrarian systems,* ed. T. Bassett and D. Crummey, 131–54. Madison: University of Wisconsin Press.

Batran, A. 1989. The nineteenth-century Islamic revolutions in West Africa. In *Africa in the nineteenth century until the 1880s,* ed. J. F. Ade Ajayi, 537–54. UNESCO general history of Africa, vol. 6. Berkeley and Los Angeles: University of California Press.

BCR (Bureau Central de Recensement). 1987. *Recensement général de la population et de l'habitat: Résultats provisoires.* Bamako: Ministère du Plan.

Bernard, H. Russell. 1994. *Research methods in anthropology: Qualitative and quantitative approaches.* 2d ed. Thousand Oaks, CA: Sage.

Berry, Sara. 1988. Concentration without privatization? Some consequences of changing patterns of rural land control in Africa. In *Land and society in contemporary Africa,* ed. R. Downs and S. Reyna, 53–75. Hanover, NH: University Press of New England for University of New Hampshire.

———. 1993. *No condition is permanent: The social dynamics of agrarian change in sub-Saharan Africa.* Madison: University of Wisconsin Press.

Bingen, R. James. 1985. *Food production and rural development in the Sahel: Lessons from Mali's Operation Riz-Segou.* Boulder, CO: Westview.

Bingen, R. James, Brent Simpson, and Adama Berthé. 1993. *Analysis of service delivery systems to farmers and village associations in the zone of the Office de la Haute Vallée du Niger.* East Lansing: Michigan State University Department of Resource Development.

Boahen, A. A. 1989. New trends and processes in Africa in the nineteenth century. In *Africa in the nineteenth century until the 1880s,* ed. J. F. Ade Ajayi, 40–63.

UNESCO general history of Africa, vol. 6. Berkeley and Los Angeles: University of California Press.

Bohannon, Paul. 1954. The migration and expansion of the Tiv. *Africa* 24:2–16.

Boserup, Ester. 1970. *Woman's role in economic development.* New York: St. Martin's Press.

Brain, James. 1976. Less than second-class: Women in rural settlement schemes in Tanzania. In *Women in Africa: Studies in social and economic change,* ed. N. Hafkin and E. Bay, 265–82. Stanford, CA: Stanford University Press.

Brain, Robert. 1975. Les problèmes sociologiques dans la zone des terres liberées de l'onchocercose. Technical report to the Government of Mali. Rome: FAO. Mimeo.

Brett-Smith, Sarah. 1985. Report on hunger, immigration and resettlement in the Third Region of Mali. Report to United States Agency for International Development, Bamako. Mimeo.

Brett-Smith, Sarah, Leland Carmichael, Gurbachan Dhillon, Cheick Drame, John Ericksen, Frank Moore, and Thomas Whitney. 1987. *Mali livestock sector project: A mid-term evaluation report.* Binghamton, NY: Institute for Development Anthropology.

Brokensha, David, and Bernard Riley. 1980. Mbeere knowledge of their vegetation and its relevance for development: A case-study from Kenya. In *Indigenous knowledge systems and development,* ed. D. Brokensha, D. M. Warren, and O. Werner, 111–27. Washington, DC: University Press of America.

Brokensha, David, D. M. Warren, and Oswald Werner, eds. 1980. *Indigenous knowledge systems and development.* Washington, DC: University Press of America.

Bruce, John. 1988. A perspective on indigenous land tenure systems and land concentration. In *Land and society in contemporary Africa,* ed. R. Downs and S. Reyna, 23–52. Hanover, NH: University Press of New England for University of New Hampshire.

Buursink, John. 1990. Environmental assessment of Mali Sud III. Report to the World Bank. Mimeo.

Cauquil, Jean, and M. Vaissayre. 1994. IPM in cotton in sub-Saharan French-speaking Africa. In *IPM implementation workshop for East/Central/Southern Africa,* 72–82. Workshop proceedings, Harare, Zimbabwe, 1993. Chatham, UK: Natural Resources Institute.

Cellule Oncho. 1984. Rapport sur le développement socio-économique des zones liberées d'onchocercose. Bamako: Ministère du Plan, Cellule de Planification et de Programmation du Développement des Zones Liberées de l'Onchocercose.

Cernea, Michael. 1991. The social actors of participatory afforestation strategies. In *Putting people first: Sociological variables in rural development.* 2d ed., ed. M. Cernea, 340–93. New York: Oxford University Press for the World Bank.

Cesara, Manda. 1982. *Reflections of a woman anthropologist: No hiding place.* London: Academic Press.

Chu, Daniel, and Elliott Skinner. 1965. *A glorious age in Africa: The story of three great African empires.* Garden City, NY: Doubleday.

CILSS (Comité Permanent Inter-états de Lutte contre la Sécheresse dans le Sahel)/Club du Sahel. 1978. La mise en valeur des "terres neuves" au Sahel. Synthèse du Séminaire de Ouagadougou. CILSS/Club du Sahel.

———. 1983. Développement des cultures pluviales au Mali. Report SAHEL D(83) 192. CILSS/Club du Sahel.

Cissé, Ibrahima, Ousmane Coulibaly, and Fatoumata Sow. 1989. *Projet Mali-Sud III: Etude socio-économique.* Rapport provisoire. Bamako: Institut d'Economie Rurale.

Cissé, Moussa Cola. 1981. Les "acquis du peuple," les sociétés et entreprises d'Etat. In *Le Mali: Le paysan et l'état,* ed. P. Jacquemot, 131–58. Paris: L'Harmattan.

Cissé, Youssouf, Amadou Camara, Abdrahamane Diallo, and Zié Sanogo. 1989. *Etude socio-économique en bordure de la forêt classée du Sounsa.* Rapport provisoire. Bamako: Institut d'Economie Rurale.

Clark, Gracia. 1994. *Onions are my husband: Survival and accumulation by West African market women.* Chicago: University of Chicago Press.

Clifford, James. 1988. *The predicament of culture: Twentieth-century ethnography, literature, and art.* Cambridge, MA: Harvard University Press.

Cohen, Abner. 1969. *Custom and politics in urban Africa: A study of Hausa migrants in Yoruba towns.* Berkeley and Los Angeles: University of California Press.

Cohen, Stan. 1981. An economic analysis of millet production in two Dogon villages in Mali, West Africa. Master's thesis, Department of Agricultural Economics, Purdue University.

Commodity Research Bureau. 1970. Cotton; Peanuts and peanut oil. *Commodity Year Book:* 130–40; 245–49.

———. 1980. Cotton; Peanuts and peanut oil. *Commodity Year Book:* 132–40; 254–58.

———. 1987. Peanuts and peanut oil. *CRB Commodity Year Book:* 177–80.

———. 1990. Cotton; Peanuts and peanut oil. *CRB Commodity Year Book:* 63–72; 176–79.

———. 1992. Peanuts and peanut oil. *CRB Commodity Year Book:* 186–89.

Coquery-Vidrovitch, Catherine. 1986. French black Africa. In *The Cambridge history of Africa.* Vol. 7, from 1905 to 1940, ed. A. D. Roberts, 329–98. Cambridge: Cambridge University Press.

Cornia, Giovanni, Richard Jolly, and Frances Stewart, eds. 1987. *Adjustment with a human face: Protecting the vulnerable and promoting growth.* Oxford: Clarendon Press.

Coulibaly, Emilie Kantara. 1986. Training of rural women with the Stock-Farming Development Project in western Sahel. In *Women farmers in Africa: Rural development in Mali and the Sahel,* ed. L. Creevey, 117–31. Syracuse, NY: Syracuse University Press.

Cronje, Suzanne. 1993. Mali. *Africa review: The economic and business report.* 17th ed., 1993–94, 108–110.

Crowder, Michael. 1970. The white chiefs of tropical Africa. In *Colonialism in Africa, 1870–1970.* Vol. 2, *The history and politics of colonialism, 1914–1960,* ed. L. Gann and P. Duignan, 320–50. Cambridge: Cambridge University Press.

D'Agostino, Victoire. 1988. Coarse grain production and transactions in Mali: Farm household strategies and government policy. Master's thesis, Department of Agricultural Economics, Michigan State University.

Dandenault, André. 1987. Rapport final: Projet relocalisation à Yanfolila. Report to CECI. Mimeo.

Dembélé, Kary. 1981. La dimension politique du développement rural. In *Le Mali: Le paysan et l'état,* ed. P. Jacquemot, 103–30. Paris: L'Harmattan.

DeWilde, John C., with Peter McLoughlin, André Guinard, Thayer Scudder, and Robert Maubouché. 1967. *Experiences with agricultural development in tropical Africa.* Vol. 2, *The case studies.* Baltimore, MD: Johns Hopkins Press for the International Bank for Reconstruction and Development.

Diagne, P. 1992. African political, economic, and social structures during this period. In *Africa from the sixteenth to the eighteenth century,* ed. B. A. Ogot, 23–45. UNESCO general history of Africa, vol 5. Berkeley and Los Angeles: University of California Press.

Diarra, Ousmane, and Dolores Koenig. 1992. Rapport de site: Dioïla, Mali. Land Settlement Review Report to Institute for Development Anthropology, Binghamton, NY.

Diarra, Tiéman. 1989. *Les innovations techniques et technologiques en milieu rural: Problèmes et perspectives.* Abidjan: CIRES/CRDI, Réseau de Recherches en Economie Agricole.

Diarra, Tiéman, Dolores Koenig, Yaouaga Félix Koné, and Fatoumata Maiga Maiga. 1995. *Reinstallation et développement dans la zone du barrage de Manantali.* Bamako: Institut des Sciences Humaines.

Diarra, Tiéman, Halimata Konaté Simaga, and Dolores Koenig. 1992. Rapport de site: Yanfolila, Mali. Land Settlement Review Report to Institute for Development Anthropology, Binghamton, NY.

Diarra, Tiéman, Moussa Sow, Félix Yaouaga Koné, Makan Fofana, Ousmane Diarra, Halimata Konaté Simaga, and Fatoumata Maiga Maiga. 1989. *Etude de l'installation des populations dans les zones liberées d'onchocercose.* Bamako: Institut des Sciences Humaines.

Diarra, Tiéman, Moussa Sow, Mamadou Sarr, and Fatoumata Maiga Maiga. 1990. *Etude de l'économie domestique dans la zone de Manantali: Rapport final.* Bamako: Institut des Sciences Humaines.

Dickerman, Carol. 1988. Urban land concentration. In *Land and society in contemporary Africa,* ed. R. Downs and S. Reyna, 76–90. Hanover, NH: University Press of New England for University of New Hampshire.

Dione, Josué. 1987. Production et transactions céréalières des producteurs agricoles: Campagne 1985/86. Working paper 87.02, Projet Sécurité Alimentaire MSU/CESA, Institut d'Economie Rurale, Bamako.

Dione, Josué, and Niama Nango Dembelé. 1987. Le programme de restructuration de marché céréalière au Mali (PRMC): Une analyse de ses objectifs, son fonctionnement et ses réalisations. Working paper 87.01, Projet Sécurité Alimentaire MSU/CESA, Institut d'Economie Rurale, Bamako.

Dione, Josué, and John Staatz. 1987. Market liberalization and food security in Mali. Working paper 87.03, Projet Sécurité Alimentaire MSU/CESA, Institut d'Economie Rurale, Bamako. Also presented at University of Zimbabwe's third annual conference on food security in southern Africa, 1–5 November, Harare.

Djibo, Hadiza, Cheibane Coulibaly, Paul Marko, and James Thomson. 1991. *Decentralization, governance, and management of renewable natural resources: Local options in the Republic of Mali.* Draft report to OECD. Burlington, VT: Associates in Rural Development.

DNAFLA (Direction Nationale de l'Alphabétisation Fonctionnelle et de la Linguistique Appliquée). 1978. *Rapport final de l'évaluation de l'alphabétisation fonctionelle dans l'OACV.* Bamako: DNAFLA.

DNAS (Direction Nationale des Affaires Sociales). 1985. Enquêtes sur les populations déplacées du fait de la sécheresse. Bamako: DNAS.

DNEF (Direction Nationale des Eaux et Forêts). 1986. *Textes forestiers.* Bamako: Imprimerie Nouvelle for the DNEF.

Dommen, Arthur. 1988. *Innovation in African agriculture.* Boulder, CO: Westview.

Eckholm, Erik. 1989. River blindness: Conquering an ancient scourge. *New York Times Magazine,* January 9, 20–27, 58–59.

Ellis, William S. 1987. Africa's Sahel: The stricken land. *National Geographic* 172(2): 140–79.

Escobar, Arturo. 1995. *Encountering development: The making and unmaking of the third world.* Princeton, NJ: Princeton University Press.

Eskelinen, Riita. 1977. Field report—Dogon Cereals Project: Demographic variables in a village population. Report to USAID, Bamako, and the Institute for Development Anthropology, Binghamton, NY.

FAO (UN Food and Agriculture Organization). 1986. *Atlas of African agriculture.* Rome: FAO.

FAO/World Bank. 1986. Projet ODIPAC: Potentiel de Développement Agricole. Working Paper. Rome: FAO/World Bank.

Ferguson, James. 1990. *The anti-politics machine: "Development," depoliticization, and bureaucratic power in Lesotho.* Cambridge: Cambridge University Press.

Finan, Timothy, and John van Willigen. 1991. The pursuit of social knowledge: Methodology and the practice of anthropology. In *Soundings: Rapid and reliable research methods for practicing anthropologists,* ed. J. van Willigen and T. Finan, 1–10. NAPA Bulletin, no. 10. Washington, DC: American Anthropological Association.

Fofana, Makan, Halimata Konaté Simaga, and Dolores Koenig. 1992. Rapport de site: Selingue, Mali. Land Settlement Review Report to Institute for Development Anthropology, Binghamton, NY.

Fortes, Meyer. 1953. The structure of unilineal descent groups. *American Anthropologist* 55:17–41.

Frank, Andre Gunder. 1967. *Capitalism and underdevelopment in Latin America: Historical studies of Chile and Brazil.* New York: Monthly Review Press.

Franke, Richard, and Barbara Chasin. 1980. *Seeds of famine: Ecological destruction and the development dilemma in the West African Sahel.* Montclair, NJ: Allenheld, Osmun.

Gabriel, Tom. 1991. *The human factor in rural development.* London: Belhaven Press.

Gladwin, Christina, ed. 1991a. *Structural adjustment and African women farmers.* Gainesville: University of Florida Press.

Gladwin, Christina. 1991b. Fertilizer subsidy removal programs and their potential impacts on women farmers in Malawi and Cameroon. In *Structural adjustment and*

*African women farmers,* ed. C. Gladwin, 191–216. Gainesville: University of Florida Press.

Goheen, Miriam. 1988. Land accumulation and local control: The manipulation of symbols and power in Nso, Cameroon. In *Land and society in contemporary Africa,* ed. R. Downs and S. Reyna, 280–308. Hanover, NH: University Press of New England for University of New Hampshire.

Gran, Guy. 1983. *Development by people: Citizen construction of a just world.* New York: Praeger.

Griaule, Marcel. 1965. *Conversations with Ogotemmêli: An introduction to Dogon religious ideas.* London: Oxford University Press for the International African Institute. Originally published in French in 1948.

Grigg, D. B. 1974. *The agricultural systems of the world: An evolutionary approach.* Cambridge: Cambridge University Press.

Grimm, Curt. 1991. Turmoil and transformation: A study of population relocation at Manantali, Mali. Ph.D. diss., Department of Anthropology, SUNY Binghamton.

GRM (République du Mali). 1987. *Code domanial et foncier.* Bamako: GRM.

Grosz-Ngaté, Maria. 1988. Monetization of bridewealth and the abandonment of "Kin Roads" to marriage in Sana, Mali. *American Ethnologist* 15(3): 501–14.

Guyer, Jane, with Olukemi Idowu. 1991. Women's agricultural work in a multimodal rural economy: Ibarapa district, Oyo state, Nigeria. In *Structural adjustment and African women farmers,* ed. C. Gladwin, 257–80. Gainesville: University of Florida Press.

Hall, Robert, Hamidou Magassa, Aliou Ba, and Jeremy Hodson. 1991. *Decentralization, service provision, and user involvement: Local level options in the Republic of Mali.* Draft. Report to CILSS and the Club du Sahel.

Hansen, Art. 1982. Self-settled rural refugees in Africa: The case of Angolans in Zambian villages. In *Involuntary migration and resettlement: The problems and responses of dislocated people,* ed. A. Hansen and A. Oliver-Smith, 13–35. Boulder, CO: Westview.

Hargreaves, J. D. 1985. Western Africa, 1886–1905. In *The Cambridge history of Africa.* Vol. 6, from 1870 to 1905, ed. R. Oliver and G. N. Sanderson, 257–97. Cambridge: Cambridge University Press.

Harrison, David. 1988. *The sociology of modernization and development.* London: Unwin Hyman.

Hazel, Robert, and André Dandenault. 1989. Rapport de fin de projet. Report to CECI. Mimeo.

Hiebsch, Clifton, and Stephen O'Hair. 1986. Major domesticated food crops. In *Food in sub-Saharan Africa,* ed. A. Hansen and D. McMillan, 177–206. Boulder, CO: Lynne Rienner.

Hill, Polly. 1986. *Development economics on trial: The anthropological case for a prosecution.* Cambridge: Cambridge University Press.

Hoben, Allan. 1986. Assessing the social feasibility of a settlement project in north Cameroon. In *Anthropology and rural development in West Africa,* ed. M. Horowitz and T. Painter, 169–94. Boulder, CO: Westview.

Holcombe, Susan. 1995. *Managing to empower: The Grameen Bank's experience of poverty alleviation.* Atlantic Highlands, NJ: Zed Books.

Hopkins, Nicholas. 1972. *Popular government in an African town (Kita, Mali)*. Chicago: University of Chicago Press.

Horowitz, Michael. 1979. *The sociology of pastoralism and African livestock projects*. AID Program Evaluation Discussion Paper, no. 6. Washington, DC: USAID.

Horowitz, Michael, Dolores Koenig, Curt Grimm, and Yacouba Konate. 1993. Resettlement at Manantali, Mali: Short-term success, Long-term problems. In *Anthropological approaches to resettlement: Policy, practice, and theory*, ed. M. Cernea and S. Guggenheim, 229–50. Boulder, CO: Westview.

Howes, Michael, and Robert Chambers. 1979. Indigenous technical knowledge (ITK): Analysis, implications, and issues. *Institute for Development Studies Bulletin* 10(2): 5–11.

Hunting Technical Services, Ltd. 1988. *Final report: Socioeconomic development studies in the onchocerciasis control programme area*. Vol. 1, *Main report*. Vol. 2, *National oncho zone development studies and development proposals*. Vol. 3, *National oncho zone development studies and development proposals*. Vol. 4, *Bibliography*. Hemel Hempstead, UK: Hunting Technical Services, Ltd.

Hyden, Goran. 1983. *No shortcuts to progress: African development management in perspective*. Berkeley and Los Angeles: University of California Press.

Hyden, Goran, and Michael Bratton, eds. 1992. *Governance and politics in Africa*. Boulder, CO: Lynne Rienner.

IER (Institut d'Economie Rurale). 1984. *Recasement des populations de Manantali: Etude agro-socio-économique*. Bamako: Institut d'Economie Rurale.

Inikori, J. E. 1992. Africa in world history: The export slave trade from Africa and the emergence of the Atlantic economic order. In *Africa from the sixteenth to the eighteenth century*, ed. B. A. Ogot, 74–112. UNESCO general history of Africa, vol 5. Berkeley and Los Angeles: University of California Press.

Izard, M., and J. Ki-Zerbo. 1992. From the Niger to the Volta. In *Africa from the sixteenth to the eighteenth century*, ed. B. A. Ogot, 327–67. UNESCO general history of Africa, vol 5. Berkeley and Los Angeles: University of California Press.

Jacobs, Susan. 1989. Zimbabwe: State, class, and gendered models of land resettlement. In *Women and the state in Africa*, ed. J. Parpart and K. Staudt, 161–84. Boulder, CO: Lynne Rienner.

Jacquemot, Pierre, ed. 1981. *Mali: Le paysan et l'état*. Paris: L'Harmattan.

Johnston, Bruce. 1991. Getting priorities right: Structural transformation and strategic notions. In *Structural adjustment and African women farmers*, ed. C. Gladwin, 81–99. Gainesville: University of Florida Press.

Jones, William I. 1976. *Planning and economic policy: Socialist Mali and her neighbors*. Washington, DC: Three Continents Press.

Kamuanga, Mulumba. 1982. Farm level study of the rice production system at the Office du Niger in Mali: An economic analysis. Ph.D. diss., Department of Agricultural Economics, Michigan State University.

Kante, Mamadou. 1993. L'Efficacité dans les institutions publiques. Draft report to USAID, Bamako. Burlington, VT: Associates in Rural Development.

Kanya-Forstner, A. S. 1971. Mali-Tukulor. In *West African resistance: The military response to colonial occupation*, ed. M. Crowder, 53–79. New York: Africana Publishing Co.

Kassogué, Armand, with Jean Dolo and Tom Ponsioen. 1990. *Traditional soil and water conservation on the Dogon plateau, Mali.* International Institute for Environment and Development Drylands Network Programme Issue Paper no. 23. London: IIED.

Kébé, Youssouf Gaye. 1981. L'agriculture malienne, le paysan, sa terre et l'Etat. In *Le Mali: Le paysan et l'état,* ed. P. Jacquemot, 21–102. Paris: L'Harmattan.

Klein, Martin. 1983. Women in slavery in the western Sudan. In *Women and slavery in Africa,* ed. C. Robertson and M. Klein, 67–92. Madison: University of Wisconsin Press.

———. 1988. Slavery and emancipation in French West Africa. *Indian Historical Review* 15(1–2): 188–211.

———. 1990. The impact of the Atlantic slave trade on the societies of the western Sudan. *Social Science History* 14(2): 231–53.

Koenig, Dolores. 1977. Sex, work and social class in Cameroon. Ph.D. diss., Department of Anthropology, Northwestern University.

———. 1986. Research for rural development: Experiences of an anthropologist in rural Mali. In *Anthropology and rural development in West Africa,* ed. M. Horowitz and T. Painter, 29–60. Boulder, CO: Westview.

———. 1987. Old stereotypes, new stereotypes: The realities for Africa's women farmers. *TransAfrica Forum* 4(4): 17–34.

———. 1988. Local politics and resettlement in Manantali, Mali. Paper presented at the thirty-first annual meeting of the African Studies Association, Chicago.

———. 1990 *Country case study: Mali.* Binghamton, NY: Institute for Development Anthropology.

———. 1992. Rapport de site: Manantali, Mali. Land Settlement Review Report to Institute for Development Anthropology, Binghamton, NY.

———. 1993. Guinea natural resources project: Women and gender issues. Report to USAID, Guinea and Chemonics. Mimeo.

———. 1995. Women and resettlement. In *Women and international development annual,* ed. R. Gallin and A. Ferguson, 4:21–49. Boulder, CO: Westview.

Konate, Yacouba. 1994. Household income and agricultural strategies in the peri-urban zone of Bamako, Mali. Ph.D. diss., Department of Anthropology, SUNY Binghamton.

Koné, Yaouaga Félix, Fatoumata Maiga Maiga, and Dolores Koenig. 1992. Rapport de site: Finkolo, Mali. Land Settlement Review Report to Institute for Development Anthropology, Binghamton, NY.

Kopytoff, Igor. 1987. The internal African frontier: The making of African political culture. In *The African frontier: The reproduction of traditional African societies,* ed. I. Kopytoff, 3–84. Bloomington: Indiana University Press.

Kopytoff, Igor, and Suzanne Miers. 1977. African "slavery" as an institution of marginality. In *Slavery in Africa: Historical and anthropological perspectives,* ed. S. Miers and I. Kopytoff, 3–81. Madison: University of Wisconsin Press.

Kottak, Conrad. 1991. When people don't come first: Some sociological lessons from completed projects. In *Putting people first: Sociological variables in rural development.* 2d ed., ed. M. Cernea, 431–64. New York: Oxford University Press for the World Bank.

Leach, Edmund. 1965. *Political systems of highland Burma.* Boston: Beacon Press. Original edition, 1954.

Lewis, John. 1978. Small farmer credit and the village production unit in rural Mali. *African Studies Review* 21:29–48.

———. 1979. Descendants and crops: Two poles of production in a Malian peasant village. Ph.D. diss., Department of Anthropology, Yale University.

Little, Peter, and Michael Horowitz. 1987. Subsistence crops *are* cash crops: Some comments with reference to eastern Africa. *Human Organization* 46(3): 254–58.

Long, Norman. 1977. *An introduction to the sociology of rural development.* Boulder, CO: Westview.

Lovejoy, Paul. 1985. The internal trade of West Africa before 1800. In *History of West Africa.* 3d ed. Vol. 1, ed. J. F. Ade Ajayi and M. Crowder, 648–90. New York: Longman.

Luery, Andrea. 1989. Women's economic activities and credit opportunities in the Opération Haute Vallée (OHV) zone, Mali. Report to USAID, Bamako. Tucson: University of Arizona.

Ly-Tall, M. 1989. Massina and the Torodbe (Tukuloor) empire until 1878. In *Africa in the nineteenth century until the 1880s,* ed. J. F. Ade Ajayi, 600–635. UNESCO general history of Africa, vol. 6. Berkeley and Los Angeles: University of California Press.

Manning, Patrick. 1988. *Francophone sub-Saharan Africa: 1880–1985.* Cambridge: Cambridge University Press.

———. 1990. *Slavery and African life: Occidental, oriental, and African slave trades.* African Studies Series, no. 67. New York: Cambridge University Press.

MATDB (Ministère de l'Administration Territoriale et du Développement à la Base). 1986. *Recensement administratif et fiscal du 2 Mai 1986: Résultats définitifs.* Bamako: MATDB.

Mazrui, Ali. 1986. *The Africans: A triple heritage.* London: BBC Publications.

McClelland, David. 1976. *The achieving society.* New York: Irvington. Original edition, Princeton, NJ: Van Nostrand, 1961.

McCorkle, Constance. 1986. *Farmers' associations study: Opération Haute Vallée II, Mali.* Washington, DC: Checchi and Company.

McMillan, Della. 1983. A resettlement project in Upper Volta. Ph.D. diss., Department of Anthropology, Northwestern University.

———. 1986. Distribution of resources and products in Mossi households. In *Food in sub-Saharan Africa,* ed. A. Hansen and D. McMillan, 260–73. Boulder, CO: Lynne Rienner.

McMillan, Della, Thomas Painter, and Thayer Scudder. 1990. *Settlement experiences and development strategies in the Onchocerciasis Control Programme areas of West Africa: Final report.* Binghamton, NY: Institute for Development Anthropology.

Meillassoux, Claude. 1981. *Maidens, meal, and money: Capitalism and the domestic community.* Cambridge: Cambridge University Press. Original edition, Paris: Maspero, 1975.

———. 1991. *The Anthropology of slavery: The womb of iron and gold.* Trans. Alide Dasnois. Chicago: University of Chicago. Original edition, Paris: Presses Universitaires de France, 1986.

Momsen, Janet. 1991. *Women and development in the third world.* London: Routledge.

Moore, Henrietta. 1988. *Feminism and anthropology.* Minneapolis: University of Minnesota Press.

Murphy, Josette, and Leendert Sprey. 1980. *The Volta Valley Authority: Socio-economic evaluation of a resettlement project in Upper Volta.* West Lafayette, IN: Purdue University Department of Agricultural Economics.

Murphy, William, and Caroline Bledsoe. 1987. Kinship and territory in the history of a Kpelle chiefdom (Liberia). In *The African frontier: The reproduction of traditional African societies,* ed. I. Kopytoff, 123–47. Bloomington: Indiana University Press.

N'Diayé, Bokar. 1970. *Groupes ethniques au Mali.* Bamako: Editions Populaires.

Netting, Robert, David Cleveland, and Frances Stier. 1980. The conditions of agricultural intensification in the West African savannah. In *Sahelian social development,* ed. S. Reyna, 187–505. Abidjan: USAID.

Newton, Alex, and David Else. 1995. *West Africa: A Lonely Planet travel survival kit.* 3d ed. Oakland, CA: Lonely Planet Publications.

Nyerere, Julius. 1968. *Ujamaa: Essays on socialism.* Dar es Salaam: Oxford University Press.

O'Brien, Stephen. 1991. Structural adjustment and structural transformation in sub-Saharan Africa. In *Structural adjustment and African women farmers,* ed. C. Gladwin, 25–45. Gainesville: University of Florida Press.

Oloruntimehin, B. O. 1972. *The Segu Tukulor empire.* New York: Humanities Press.

PADEM. 1988. *Enquête agricole de conjoncture: Campagne 1987–88.* Résultats définitifs. Bamako: Direction Nationale de la Statistique et de l'Informatique.

Painter, Thomas. 1986. In search of the peasant connection: Spontaneous cooperation, introduced cooperatives, and agricultural development in southwestern Niger. In *Anthropology and rural development in West Africa,* ed. M. Horowitz and T. Painter, 197–219. Boulder, CO: Westview.

Palau Marti, Montserrat. 1957. *Les Dogon.* Paris: Presses universitaires de France.

Person, Yves. 1968–75. *Samori: Une révolution dyula.* 3 vols. Dakar: IFAN.

———. 1971. Guinea-Samori. In *West African resistance: The military response to colonial occupation,* ed. M. Crowder, 111–43. New York: Africana Publishing Co.

———. 1985. Western Africa, 1870–1886. In *The Cambridge history of Africa.* Vol. 6, from 1870 to 1905, ed. R. Oliver and G. N. Sanderson, 208–56. Cambridge: Cambridge University Press.

———. 1989. States and peoples of Senegambia and Upper Guinea. In *Africa in the nineteenth century until the 1880s,* ed. J. F. Ade Ajayi, 636–61. UNESCO general history of Africa, vol. 6. Berkeley and Los Angeles: University of California Press.

PIRT (Projet Inventaire des Ressources Terrestres). 1986. *Zonage agro-écologique du Mali.* Bamako: PIRT.

———. 1989. *Etude et inventaire des potentialités de la région CMDT de Bougouni.* Vol. 1, *Ressources terrestres.* Vol. 2, *Elevage.* Vol. 3, *Monographie.* Bamako: PIRT.

Porter, Philip. 1995. A note on cotton and climate: A colonial conundrum. In *Cotton, colonialism, and social history in sub-Saharan Africa,* ed. A. Isaacman and R. Roberts, 43–49. Portsmouth, NH: Heinemann.

Raynaut, Claude. 1988. Aspects of the problem of land concentration in Niger. In *Land*

*and society in contemporary Africa,* ed. R. Downs and S. Reyna, 221–42. Hanover, NH: University Press of New England for University of New Hampshire.

Reardon, Thomas, Valerie Kelly, Bocar Diagana, Josué Dione, Eric Crawford, Kimseyinga Savadogo, and Duncan Broughton. 1995. Capital-led intensification in Sahel agriculture: Addressing structural constraints after macroeconomic policy reform. Paper presented at the ninety-fourth meeting of the American Anthropological Association. 15–19 November, Washington, DC.

Reyna, S., and R. Downs. 1988. Introduction. In *Land and society in contemporary Africa,* ed. R. Downs and S. Reyna, 1–22. Hanover, NH: University Press of New England for University of New Hampshire.

Richards, Paul. 1985. *Indigenous agricultural revolution: Ecology and food production in West Africa.* London: Hutchison, and Boulder, CO: Westview.

Roberts, Andrew. 1986. African cross-currents. In *The Cambridge history of Africa.* Vol. 7, from 1905 to 1940, ed. A. D. Roberts, 223–66. Cambridge: Cambridge University Press.

Roberts, Richard. 1987. *Warriors, merchants, and slaves: The state and the economy in the middle Niger valley, 1700–1914.* Stanford, CA: Stanford University Press.

———. 1995. The coercion of free markets: Cotton, peasants, and the colonial state in the French Soudan, 1924–1932. In *Cotton, colonialism, and social history in sub-Saharan Africa,* ed. A. Isaacman and R. Roberts, 221–43. Portsmouth, NH: Heinemann.

Robinson, David. 1985. *The holy war of Umar Tal: The western Sudan in the mid-nineteenth century.* Oxford: Clarendon Press.

Robinson, Kathryn. 1986. *Stepchildren of progress: The political economy of development in an Indonesian mining town.* Albany: State University of New York Press.

Rogers, Barbara. 1980. *The domestication of women: Discrimination in developing societies.* New York: St. Martin's.

Rogers, Patricia. 1993. The mainstreaming of African style. *Washington Post,* 4 November 1993, Washington Home.

Roseberry, William. 1988. Political economy. *Annual Review of Anthropology* 17:161–85.

Rosen, Lawrence. 1984. *Bargaining for reality: The construction of social relations in a Muslim community.* Chicago: University of Chicago Press.

Russell, Sharon Stanton, Karen Jacobsen, and William Deane Stanley. 1990. *International migration and development in sub-Saharan Africa.* Vol. 1, *Overview.* Vol. 2, *Country Analyses.* World Bank discussion papers, Africa technical department series, nos. 101 and 102. Washington, DC: World Bank.

SARSA (Systems Approach to Regional Income and Sustainable Resources Assistance)/USAID. 1994. *Opportunities for success in integrated pest management: Socioeconomic conditions of farmers in Mali.* Technical Paper, Office of Sustainable Development, Bureau for Africa. Washington, DC: USAID.

SATEC (Sodeteg Aide Technique pour la Coopération et le Développement). 1984–85. *Etude des opérations de développement rural (ODR) et des organismes similaires.* Vol. 1, *Missions, fonctions, statuts juridiques, gestion administrative et financière, zones d'interventions* (September 1984). Vol. 2, *Méthodes et dispositifs d'inter-*

*vention, transfert des activités, besoins en moyens humains, en matériels et en fonction* (November 1984). Vol. 3, *Programme de relance et plan d'action* (January 1985). Paris and Bamako: SATEC et Ministère du Plan.

Saul, Mahir. 1988. Money and land tenure as factors in farm size differentiation in Burkina Faso. In *Land and society in contemporary Africa,* ed. R. Downs and S. Reyna, 243–79. Hanover, NH: University Press of New England for University of New Hampshire.

———. 1993. Land custom in Bare: Agnatic corporation and rural capitalism in western Burkina. In *Land in African agrarian systems,* ed. T. Bassett and D. Crummey, 75–100. Madison: University of Wisconsin Press.

Scott, James. 1985. *Weapons of the weak: Everyday forms of peasant resistance.* New Haven, CT: Yale University Press.

Scudder, Thayer. 1991. A sociological framework for the analysis of new land settlements. In *Putting people first: Sociological variables in rural development.* 2d ed., ed. M. Cernea, 148–87. New York: Oxford University Press for the World Bank.

Scudder, Thayer, and Elizabeth Colson. 1979. Long-term research in Gwembe valley, Zambia. In *Long-term field research in social anthropology,* ed. G. Foster, T. Scudder, E. Colson, and R. Kemper, 227–54. New York: Academic Press.

Shea, Yvan. 1986. *Privatisation study: Opération Haute Vallée II, Mali.* Washington, DC: Checchi and Co.

Shipton, Parker, and Mitzi Goheen. 1992. Understanding African land-holding: Power, wealth, and meaning. *Africa* 62(3): 307–25.

Sidibé, Hamadoun. 1978. Field report—Dogon Cereals Project: The destinations of products. Report to USAID, Bamako, and the Institute for Development Anthropology, Binghamton, NY.

Sissoko, Naminata Dembele, Soumaila Diakité, Hinna Haidara, Mamadou Nadio, and Ousmane Sokona. 1986. *Population—santé—développement dans la zone du barrage hydro-électrique de Selingue.* Bamako: Institut d'Economie Rurale.

Smelser, Neil. 1959. *Social change in the industrial revolution: An application of theory to the British cotton industry.* Chicago: University of Chicago Press.

Somerville, Carolyn. 1986. *Drought and aid in the Sahel: A decade of development cooperation.* Boulder, CO: Westview.

Sow, Moussa, and Dolores Koenig. 1992. Rapport de site: Tienfala, Mali. Land Settlement Review Report to Institute for Development Anthropology, Binghamton, NY.

Steedman, Charles, Thomas Daves, Marlin Johnson, and John Sutter. 1976. *Mali: Agricultural sector assessment.* Ann Arbor: University of Michigan Center for Research on Economic Development.

Stewart, C. C. 1986. Islam. In *The Cambridge history of Africa.* Vol. 7, from 1905 to 1940, ed. A. D. Roberts, 191–222. Cambridge: Cambridge University Press.

Sundberg, Shelly. 1988. *An overview of the food consumption and nutrition situation in Mali.* Report to USAID, Bamako. Mimeo.

Swanson, Richard. 1980. Development interventions and self-realization among the Gourma. In *Indigenous knowledge systems and development,* ed. D. Brokensha, D. M. Warren, and O. Werner, 67–91. Washington, DC: University Press of America.

Swift, Jeremy. 1979. Notes on traditional knowledge, modern knowledge, and rural development. *Institute for Development Studies Bulletin* 10(2): 41–43.

TAMS (Tippetts-Abbett-McCarthy-Stratton). 1983. *Les ressources terrestres au Mali.* Vol. 2, *Rapport technique.* Bamako: Ministère Chargé du Développement Rural.

Toulmin, Camilla. 1992. *Cattle, women, and wells: Managing household survival in the Sahel.* Oxford: Clarendon Press.

Traoré, Mamadou, ed. 1980. *Atlas du Mali.* Paris: Editions Jeune Afrique.

Traoré, Soumana. 1989. Développement durable au Sahel: Le rôle des organisations rurales. Document de synthèse, CILSS/Club du Sahel meeting on the Gestion des Terroirs Villageois au Sahel, 22–27 May, Segou, Mali.

UN (United Nations). 1964. *The economic development of Latin America in the postwar period.* New York: United Nations.

Uphoff, Norman. 1991. Fitting projects to people. In *Putting people first: Sociological variables in rural development.* 2d ed., ed. M. Cernea, 467–511. New York: Oxford University Press for the World Bank.

USAID (United States Agency for International Development). 1988. *Request for proposal number REDSO/WCA/Mali 89-004: Development of the Haute Vallée Project (688-0233).* Washington, DC: USAID.

———. 1993 *Africa: Growth renewed, hope rekindled.* Washington, DC: USAID.

Van Campen, Wim, Jan Hijkoop, and Piet van der Poel. 1988. D'un aménagement anti-érosif des champs à la gestion de l'espace rural. Bamako: CMDT, Institut d'Economie Rurale, and Institut Royal des Régions Tropicales, Amsterdam.

Venema, Bernard. 1986. The changing role of women in Sahelian agriculture. In *Women farmers in Africa: Rural development in Mali and the Sahel,* ed. L. Creevey, 81–94. Syracuse, NY: Syracuse University Press.

Waldstein, Alfred S. 1986. Irrigated agriculture as an archetypal development project: Senegal. In *Anthropology and rural development in West Africa,* ed. M. Horowitz and T. Painter, 119–43. Boulder, CO: Westview.

Wallerstein, Immanuel. 1979. *The capitalist world-economy.* Cambridge: Cambridge University Press.

Warshall, Peter. 1989. *Mali: Biological diversity assessment.* Tucson: University of Arizona, Office of Arid Lands Studies.

Whitney, Thomas. 1981. Changing patterns of labor utilization, productivity, and income: The effects of draft animal technology on small farms in southeastern Mali. Master's thesis, Department of Agricultural Economics, Purdue University.

Willis, John Ralph. 1985. The western Sudan from the Moroccan invasion (1591) to the death of Al-Mukhtar Al-Kunti (1811). In *History of West Africa.* 3d ed. Vol. 1, ed. J. F. Ade Ajayi and M. Crowder, 531–76. New York: Longman.

Wolf, Eric. 1982. *Europe and the people without history.* Berkeley and Los Angeles: University of California Press.

World Bank. 1981a. *Accelerated development in sub-Saharan Africa: An agenda for action.* Washington, DC: World Bank.

———. 1981b. *World Development Report.* Washington, DC: World Bank.

———. 1989. *Sub-Saharan Africa: From crisis to sustainable growth.* Washington, DC: World Bank.

———. 1992. *World Development Report.* Washington, DC: Oxford University Press for the World Bank.

———. 1993. *World Development Report.* Washington, DC: Oxford University Press for the World Bank.

———. 1994a. *Adjustment in Africa: Reform, results, and the road ahead.* New York: Oxford University Press for the World Bank.

———. 1994b. *Programme de la Coopération Mali-Banque Mondiale.* Bamako: Mission Residente de la Banque Mondiale au Mali.

———. 1995. *World Development Report.* Washington, DC: Oxford University Press for the World Bank.

Wrigley, C. C. 1986. Aspects of economic history. In *The Cambridge history of Africa.* Vol. 7, from 1905 to 1940, ed. A. D. Roberts, 77–139. Cambridge: Cambridge University Press.

# Index

Note: Contemporary Malians are listed in the index by last name first (e.g., Keita, Modibo; Traoré, Moussa); precolonial Malians are listed by given name first (e.g., Samory Toure, Umar Tall).

vegetables. *See* fruit and vegetable production
villages: fission, 21, 100, 219; hamlet-
village relations, 86–87; social and political organization, 85–87, 219–21.
*See also* hamlets

wage labor, 52, 90, 99, 148–49; Finkolo,
106, 165, 190–91; Manantali, 195; and
migration, 23, 49, 102–3, 196, 241;
Selingue, 121; Tienfala, 105, 119,
191–92, 213; Yanfolila, 126
Wahabiyya, 110, 122–23, 147, 211,
213
Wassulu: colonial population growth,
50; contemporary population, 126–
28

WFP (World Food Programme), 126,
161, 171, 212, 223
women. *See* gender
Wuru Wuru, 125–26, 128, 140, 148, 153,
167, 197–98, 201, 217. *See also*
Yanfolila

Yanfolila, 123–28; cotton, 170; equipment cooperatives, 153; gender issues,
migrants, 210–11; grain production,
164; land access, 138–40; livestock,
indigenous, 185–86; livestock, migrants, 187–89; nonagricultural activities, 197–99; relations with indigenous
population, 215–17; sample, 128;
town, 127; variation in production,
167–68